IMAGES
of America

BRIGHTON

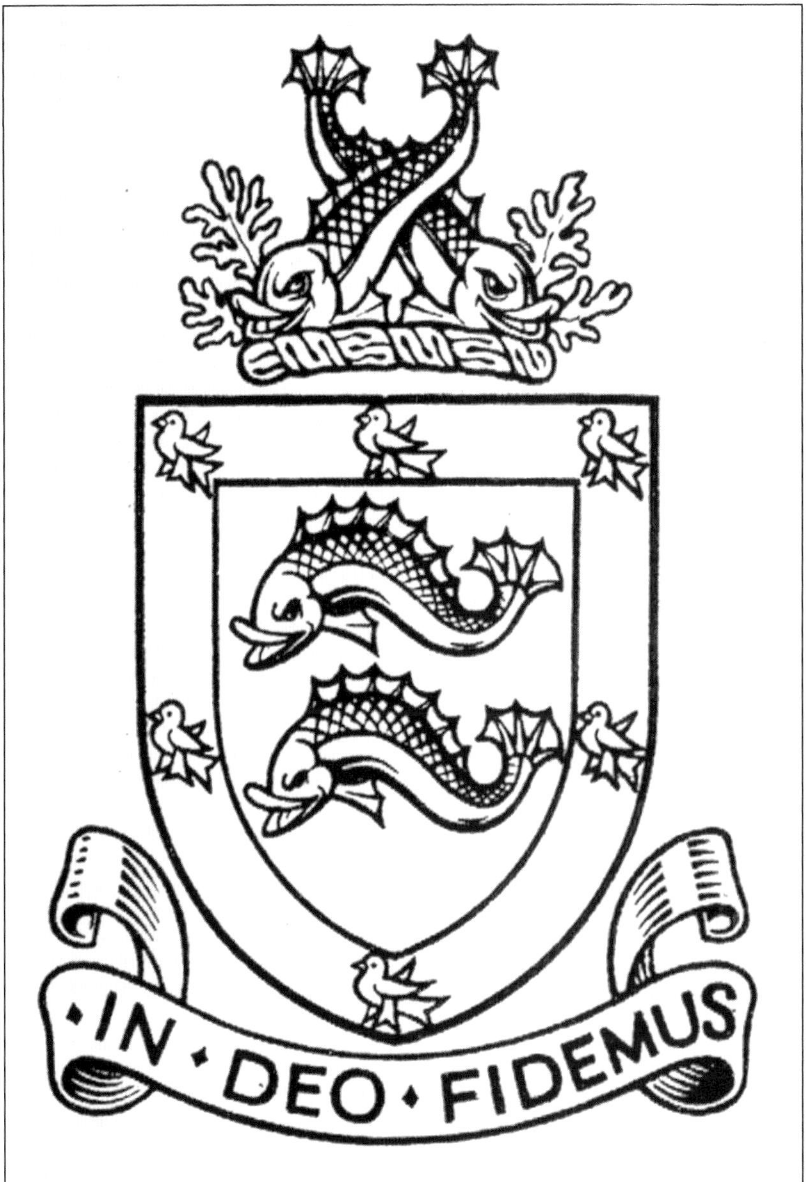

Brighton Coat of Arms. Nearly every state in the United States has a town or city named after the popular seaside resort of Brighton, England, as was the city of Brighton, Colorado, if only indirectly. The Brighton coat of arms reflects the origin of the name, meaning "the town on the bright" (an archaic term for a bay).

On the Cover: The Brighton Boosters Baseball Team posed for its portrait on August 22, 1920, in front of the grandstand at the Adams County Fairgrounds on South Fourth Avenue in Brighton (now the site of the Adams County Administration). See page 118. (Courtesy of the Brighton Historical Preservation Commission.)

IMAGES
of America

BRIGHTON

Albin Wagner

ARCADIA
PUBLISHING

ISBN 978-0-7385-6941-3

Published by Arcadia Publishing
Charleston, South Carolina

Printed in the United States of America

Library of Congress Control Number: 2008940182

For all general information contact Arcadia Publishing at:
Telephone 843-853-2070
Fax 843-853-0044
E-mail sales@arcadiapublishing.com
For customer service and orders:
Toll-Free 1-888-313-2665

Visit us on the Internet at www.arcadiapublishing.com

This book is dedicated to the people of Brighton—past, present, and future—who share a proud past and bright future.

Contents

ACKNOWLEDGMENTS

A book such as this is built on the generosity of others. Teachers, scholars, researchers, editors, photographers, and residents of Brighton contributed to this work, many of who may never know the role they played. Regretfully, I cannot acknowledge or even remember all of them, but I am profoundly grateful to each one.

Long ago, the seed that grew into this book was planted by W. Carl Dorr, editor of the *Brighton Blade*, whose *History of Adams County, Brighton and Fort Lupton* (1955)—to my knowledge, the first history of Brighton ever published—and Maude Linstrom Fransen's book, *All the Way: An Account of the Development of a City and a Church: First Methodist Church* (1963), were my first introductions to the history of Brighton.

My greatest debt is to Patricia Reithman and the Brighton Historical Preservation Commission. Pat Reithman has picked up the torch as Brighton historian and advocate. The Brighton Historical Preservation Commission contributed the majority of the photographs in this book, many donated by Ron Money, manager of Brighton Federal Savings.

A wide variety of historical societies and institutions hold a treasure trove of historic photographs, only a few of which, due to space and finances, could be reproduced in this book. They include the Adams County Historical Society, South Platte Valley Historical Society, Colorado Historical Society, Denver Public Library Western History and Genealogy Department, University of Denver Penrose Library, Colorado State Archives, Smithsonian Institution, Library of Congress, and National Archives and Records Administration.

I am especially grateful to the individuals who contributed photographs from their own collections, in particular Evelyn Tepe, Beulah Barnard, Kenneth Wagner, Kathy Granlund, Ester and Bruce Canterbury, and Kenneth and Lou Ellen Bromley.

I acknowledge the support that the Adams County Commissioners have given to promote regional history with *Adams County: Crossroads of the West* (1977) and *Adams County: A Centennial History* (2002), which I authored. Joan Johnson, Kay Dreyer, Ruth Kedzior, and Linda Hawkins assisted on those projects.

I also express gratitude to Jerry Roberts and Arcadia Publishing for support and guidance in the production of this book.

This is not a definitive history but a collection of snapshots of Brighton's colorful past. The history of Brighton is a work in progress. All the members of the community can be proud of their history and have a role to play in preserving this legacy for future generations.

Note: The author has made every effort to give credit for the original sources of photographs and images that appear in this book, although over the years a large number of them have become available from many different sources. Any photographs or images that do not carry a credit line are from the author's own collection of historical material on Brighton and the surrounding area.

INTRODUCTION

The city of Brighton is located on the Great Plains of northern Colorado, just east of the Front Range of the Rocky Mountains. The city lies in the valley of the South Platte River, which flows northward along the mountains before turning east to join the North Platte River, then the Missouri, and finally the mighty Mississippi. Thus the Platte River formed a natural highway pointing directly to the heart of the Rocky Mountains for the Native Americans, the early fur trappers, explorers, miners, farmers, settlers, and railroad men who followed its course westward.

The Platte River got its name from French explorers and fur trappers from the French adjective *plat(e)*, meaning flat, an appropriate description of the river that early travelers said was "a mile wide and an inch deep, too thin to plow and too thick to drink." Before that, the South Platte was known as the Rio Jesus Maria by the Spanish officials of New Mexico, who originally claimed the area as part of the Providence of San Luis and the Padouca River for the Padouca tribe of Plains Apaches farming the valley when the French and Spanish first entered the region.

Disruption from European influence and the advancing American frontier caused the Padouca to be forced off the Great Plains by, first, the Comanche and Kiowa and, in turn, the Arapahoe and Cheyenne tribes. Demand for furs—especially beaver skins—in the early decades of the 19th century brought mountain men and fur trappers from Canada, the United States, and New Mexico to the Rocky Mountains. As the trade in buffalo hides gradually replaced beaver skins and other furs, a string of fur trading posts sprung up along the South Platte, first Fort Convenience in 1834 by Louis Vasquez and his partner Andrew Sublette south of present-day Brighton, then to the north: Fort Vasquez in 1835 by Vasquez and Sublette, Fort Lupton in 1836 by Lancaster P. Lupton, and Fort St. Vrain in 1837 by Ceran St. Vrain in partnership with Bent's Fort on the Santa Fe Trail along the Arkansas River.

Red River carts carried to the forts trade goods and supplies brought west on the Santa Fe Trail. The caravans traveled north from Santa Fe and Taos, New Mexico, along the Trappers Trail, following the tributaries of the Arkansas and South Platte Rivers along the mountains to the forts. The carts returned south with heavy buffalo hides and other furs bound for the markets back East.

Before the forts closed one by one, a large number of well-known mountain men, military figures, explorers, and early-day tourists traveling along the South Platte visited the forts and passed through the present site of Brighton. Included in the string of visitors were mountain man Kit Carson; John Fremont, the "Great Pathfinder" and first presidential candidate for the Republican Party, on his first and second western expeditions in 1842 and 1843; and Maj. Stephen Long, civil engineer, explorer, and inventor, who labeled the region the "Great American Desert" and held the first recorded Fourth of July celebration on the present location of Brighton in 1845. Lancaster P. Lupton finally abandoned Fort Lupton in 1846, eventually settling in California. Fort St. Vrain was the last of the forts to close in 1848, but the location of the former forts continued to serve as landmarks and the focus of new communities for later settlers.

The first permanent settlement in the Brighton area was established by Col. Jack Henderson on a large island in the South Platte River about 7 miles south of present-day downtown Brighton. The Henderson area soon became home to a number of settlers, many of whom had come west to strike it rich during the 1859 Pikes Peak Gold Rush. These first residents of the county soon discovered there was more money in raising crops and livestock to supply the prospectors in the mountains and the residents of new city of Denver than there was in gold mining. Previously, food had to be shipped in from New Mexico or points east. The early farmers of Adams County helped the growth of Denver and established the agricultural economy that much of the county still depends on today.

With the construction of the transcontinental railroad after the Civil War, the people of Colorado Territory expected the main line of the Union Pacific to pass through this area, but the shorter route across Wyoming was chosen. So Denver organized the Denver Pacific Railway and Telegraph Company to construct a branch line between Cheyenne and Denver. The company started grading north from Denver in May 1868 and laying rails south from Cheyenne in 1869. The rails reached present-day Brighton on June 9, 1870, and Denver on June 22, 1870.

The town of Brighton was founded by railroad man and real estate developer Daniel F. Carmichael at the junction of the Denver Pacific (now Union Pacific) and the Denver and Boulder Valley Railroads. Carmichael determined, "There should be a town here that would do credit to the splendid valley." The junction, originally named Hughes after the first president of the Denver Pacific Railroad, had a long history as a crossroads of the West. The name was later changed from "Hughes" to "Brighton" when Carmichael filed the first plat for the town of Brighton on February 16, 1881. Then Brighton was incorporated as a town in 1887.

In 1902, voters approved the creation of three new counties, including Adams County, all of which, prior to that time, had been part of enormous Arapahoe County, which included the city of Denver and stretched east all the way to Kansas. The new county was named after Alva Adams, a popular governor of Colorado. The county government was temporarily located in Brighton, where the former residence of Daniel Carmichael was rented as the first county courthouse. A fire destroyed these offices in January 1904. Brighton was chosen as the permanent county seat in an election held November 8, 1904. Brighton defeated the towns of Harris (now Westminster), Fletcher (now Aurora), Hazeltine, and Adams City, then a brand-new real estate development. Brighton had promised the county a new courthouse if they won the election. A new courthouse befitting a growing and prosperous county was built at Fourth and Bridge Streets in 1906. That building still stands as the eastern half of the Brighton City Hall.

With the development of large irrigation projects, the town grew into an agricultural center for the Platte River Valley with a thriving sugar beet industry, dairies, and canning factories. These agricultural industries attracted a diverse community, including Germans from Russia and Japanese and Hispanic farmers and factory workers. Along with these groups, a rich community life developed, including a variety of churches, clubs, social and fraternal organizations, and sports.

But the impact of the changing economy transformed Brighton first into a suburban community and now into one of the fastest growing cities in the United States. Brighton placed second in the Gadberry Group's "Seven from 2007." The Gadberry Group, a national firm, lists the most notable high-growth places in the United States for the nation's top retail corporations, many of whom have now located in Brighton.

One

Crossroads of the West

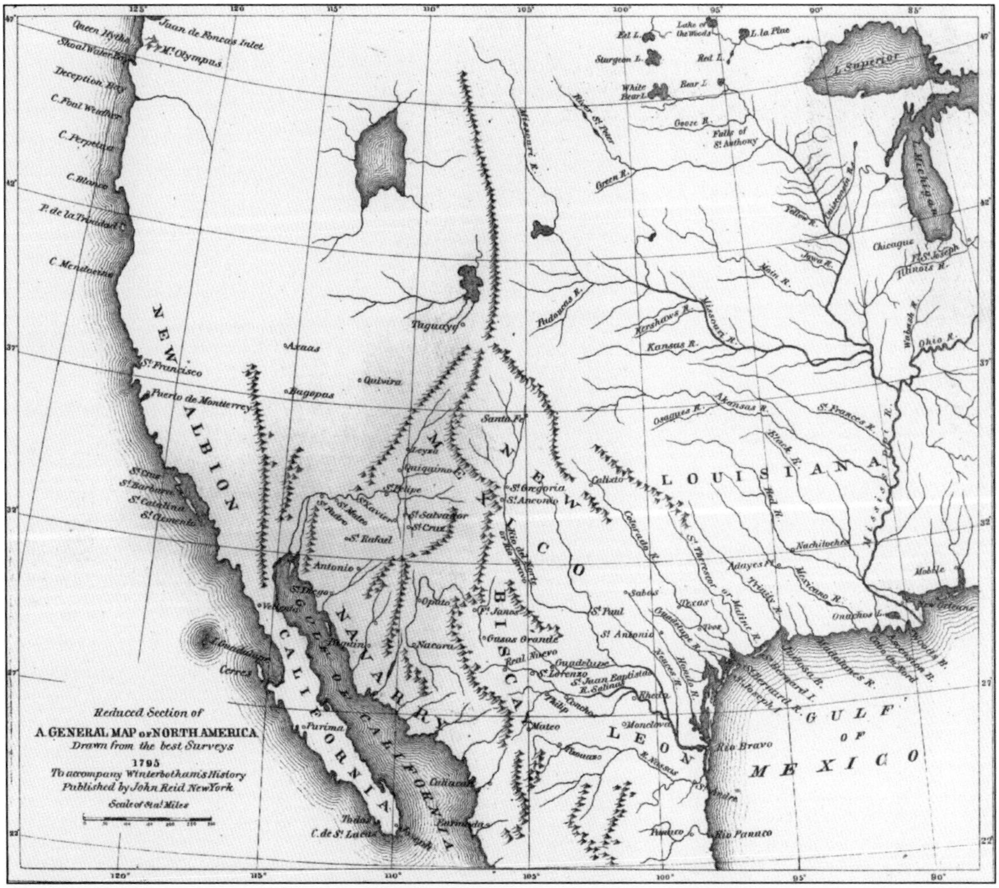

North America, 1795. "A General Map of North America" published by John Reid of New York in 1795 shows only a vague idea of the Platte River and the Rocky Mountain West. The South Platte River, located roughly in the center of this map, is called the "Padoucas River" for the Padouca tribe of Plains Apaches who inhabited the river valley when the Spanish first came to the area.

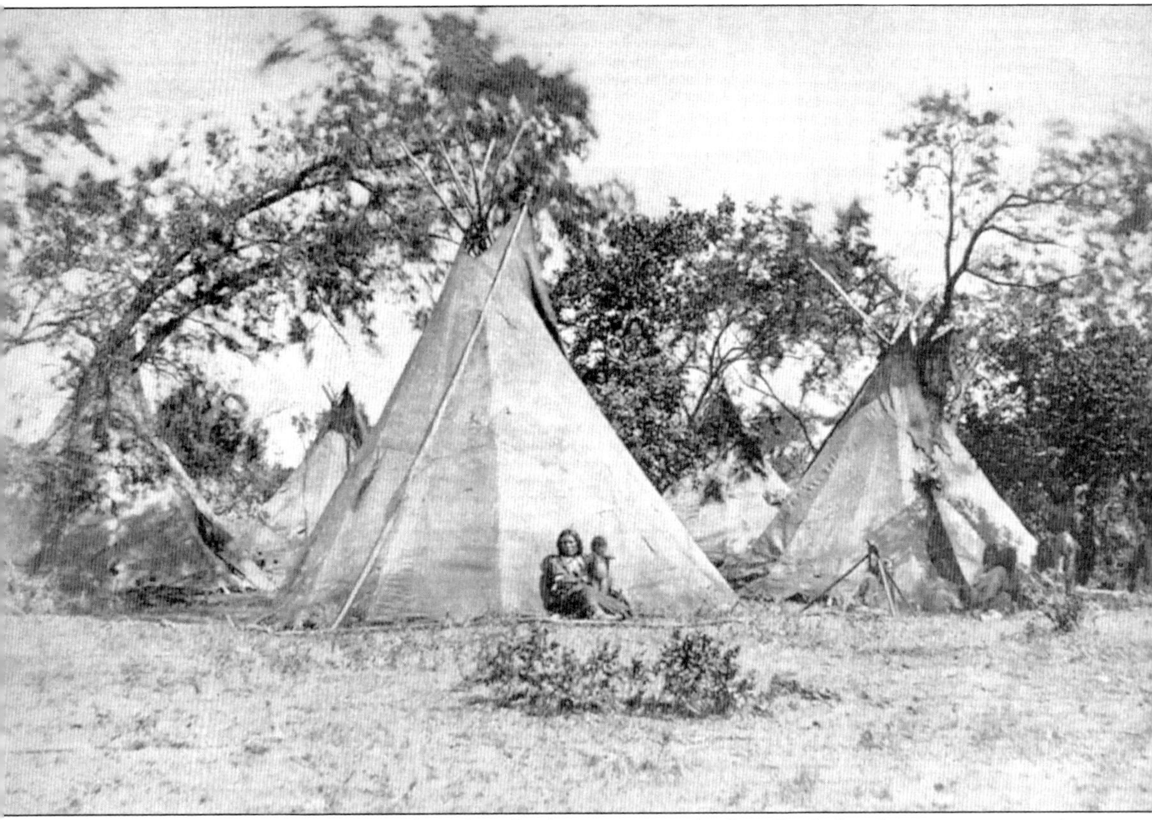

ARAPAHO INDIAN VILLAGE. Three hundred years ago, as the first English colonies were struggling to gain a foothold on the Atlantic coast, New Mexico was colonized by the Spanish, beginning in 1590. Santa Fe was founded in 1620, the same year the Pilgrims landed on Plymouth Rock. New Mexico claimed present-day Colorado as part of the Provence of San Luis. They named the South Platte River the "Rio Santa Maria." The river was also known as the "Padouca River" for the tribe of Plains Apaches who had permanent settlements and farmed the river valley. The Plains Apaches allied themselves with the Spanish, but disruptions caused by European influences and the resulting movement of first the Comanche and Kiowa, and later the Arapaho and Cheyenne tribes, on to the Great Plains forced the Apaches to migrate to the desert Southwest. The Arapaho Indians were of Algonquin linguistic stock. There are divided into three main branches or tribes, the Gros Ventre (allied with the Blackfeet), the Southern Arapaho (allied with the Cheyenne), and the Northern Arapaho (considered the parent group). (Courtesy of the Library of Congress.)

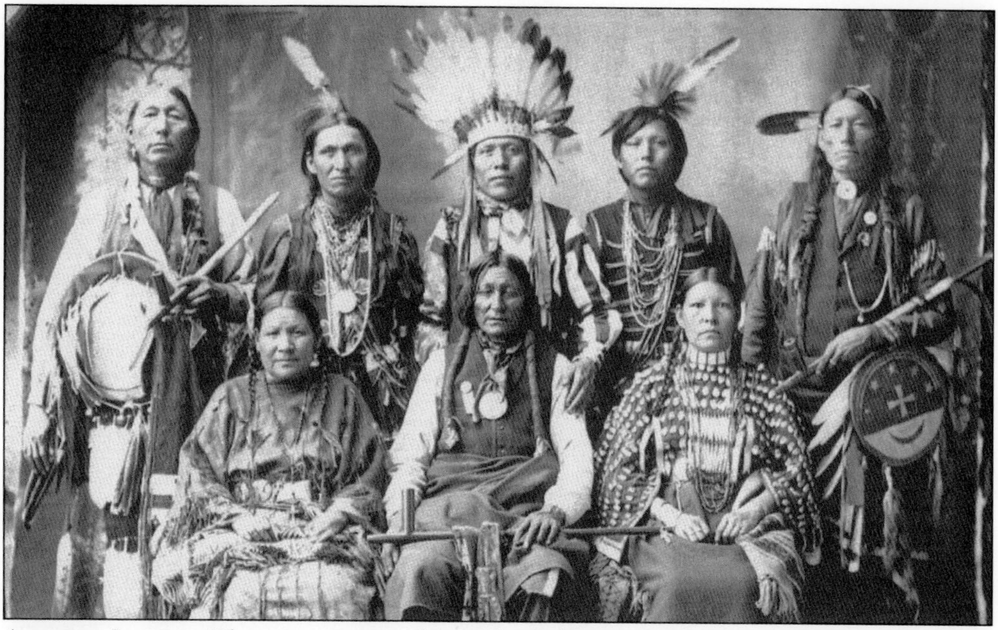

Arapaho Indians. These two groups of Arapaho Indians are part of a series of photographs of Arapaho and Cheyenne Indians taken by photographer Frank Albert Rinehart at the Omaha Exposition in 1898. The glass negatives were collected by the U.S. Bureau of American Ethnology and have been preserved by the National Anthropological Archive at the Smithsonian Institution. Note the mixture of native and European dress and shields held by several of the men, a characteristic item for the Arapaho warriors, which often carried elaborate designs. The Arapaho bands moved out onto the Plains to hunt buffalo. Later they became great traders of furs and other trade items. The name Arapaho might have come from the Pawnee word for traders. Their name for themselves is Inuna-ina ("our people"). (Both courtesy of the Smithsonian Institution.)

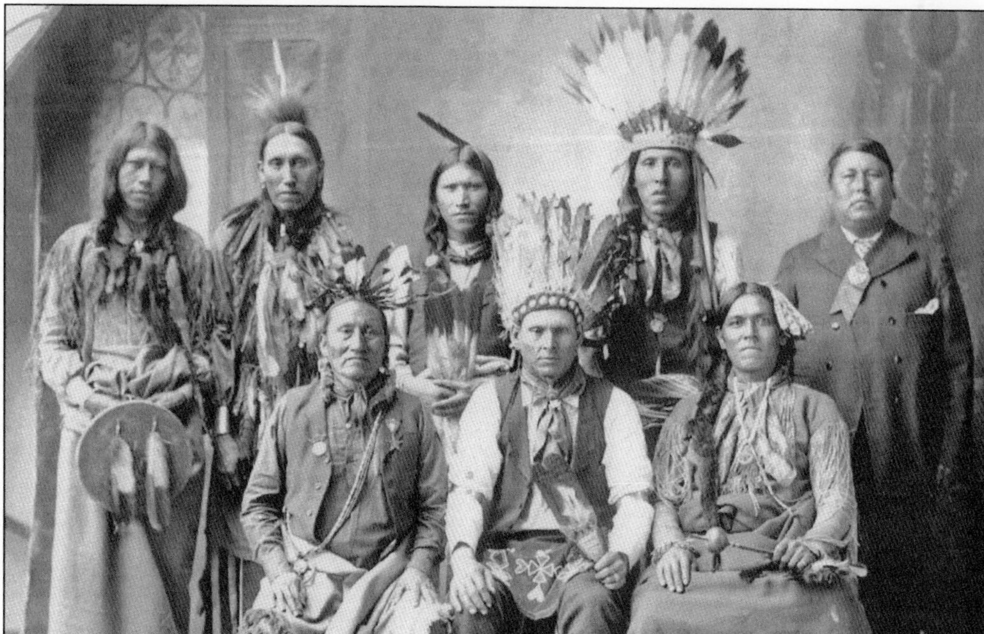

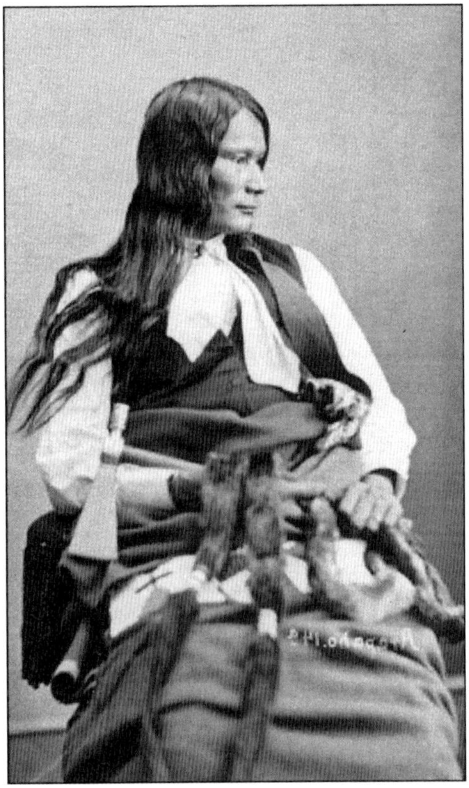

Chief Left Hand (Niwot). Left Hand (Niwot, or Nawat), photographed in Washington, D.C., in 1872 as part of a delegation of Arapaho and Cheyenne Indians, was chief of the Arapaho that lived and hunted in the South Platte valley. Left Hand Canyon and the community of Niwot west of Brighton are named after him. The bluffs opposite the mouth of Clear Creek on the South Platte (now the site of Adams County office buildings) were a favorite camping place. The confluence of Clear Creek and the Platte was the location of an annual rendezvous (trade meet) between the Native Americans and traders and trappers from New Mexico. Louis Vasquez chose the location for his first fur trading post along the Platte in 1834, and John C. Fremont encountered a large Arapaho village there during his explorations of the Rocky Mountain West in 1843. Left Hand was friendly with the early settlers and often visited and camped near the homesteads and communities along the South Platte until the Sand Creek Massacre set off the Indian Wars in 1864. (Both courtesy of the Smithsonian Institution.)

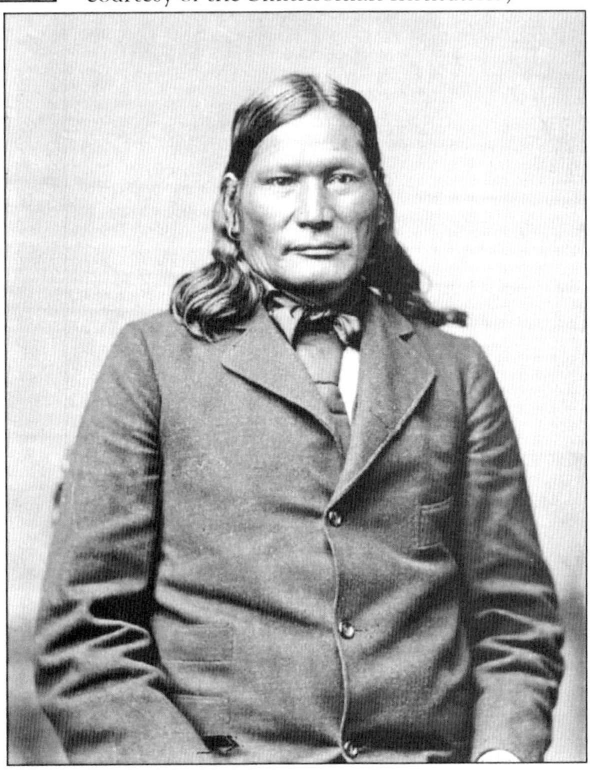

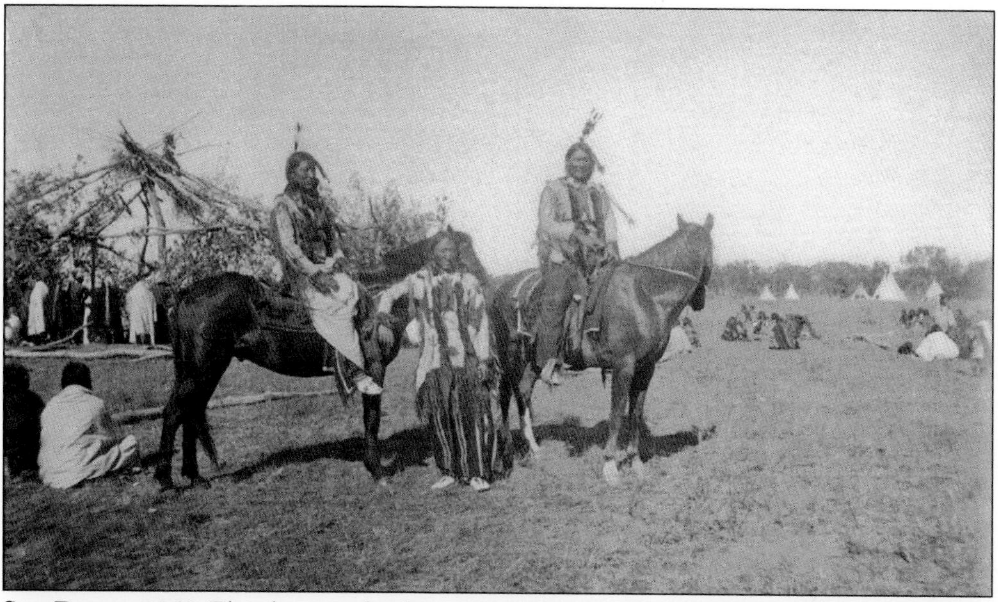

Sun Dance, 1869. The photograph of Arapaho Indians at the Sun Dance ceremony in 1869 is from glass negatives collected by the Bureau of American Ethnology. The men in the foreground were identified as, from left to right, Hail, Black Man (standing), and Fingernail. Note the Sun Dance pole and surrounding structure to the left. The Arapaho placed some emphasis on age grades mainly for ceremonial purposes. They were known for their religious ceremonies and elaborate artwork. Their annual Sun Dance was a major tribal event. Later the Arapaho adopted the Ghost Dance religion. The Northern Arapaho retain all of the sacred tribal stone articles. Since 1876, they have lived with their former enemies, the Shoshone, on the Wind River Reservation in Wyoming. (Courtesy of the Smithsonian Institution.)

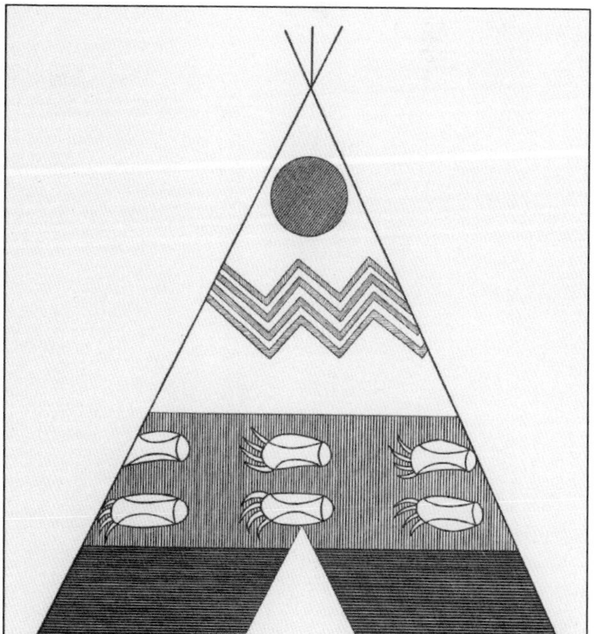

Arapaho Tepee Design. The tent of Agaha Wacuce, an Arapaho chief, was published in the 1882 *Annual Report of the U.S. Bureau of Ethnology*. The designs are characteristic of the Arapaho.

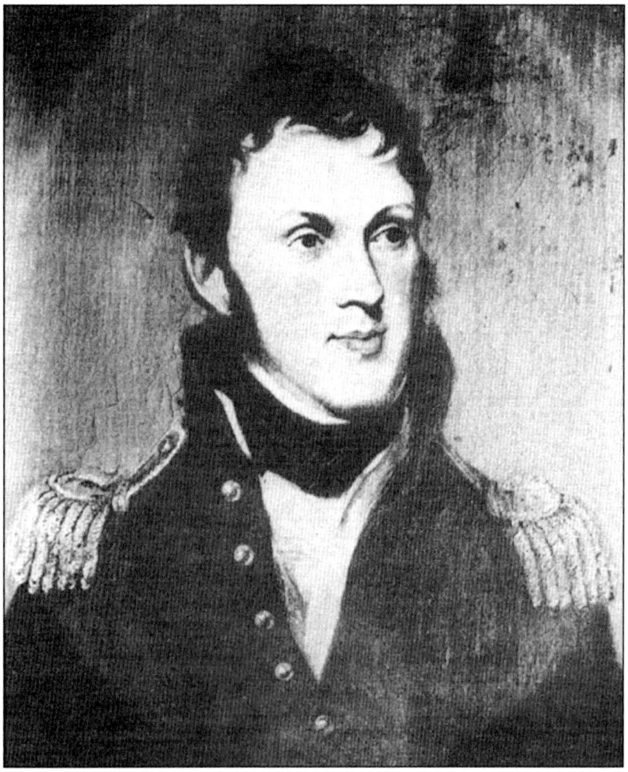

MAJ. STEPHEN H. LONG. A civil engineer and American explorer, Maj. Stephen Harriman Long (1784–1864) explored the upper Mississippi region in 1817. In 1819–1820, he explored the Rocky Mountains, including modern-day Adams County. His expedition left its mark on the area in such names as Long's Peak, Longmont, Bijou Creek, and "The Great American Desert." Explorers Stephen Long in 1819–1820 and Zebulon Pike in 1806–1807 (for whom Pikes Peak is named) encountered American trappers already in the Rocky Mountains trapping beaver and other animals. Beaver pelts were especially valuable, used for making hats. It was these wild mountain men who served as guides for Long and other later official explorers.

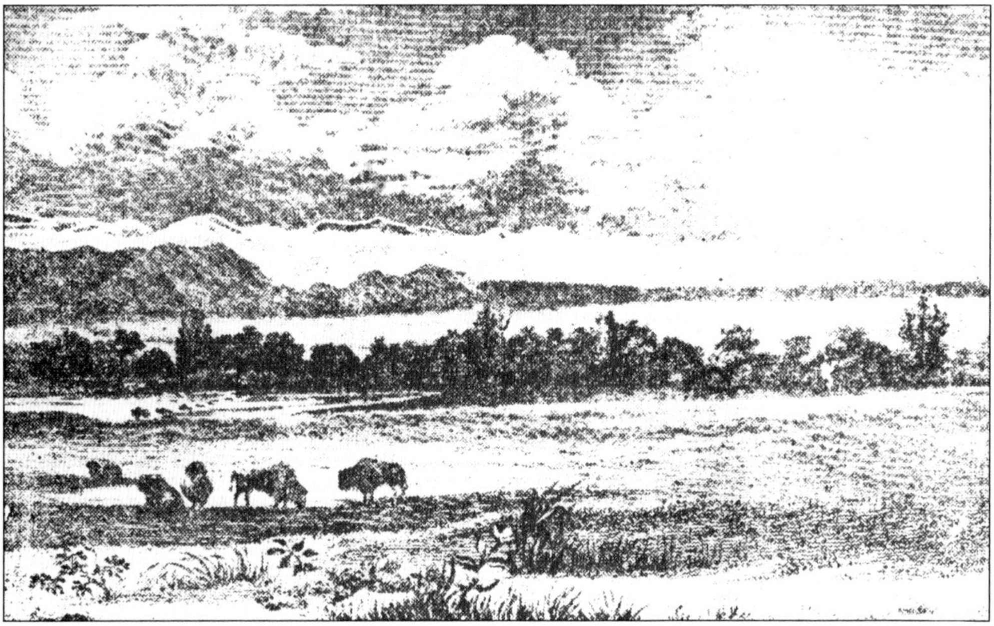

BUFFALO CROSSING THE SOUTH PLATTE. This drawing, "Buffalo Crossing the South Platte," may have been the first view of what is now Adams County that was ever published. The print by Samuel Seymour, the artist for the expedition, appeared in the official report of Maj. Stephen Long's expedition through present-day Adams County in 1820. The report, *Account of the Expedition from Pittsburgh to the Rocky Mountains*, by Edwin James, was published in 1823.

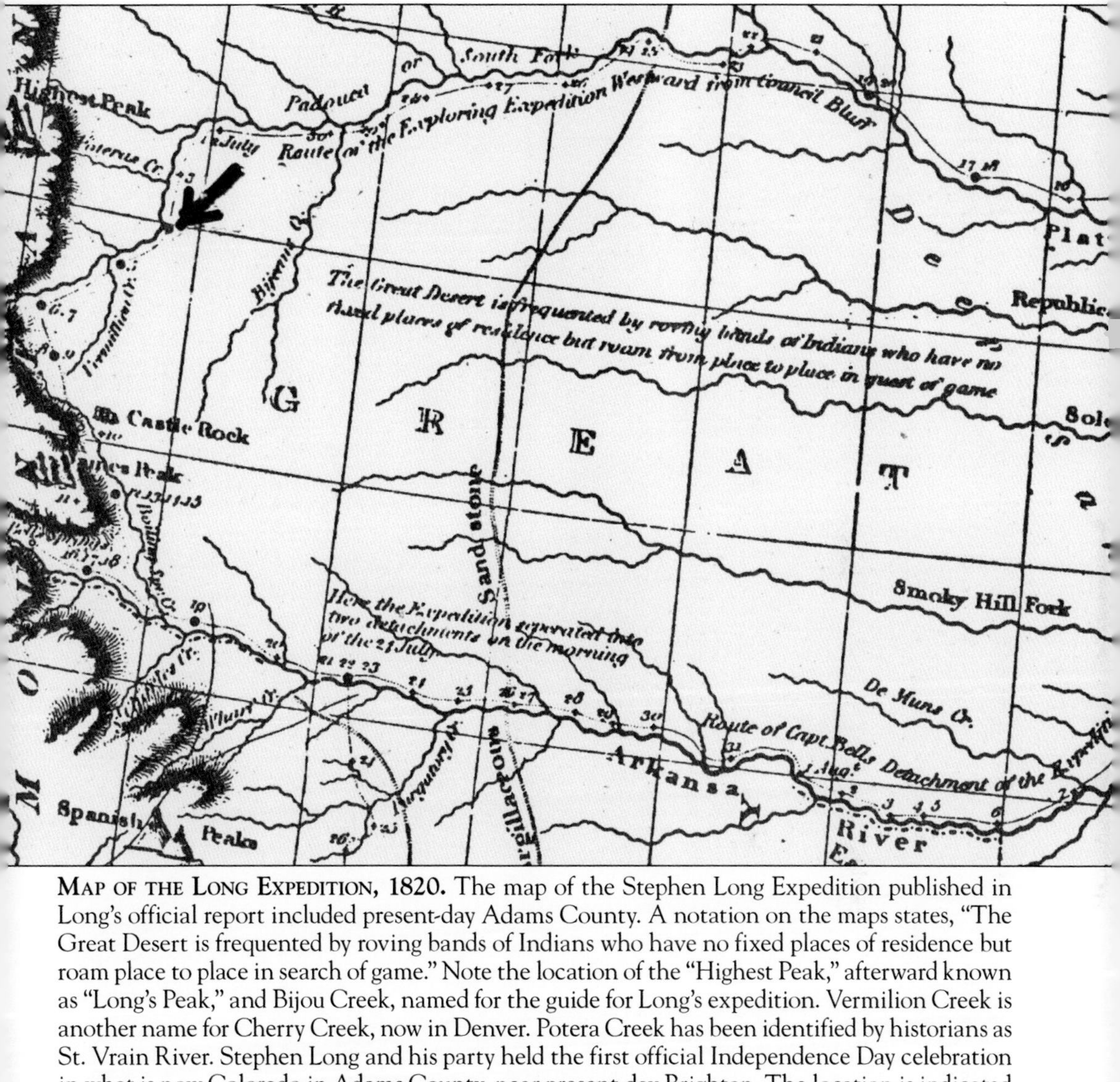

Map of the Long Expedition, 1820. The map of the Stephen Long Expedition published in Long's official report included present-day Adams County. A notation on the maps states, "The Great Desert is frequented by roving bands of Indians who have no fixed places of residence but roam place to place in search of game." Note the location of the "Highest Peak," afterward known as "Long's Peak," and Bijou Creek, named for the guide for Long's expedition. Vermilion Creek is another name for Cherry Creek, now in Denver. Potera Creek has been identified by historians as St. Vrain River. Stephen Long and his party held the first official Independence Day celebration in what is now Colorado in Adams County, near present-day Brighton. The location is indicated on the map with the number four where the 40th Parallel and the South Platte River intersect at the party's campsite on July 4, 1820. The 40th Parallel (now marked by Baseline Road) later became the boundary between Kansas and Nebraska Territories and now serves as the boundary between Adams and Weld Counties.

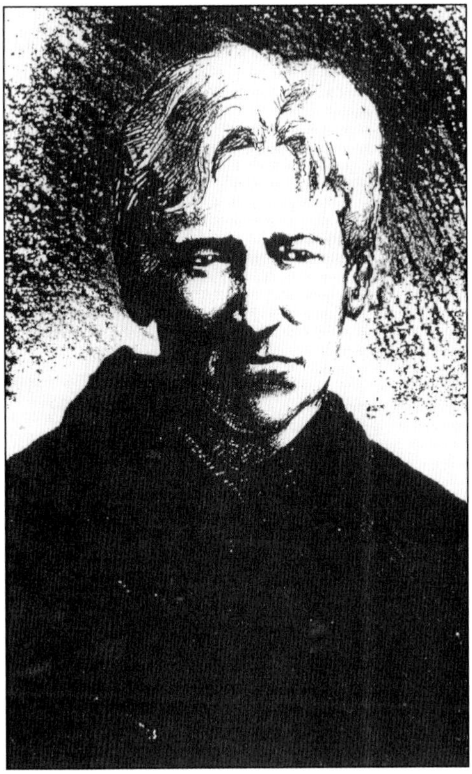

Lancaster P. Lupton. Four trading posts on the South Platte River (Fort Lupton, Fort Jackson, Fort Vasquez, and Fort St. Vrain) competed against one another and their larger rivals (Bent's Fort on the Arkansas River and Fort Laramie on the North Platte) for the fur trade along the Front Range during the 1830s. Lancaster Platt Lupton (1825–1885), a West Point graduate, came west as a first lieutenant in the U.S. Army. Impressed with the opportunities of the fur trade on the South Platte, after he resigned his commission in the Dragoons, he built a trading post near the present town of Fort Lupton, Colorado, in 1836–1837. The drawing of Lancaster P. Lupton as a young man was extrapolated from the photograph of him taken in California around 1884 when he was almost 77 years old. Lupton moved to California during the California Gold Rush after abandoning Fort Lupton in 1845. The drawing was created in the Forensic Science Lab of Prof. Michael Charney at Colorado State University in 1994. (Above courtesy of the South Platte Valley Historical Society; below courtesy of the Colorado Historical Society.)

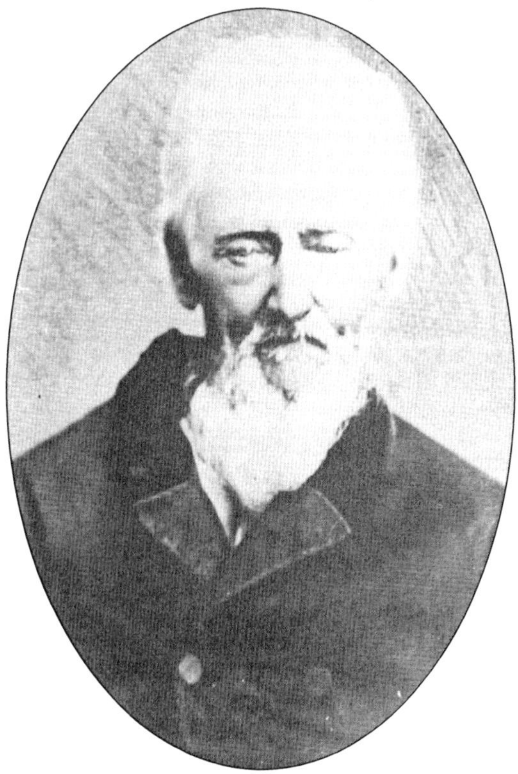

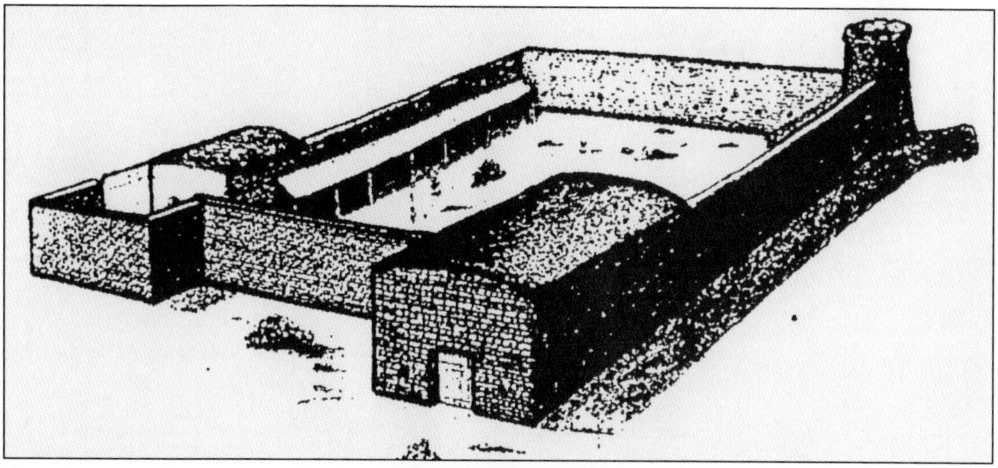

Fort Lupton. Fort Lupton, built in 1836–1837, was also known as Fort Lancaster, named after the first name of the proprietor, Lancaster P. Lupton. A portion of the fort, seen here in a sketch of Fort Lupton by an early settler in the area, still stands on the north edge of the town of Fort Lupton, just west of U.S. 85, where it was used as a barn. The fort or its ruins was visited by early travelers. It was later used as a stage station and a fortification during the Native American uprising of 1864–1865. Local residents are now restoring the fort as a historic site. (Courtesy of the South Platte Valley Historical Society.)

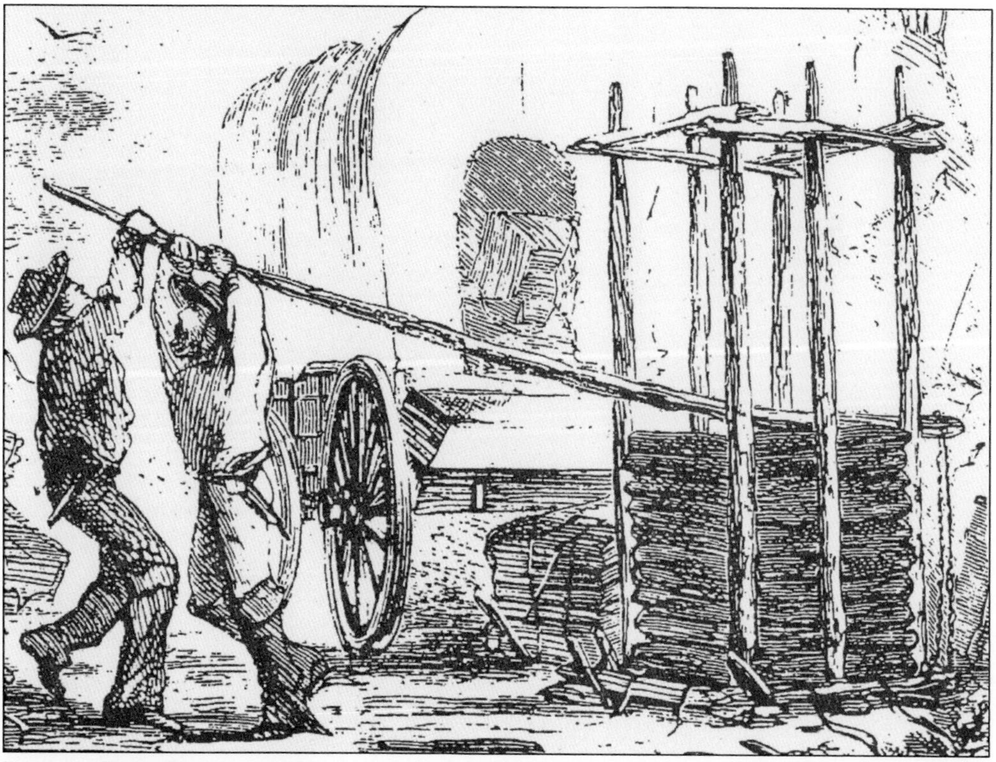

Buffalo Robe Press. An illustration of an essential piece of equipment at the trading post on the South Platte, the buffalo robe press, was published in *Harper's Weekly* in 1869. The press was used to bail furs into packs before transporting them to the markets in the East, usually consisting of 10 buffalo robes, 14 bear skins, 60 otter, 80 raccoon, 120 fox hides, or 600 muskrat skins.

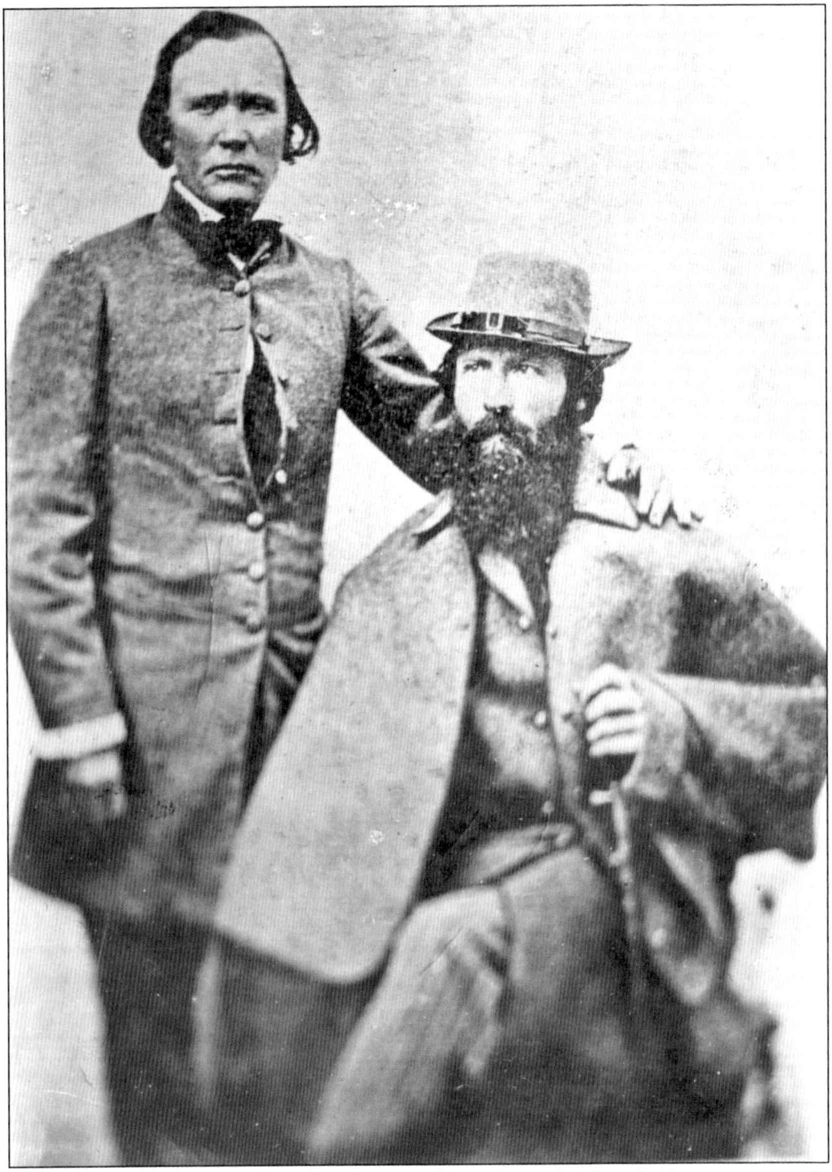

KIT CARSON AND JOHN C. FREMONT, 1849. The forts along the South Platte attracted not only Native Americans and trappers, but also explorers, immigrants, and early tourists, including Rufus B. Sage from 1841 to 1844, Gen. Stephen Watts Kearney in 1845, and Harvard historian Francis Parkman in 1846. They left many excellent descriptions of the four forts along the South Platte and the area just to the north that is today Adams County. During this period, the most famous visitor to present-day Adams County was John Charles Fremont (1813–1890), explorer, Civil War general, and the first presidential candidate for the Republican Party. Mountain man Kit Carson (1809–1868), on the left, and his friend John C. Fremont, "The Great Pathfinder," on the right, were photographed together in Taos in 1849. Both passed through what is now Adams County on Fremont's second expedition of exploration in 1843, following the South Platte. Fremont camped at the present site of Brighton, where he encountered a grizzly bear. Carson was also a frequent visitor to what is now Adams County. (Courtesy of the Denver Public Library Western History and Genealogy Department.)

Two

THE FIFTY-NINERS

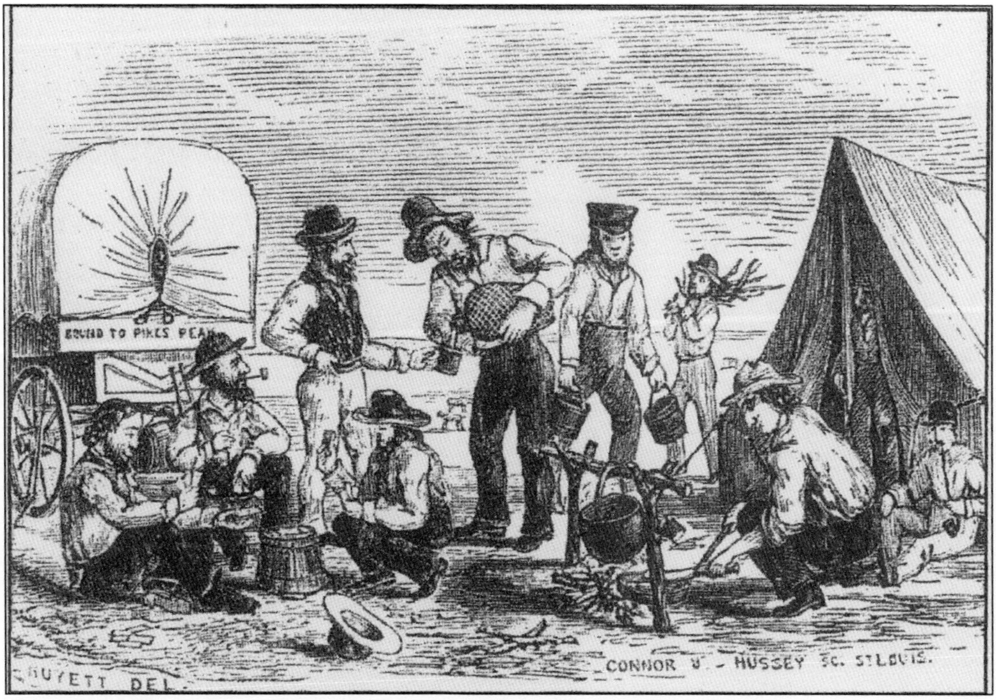

PIKES PEAK GOLD RUSH, 1859. The discovery of gold in 1858–1859 in what is now Colorado brought a flood of gold seekers. After trying their hand at mining, some who found farming more profitable settled on farms along the South Platte River, just south of present-day Brighton in 1859 and 1860, were Emil J. Reithmann, Fred Reithmann, William Blundell, Frank Aichelman, George C. Griffin, Andrew Hagus, and George W. Hazzard.

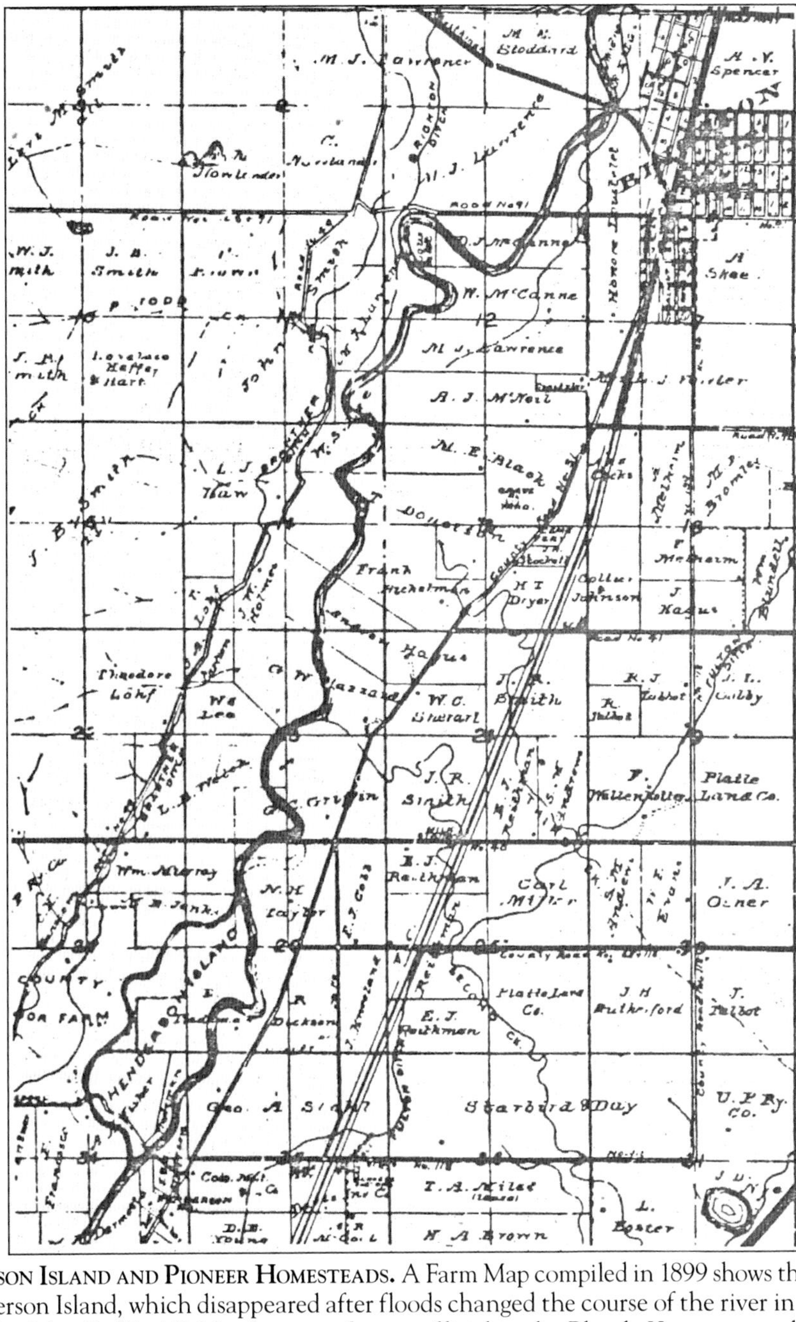

Henderson Island and Pioneer Homesteads. A Farm Map compiled in 1899 shows the location of Henderson Island, which disappeared after floods changed the course of the river in the 1940s and 1950s. John D. ("Jack") Henderson, a former official in the Bloody Kansas struggle to make Kansas a slave state, came to Denver to sell supplies to the miners in 1859. He bought the Sanders Ranch at Henderson Island and established the first major cattle ranch in the region. Despite being a pro-slavery man, he returned to Kansas to join the Union army at the beginning of the Civil War. The farms of George Hazzard, Andrew Hagus, Frank Aichelman, Thomas Donelson, and George Griffin, the early pioneers who settled just north of Henderson, can be identified by the boundaries that run perpendicular to the river since they were established before the area was officially surveyed. (Courtesy of the County Clerk of Adams County, Colorado.)

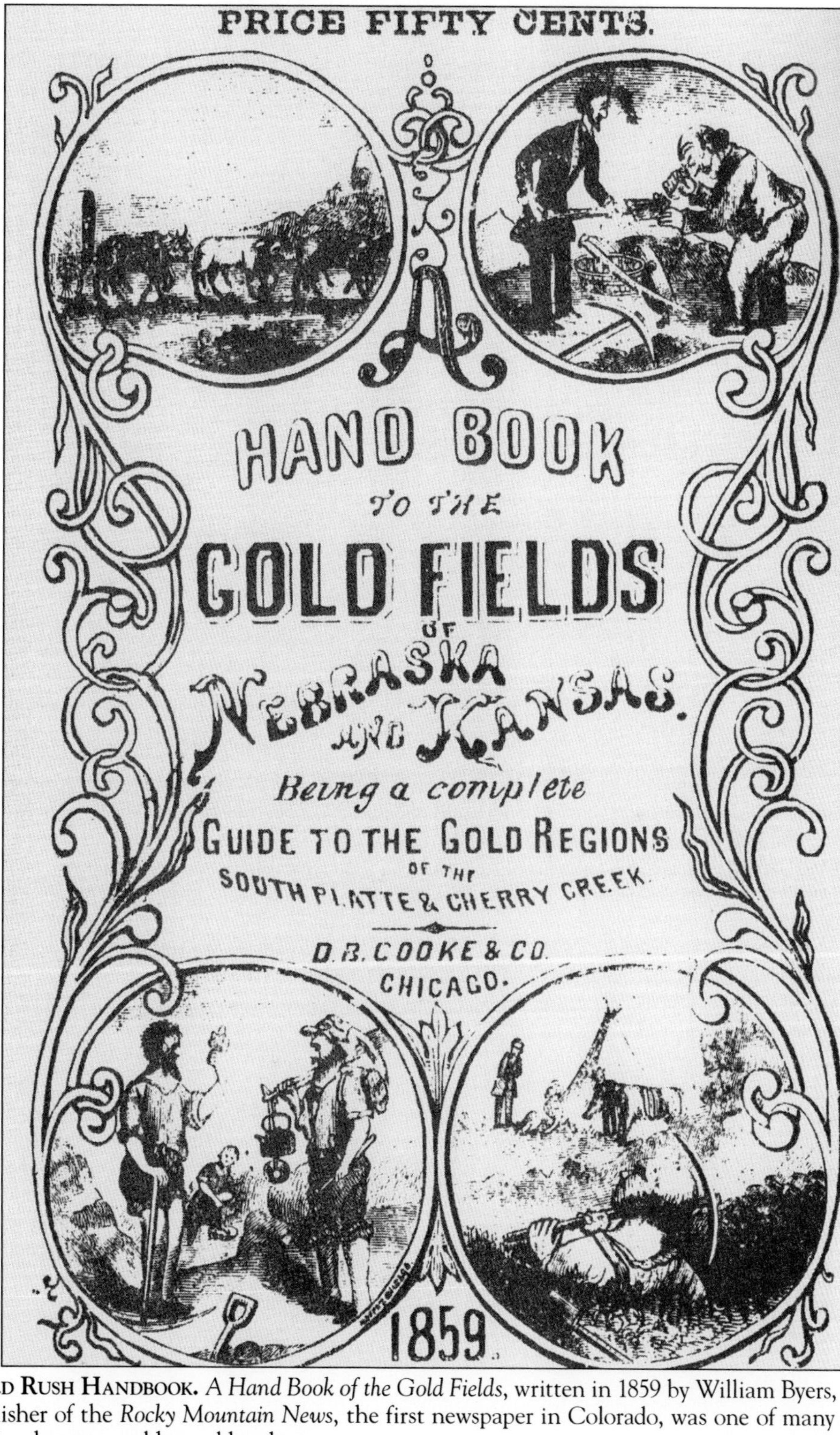

GOLD RUSH HANDBOOK. A *Hand Book of the Gold Fields*, written in 1859 by William Byers, later publisher of the *Rocky Mountain News*, the first newspaper in Colorado, was one of many such guides that were sold to gold seekers.

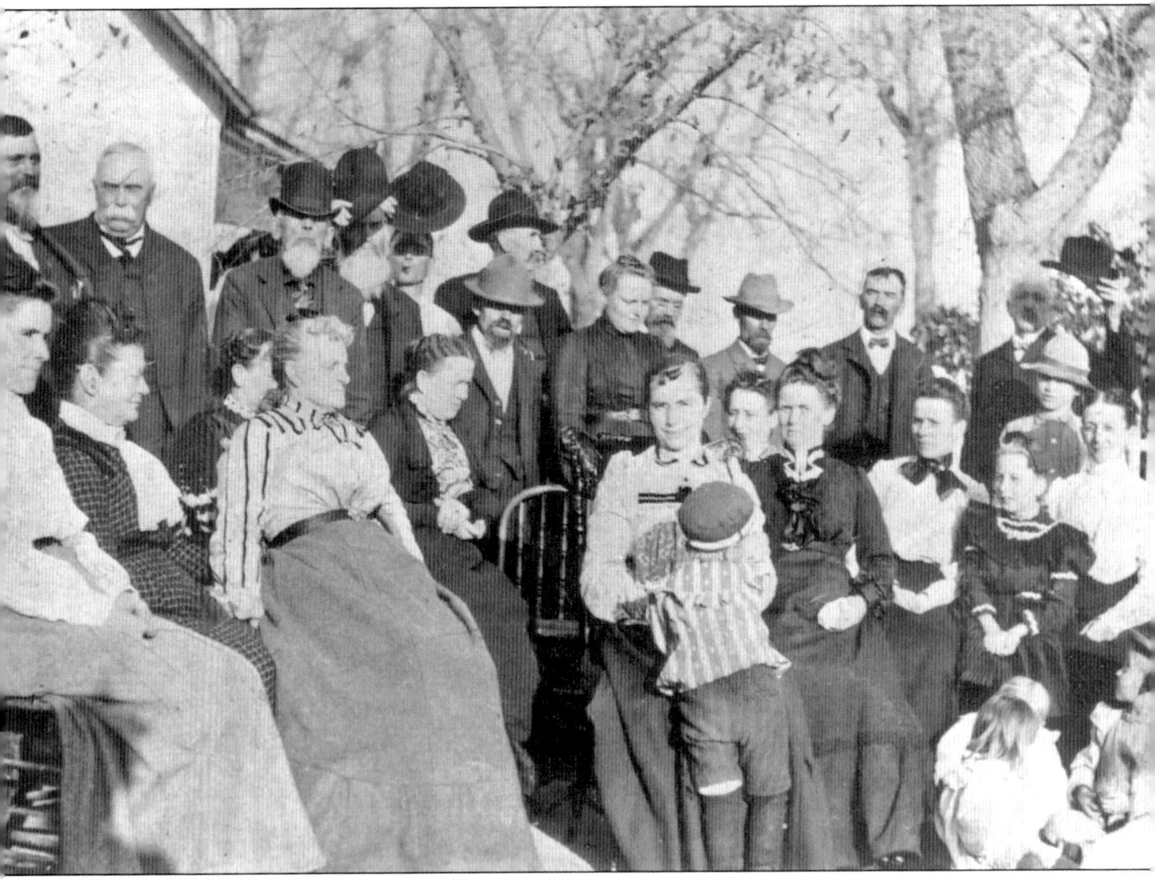

Platte Valley Pioneers, 1899. The Platte Valley pioneers who settled in the vicinity of Brighton, Colorado, in 1859 and 1860 and their families held their annual picnics at their various farms. This photograph was probably taken at their 40th anniversary reunion in 1899 that was held at Emil J. Reithmann's farm 3 miles south of Brighton. In the first row are, from left to right, Mrs. George (Barbara) Gaylor, sister of Mrs. Andrew (Magdalena) Hagus; the next two ladies and the one in back of her are unidentified, but the latter probably is Mrs. George C. (Lucelia) Griffin; Mrs. Frank (Mary) Aichelman; Mrs. Andrew (Magdalena) Hagus; "a naughty boy who would not face the camera," John Joseph (Jack) Hagus II, son of Andrew and Magdalena Hagus. Lady to the back, Mrs. Lewis (Josephine) Hagus; Mrs. George W. (Mary Blundell) Hazzard; next lady is probably Mrs. Fred (Margaret Morris) Reithmann; Lucille Marie Grams, granddaughter of the Emil J. Reithmann; unidentified boy in back of her; Mrs. Emil J. (Mary) Reithmann. Children in front unidentified. Back row, left to right: Nick Taylor; unidentified man; George W. Hazzard (came to Colorado in 1859); George C. Griffin (1860); Fred Andrew Hagus, son of Andrew Hagus; the next man probably Thomas Donelson (1859); Andrew Hagus (1859); standing in front of Donelson; Louise Ritter, daughter of Andrew Hagus; Frank Aichelman (1860); Lewis Hagus (1863), brother of Andrew Hagus; Fred Reithmann (1860) and brother, Emil J. Reithmann (1860). Not pictured, James Blundell (1859). Identification was supplied by Lucille Hagus Imherr, December 6, 1967. (Courtesy of the Adams County Historical Society.)

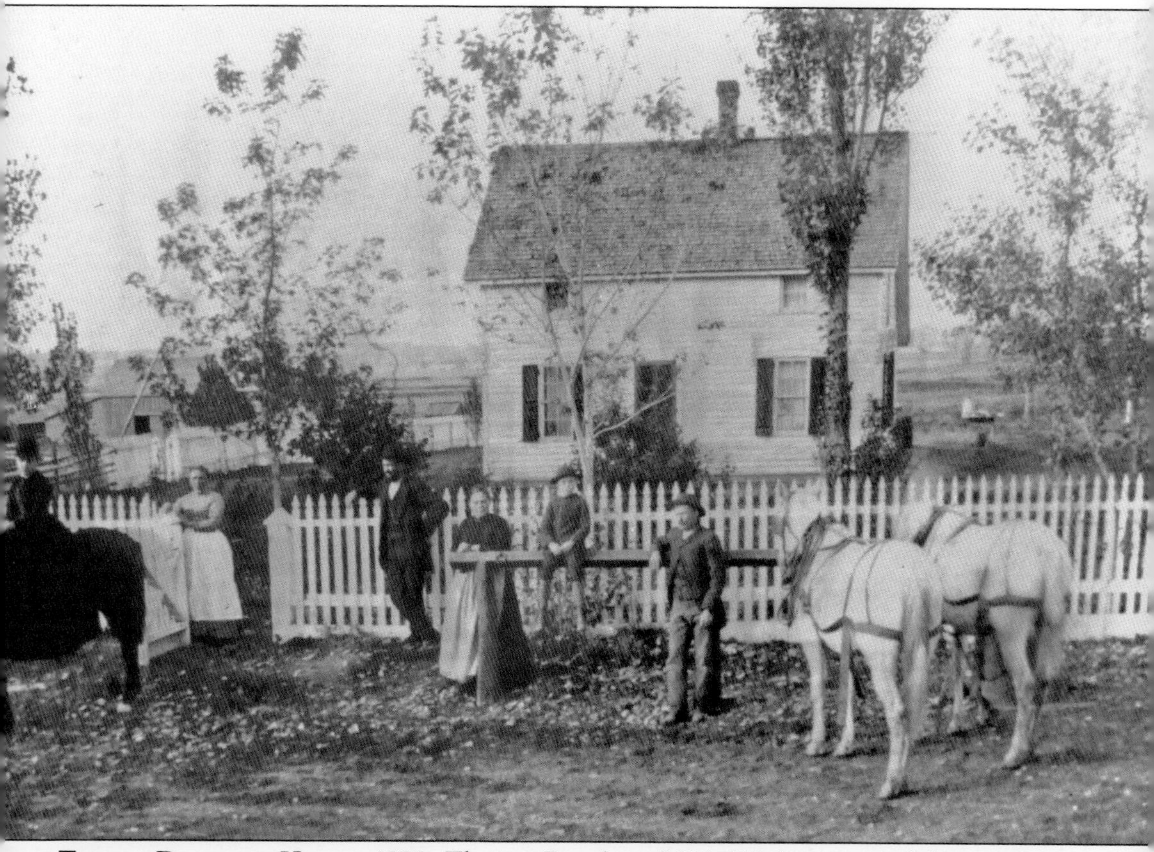

Thomas Donelson House, 1893. Thomas Donelson (1824–1904) was one of the original homesteaders along the South Platte River in 1859. Donelson returned to Wisconsin and brought his wife Laura and five children (Mary Maria, Eleanor, Thomas, John, and James) to Colorado in 1860. Donelson built the present house after a flood destroyed the family's log cabin the summer of 1864. Their home is reputed to have been the first frame house built north of Denver. It stood about a half-mile west of Brighton Road and 148th Avenue. In November 1997, the house was moved to the Fort Lupton Historic Park. James and Barbara White donated the house to the South Platte Valley Historical Society to avoid its demolition for a new housing project. Pictured in this 1893 photograph are Thomas Donelson leaning on the fence; his third wife, Mary Ann, standing at the gate; Bea Donelson on John's old horse Nig; Mary E. Donelson at the hitching rail; Thomas ("Tommy") Donelson sitting on the hitching rail; and John Donelson, next to the old farm team, Dick and Salem. (Courtesy of the Adams County Historical Society.)

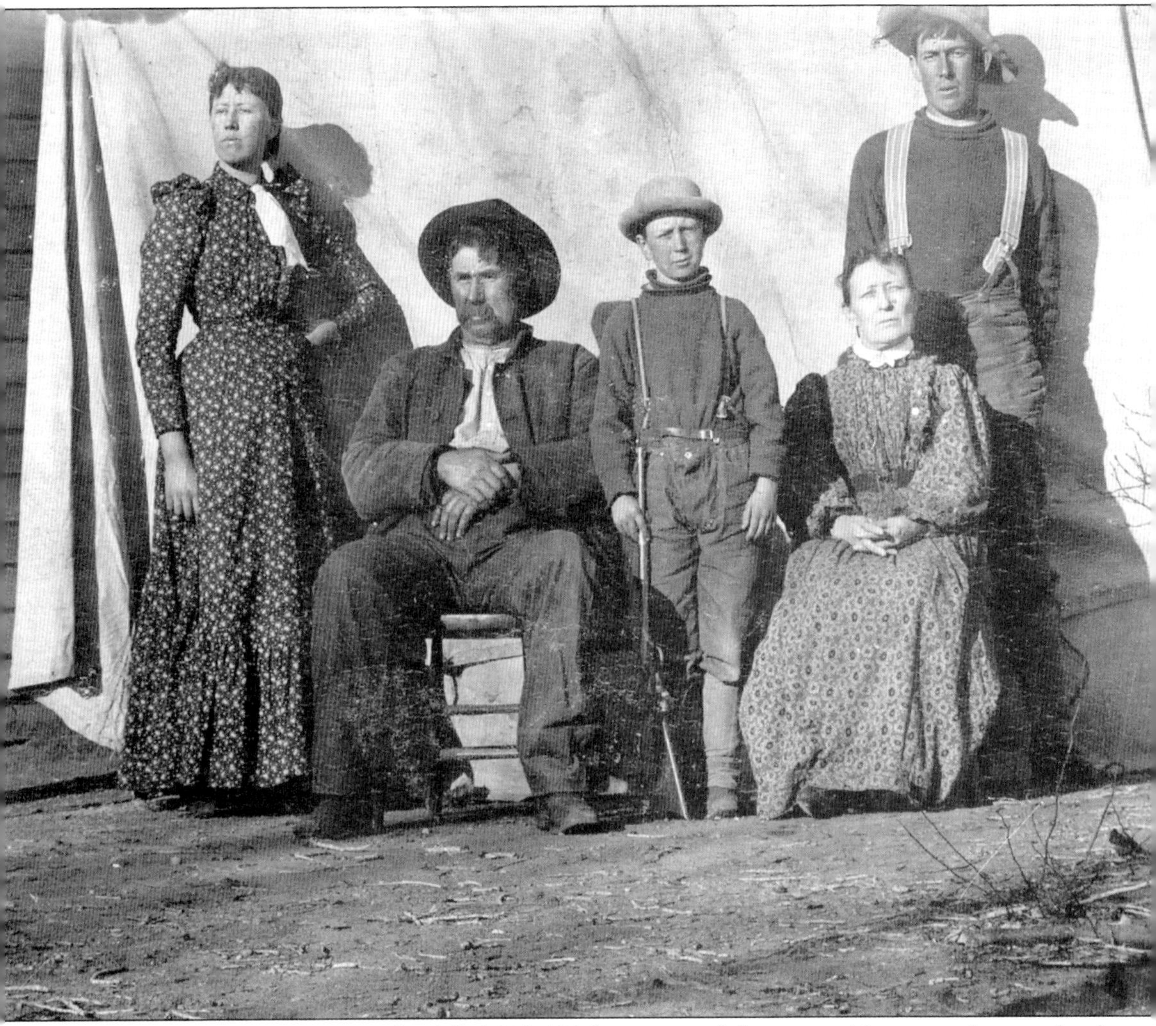

BLUNDELL FAMILY. James Blundell (1815–1884) was one of the original homesteaders south of Brighton in 1859. A year later, his son, William Blundell, moved to Colorado with the family. They raised crops and harvested sweet grass hay to sell in Denver and the mining camps in the mountains. William worked for the Overland Stage Company, hunting game for the nearby stage station. He farmed with his father and father-in-law, Thomas Donelson, before homesteading his own farm, one-half mile south of Bromley Lane on Chambers Road. He helped dig the Fulton Ditch and served as a justice of the peace. The photograph of the William Blundell family includes, from left to right, Carrie Lulubell (William and Mary Blundell's daughter, married three times and died in 1947), William Blundell (1843–1911), his son William Arthur (1889–1984), Blundell's wife, Mary Maria (née Donelson), and Hugh Bertram (who lived on the home farm and died of the flu in 1984). Not present for this photograph were Blundell's daughter Mary Laura (who married John Albert Carlson and died in 1904), and son Ira Wilfred (1876–1948). (Courtesy of the Adams County Historical Society.)

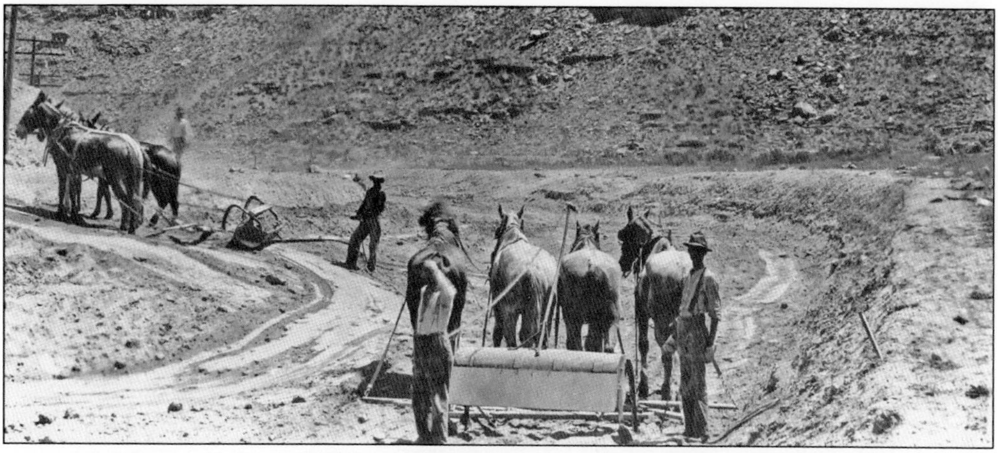

Irrigation Ditches. To provide water for their crops, the settlers on the bottomlands along the South Platte turned to irrigation. Eight farmers joined Samuel Brantner in 1860 to build the Brantner Ditch, the first in the area. The Fulton Ditch Company was organized on February 16, 1865. The Fulton Ditch became one of the major irrigation canals in the area. The ditches were constructed using horse-drawn scoops (above), called fresnos. (Courtesy of the Library of Congress.)

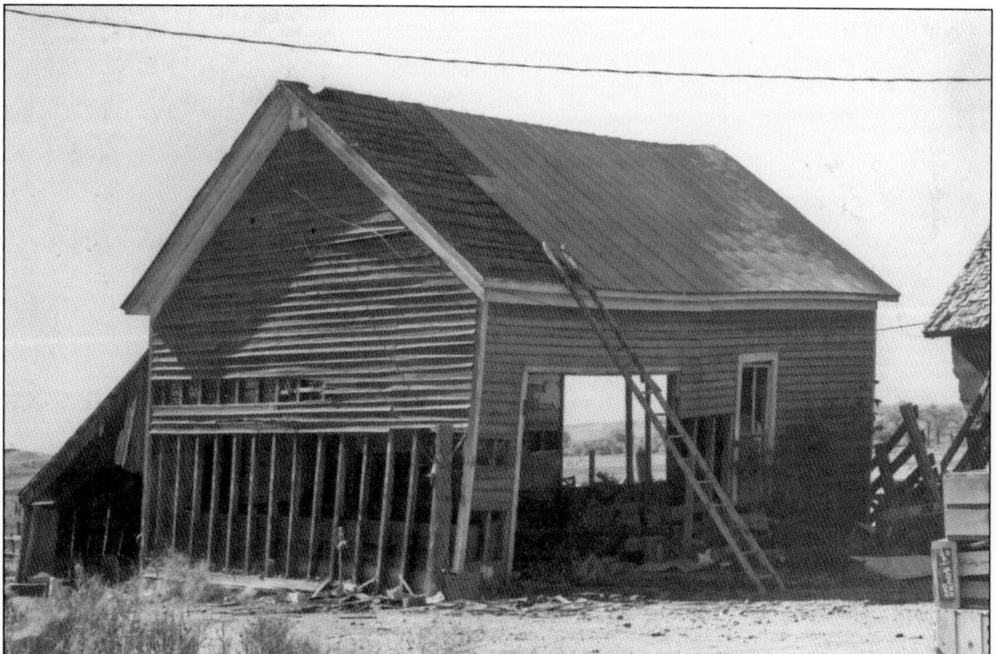

Aichelman School. The pioneer families soon set out to reproduce the culture they left back East. This building, on the Frank Aichelman farm south of Brighton, was built in 1872. Mary Ross was the first teacher. This photograph was taken in October 1977, shortly before the building was demolished. In 1891, Arapahoe County (later Adams County) School District No. 10 was organized and a brick school building was constructed on a new site.

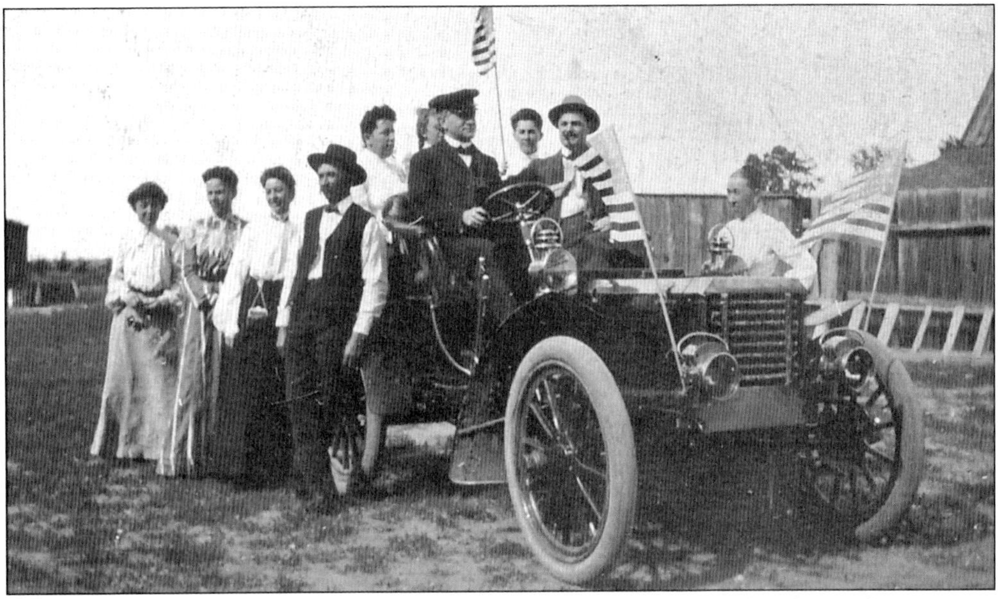

Reithmann Fourth of July Reunion. The Reithmann family gathered each year for a reunion on the Fourth of July. They were memorialized along with the other fifty-niners by the Pioneer Monument, erected by the Fort Vasquez Chapter of the Daughters of the American Revolution at the intersection of South Main Street and South First Avenue in Brighton. (Courtesy of the Brighton Historical Preservation Commission.)

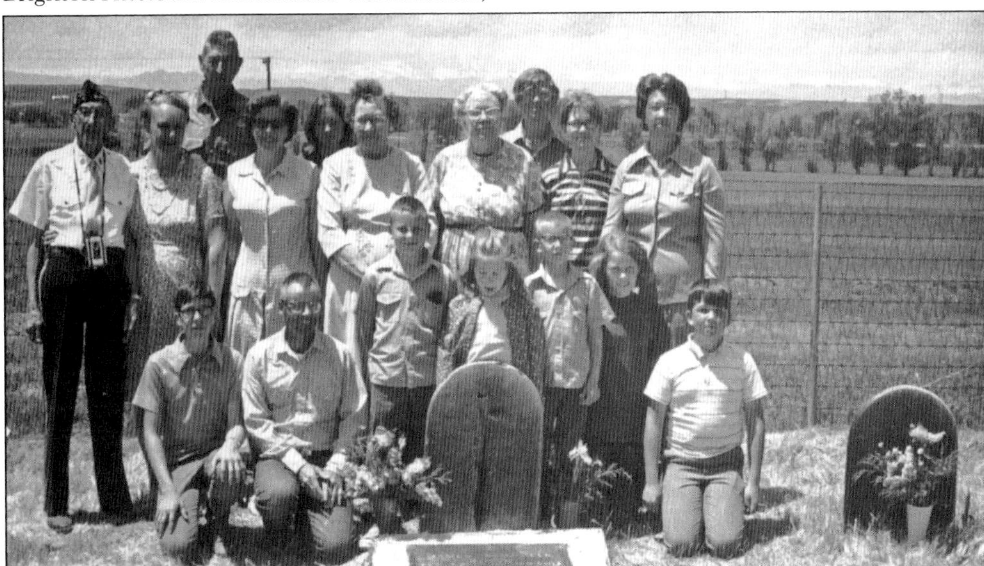

Descendants of James Blundell. The descendants of James Blundell (1815–1884) gathered on June 3, 1971, at the Pioneer Cemetery south of Brighton for the dedication of his military grave marker as a veteran of the Black Hawk War in 1832. From left to right are (first row) Bradley Haake, James Carlson, Mike Carlson, Sarah McCoy, Mark Haake, and Audi Haake; (second row) William Blundell, Phyllis Blundell, Mazel Haake, Mabel Kavick, Margaret Kramer, Rosanna McCoy, and Hattie McCoy; (third row) Albert Carlson, Mary McCoy, and Moody McCoy. (Courtesy of the Adams County Historical Society.)

Three

STAGECOACHES, RAILROADS, AND CATTLE

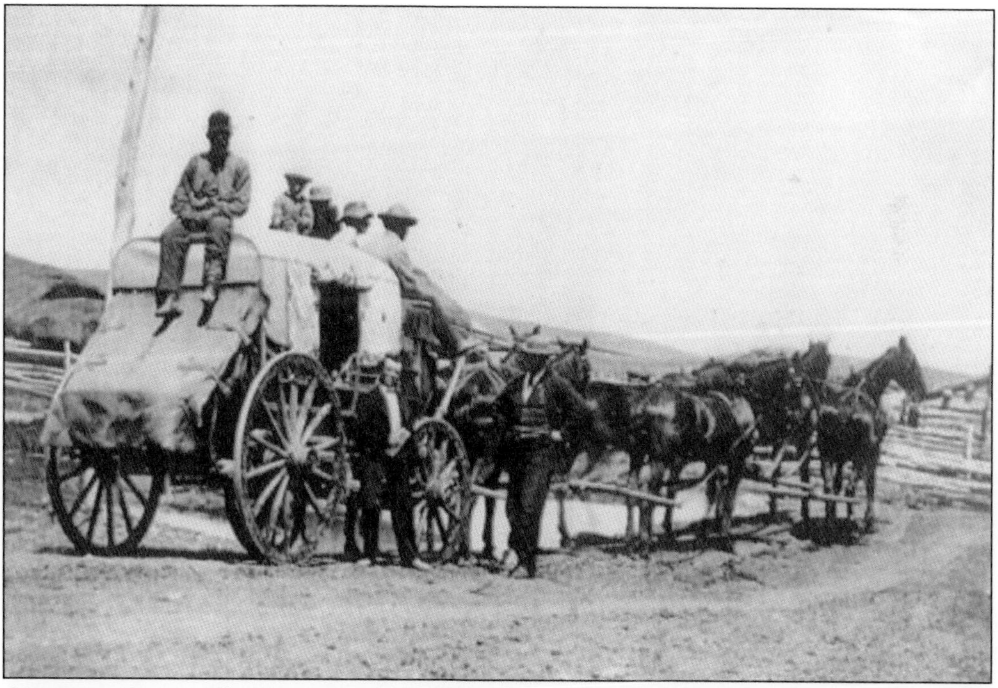

OVERLAND STAGE. The Leavenworth and Pikes Peak Express Company was organized in 1858 on the strength of the first rumors of the Pikes Peak gold strike. Bankrupt in less than a year, it was replaced in 1859 by the Central Overland, California, and Pikes Peak Express Company with triweekly service to Denver through present-day Brighton. Ben Holladay purchased the stage line in 1862. He sold out to Wells Fargo in 1866. Within four years, the stage lines were replaced by railroads. (Courtesy of the Library of Congress.)

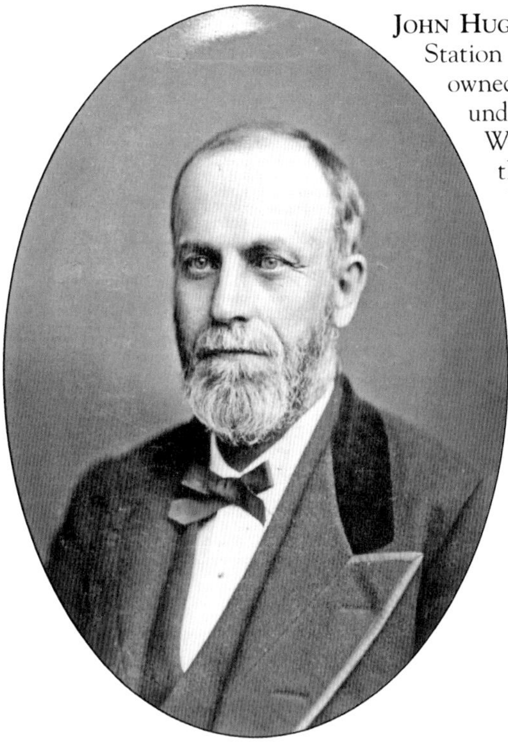

John Hughes. Some old-timers claimed that Hughes Station was named after John Hughes. John Hughes owned the stage line between Denver and Cheyenne under the name of John Hughes and Company after Wells Fargo sold the line in 1869. As a result, the stage stop at Pierson Ranch was known locally as Hughes Station. (Courtesy of the Denver Public Library Western History and Genealogy Department.)

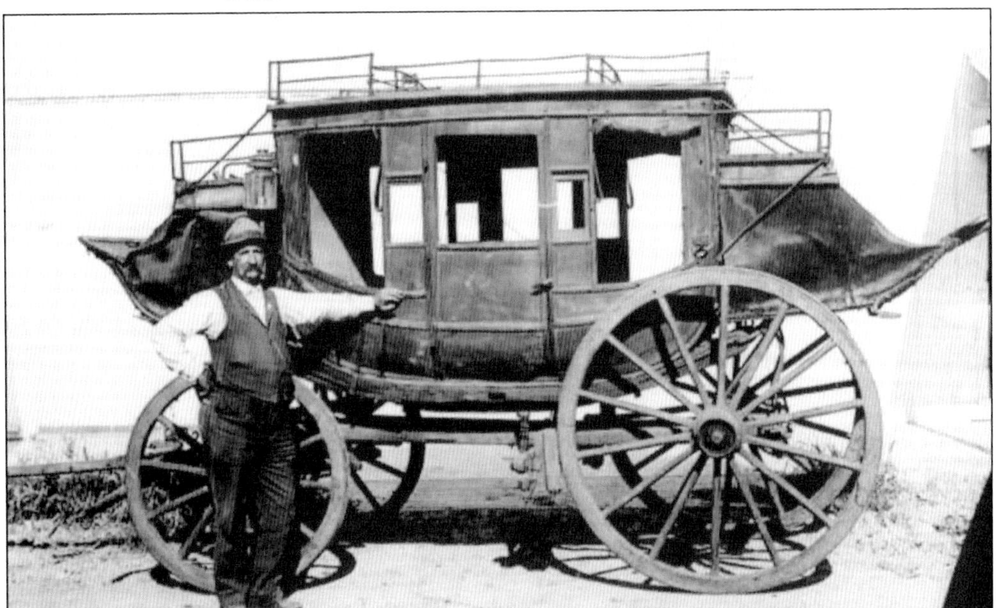

Last Overland Stage, 1870. On, June 10, 1870, the last stage arrived in Denver from Hughes (present-day Brighton). The stage line had gradually retreated with the advance of the railroad. John Hughes and Company stages abandoned their stage stations as the railhead of the Denver Pacific moved southward from Cheyenne. Alexander Majors, founder of the Overland Stage Company, later credited this last trip of the stage between Hughes (Brighton) and Denver as the last run of the once great Overland Stage. (Courtesy of the Colorado Historical Society.)

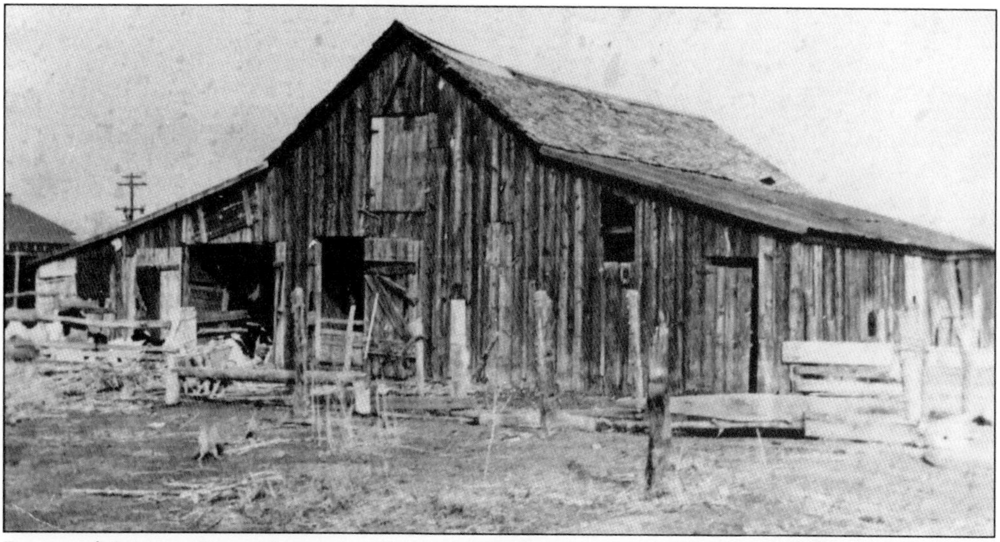

Pierson/Hughes Stage Station. Margaret Long in her book *The Smoky Hill Trail* identified the barn on this postcard as the Pierson Ranch Stage Station, also known as the Hughes Station (after the popular owner of the stage line, John Hughes). She described it as an unpainted wooden building with a sloping roof just west of Old Brighton Road, exactly 3.7 miles south of Pioneer Monument at the corner of South Main and South First Streets in Brighton. The area is now a gravel pit and the barn has since disappeared. The stage station was the last major stage stop north of Denver. The stage stations were spaced approximately 20 miles apart. The teams of horses were often exchanged at these stations. Some minor stage stops were often placed between them, such as the Sand Creek or Nine Mile House in present-day Commerce City.

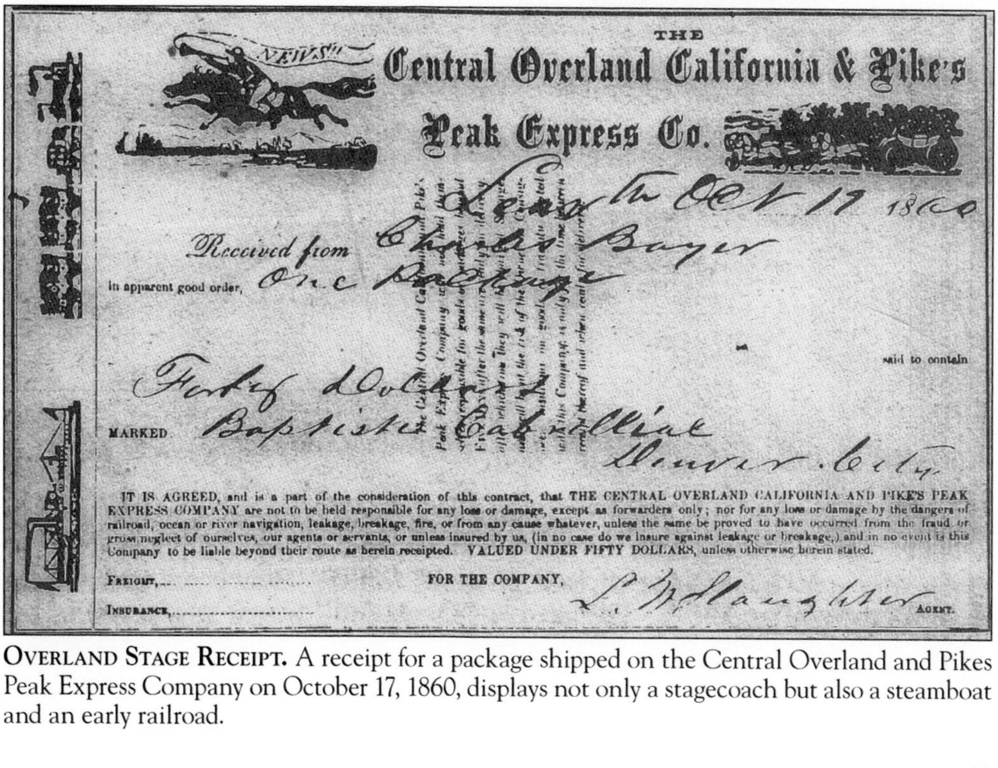

NEWS!!!

THE Central Overland California & Pike's Peak Express Co.

Leavenworth Oct 17 1860

Received from Charles Bayer

in apparent good order, One package

said to contain

Forty dollars

MARKED Baptiste Cabrilline

Denver City

IT IS AGREED, and is a part of the consideration of this contract, that THE CENTRAL OVERLAND CALIFORNIA AND PIKE'S PEAK EXPRESS COMPANY are not to be held responsible for any loss or damage, except as forwarders only; nor for any loss or damage by the dangers of railroad, ocean or river navigation, leakage, breakage, fire, or from any cause whatever, unless the same be proved to have occurred from the fraud or gross neglect of ourselves, our agents or servants, or unless insured by us, (in no case do we insure against leakage or breakage,) and in no event is this Company to be liable beyond their route as herein receipted. VALUED UNDER FIFTY DOLLARS, unless otherwise herein stated.

FREIGHT,..........

FOR THE COMPANY, L. W. Slaughter AGENT.

INSURANCE,..........

Overland Stage Receipt. A receipt for a package shipped on the Central Overland and Pikes Peak Express Company on October 17, 1860, displays not only a stagecoach but also a steamboat and an early railroad.

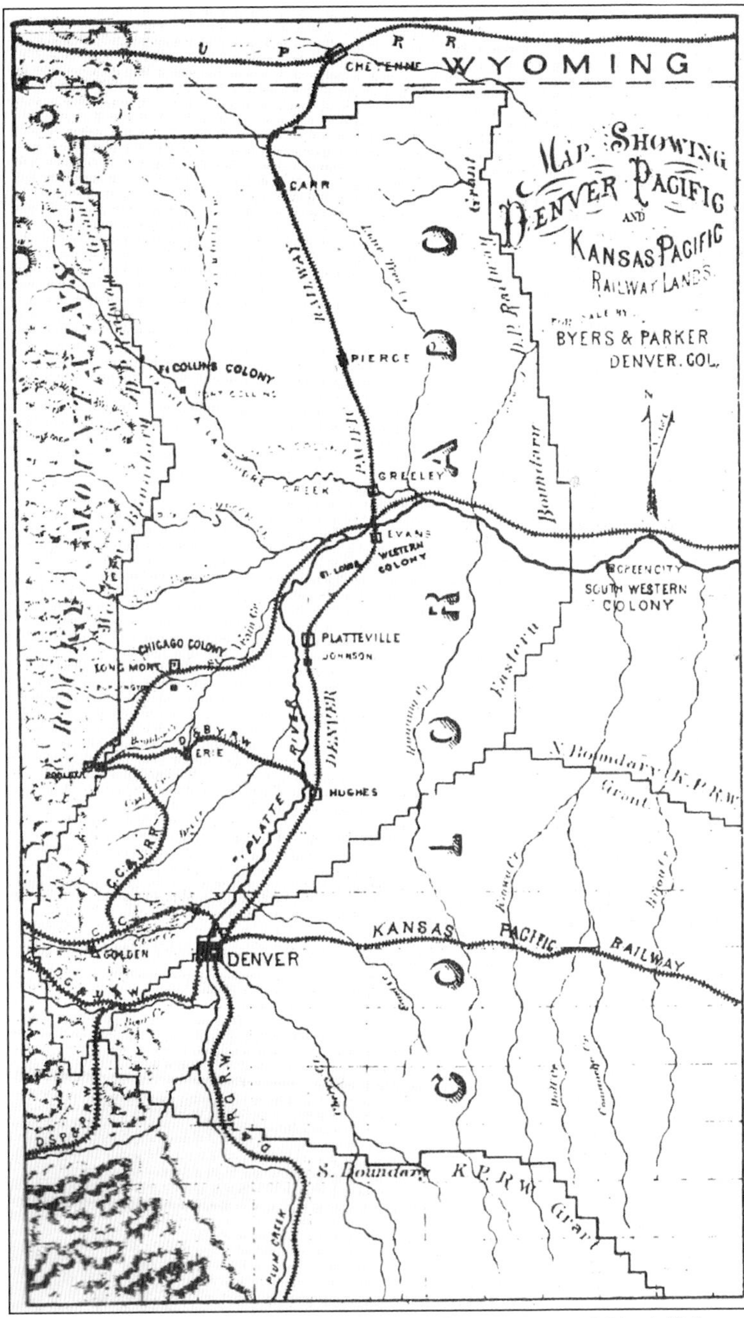

Denver Pacific and Denver and Boulder Valley Railroads, 1870. A "Map of the Denver Pacific and Kansas Pacific Railway Lands," published in Denver by Byers and Parker in 1870, shows the location of Hughes (renamed Brighton in 1879), at the junction of the Denver Pacific Railway and the D&BVRW (Denver and Boulder Valley Railway). Note the other Denver Pacific railroad stations: Johnson (near Platteville), Evans, Pierce, and Carr, all named for presidents of the Denver Pacific. The Chicago Colony (Longmont), Fort Collins Colony, Platteville, Greeley, and Western Colony (Evans) were all colonization efforts to create new communities along the South Platte and its tributaries.

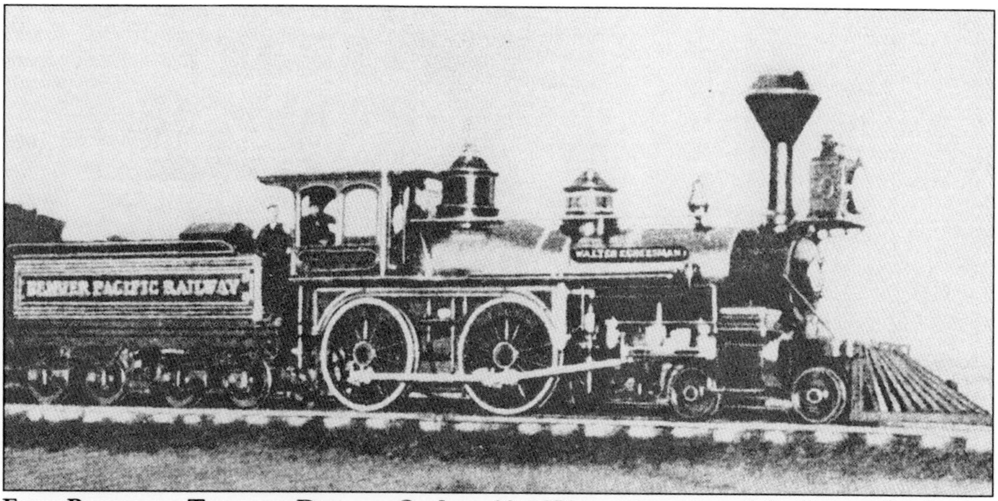

First Passenger Train to Denver. On June 22, 1870, construction of the Denver Pacific was completed into Denver. Engine No. 124, *The Walter S. Cheeseman*, pulled the first passenger train to reach Denver on June 22, 1870. The engine was one of the first four locomotives purchased by the Denver Pacific. A special train, drawn by the bedecked locomotive *The D. H. Moffat* (named after another principal backer of the Denver Pacific, who would later become famous for construction of the Moffat Tunnel), brought 200 Freemasons and other officials from Cheyenne to Hughes for the occasion. W. S. Cheeseman, David Moffat, and Gov. John Evans had the contract to build the railroad. (Courtesy of the Denver Public Library Western History and Genealogy Department.)

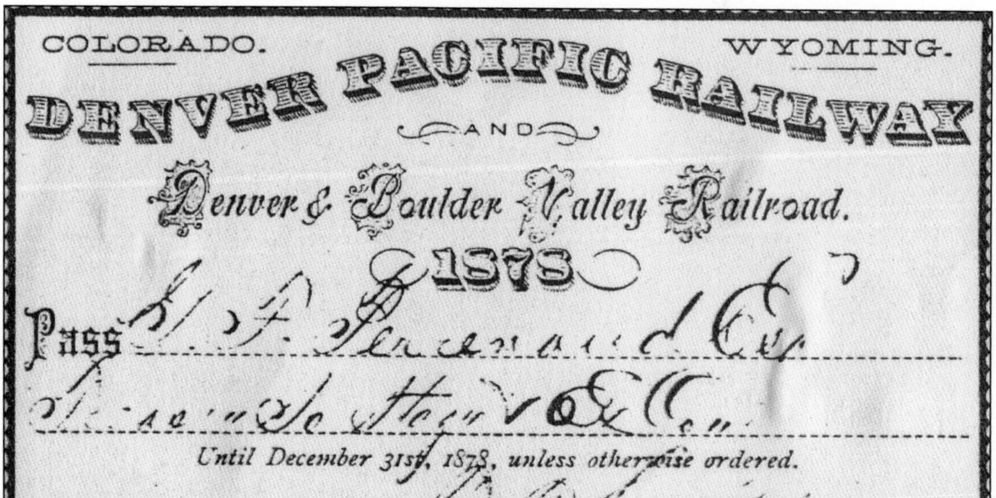
COLORADO. WYOMING.

DENVER PACIFIC RAILWAY

AND

Denver & Boulder Valley Railroad.

1878

Pass

Until December 31st, 1878, unless otherwise ordered.

No.

General Superintendent.

Denver and Boulder Valley Railroad. Railroad passes, like this 1878 pass for the Denver Pacific Railway and the Denver and Boulder Valley Railroad, were used to promote the railroads. Hughes (now Brighton) was established at the junction of the two railways.

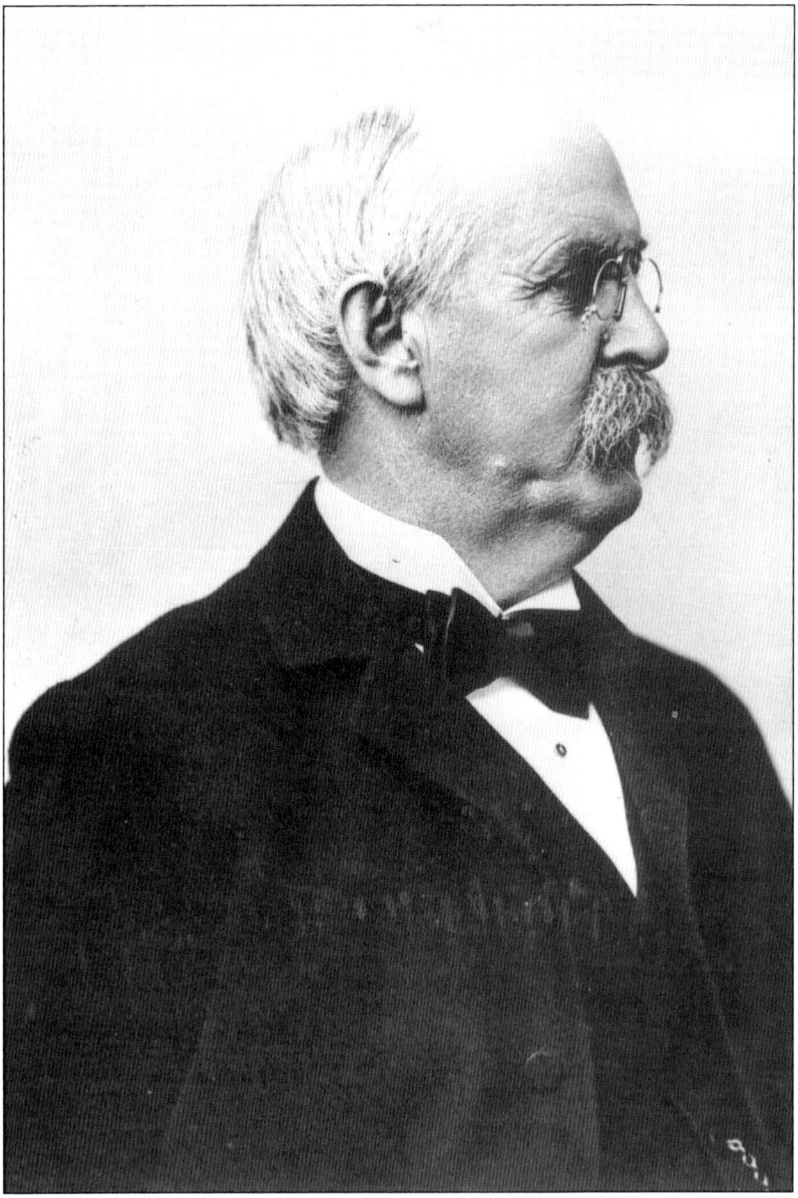

Bela Metcalf Hughes (1817–1902). Bela Metcalf Hughes was born in Nicholas County, Kentucky, in 1817, a nephew of Thomas Metcalfe (1780–1855), U.S. senator, representative, and 10th governor of that state. He was admitted to the bar in Missouri, where he practiced for years in St. Joseph, Missouri, and later in Atchison, Kansas. Since he served as an officer in the Missouri State Militia, he was often referred to as General Hughes. With his cousin, Benjamin ("Ben") Holliday, and others, he started the Overland Stage Line between Atchison, Denver, and Salt Lake and served as the president and attorney of the stage line for some years. In 1864, he came to Denver, where he continued this law practice. He was one of the most active promoters of the Denver Pacific Railroad between Denver and Cheyenne and was the first president of the company. The first railroad station north of Denver (at present-day Brighton) was named Hughes after him. A Democrat, he was a member of the first state senate of Colorado. He died in 1902. (Courtesy of the Denver Public Library Western History and Genealogy Department.)

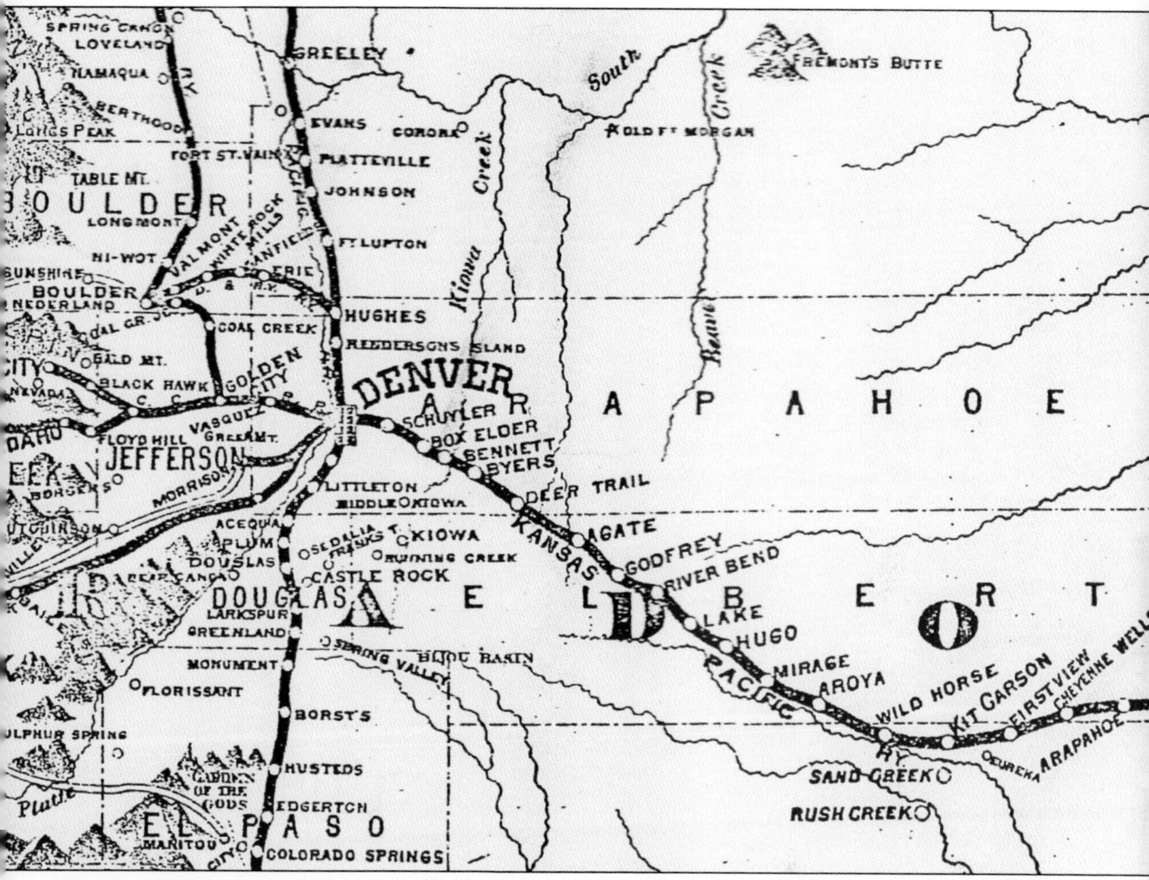

Hughes Station. Hughes, also called Hughes Station or Hughes Junction, was named for Bela Metcalf Hughes (1817–1902), the first president of the Denver Pacific, who had formerly been associated with the Overland Stage Company. The name first appeared on the railroad's map in June 1868 but remained only on paper until the railroad reached there two years later, in June 1870. On June 9, 1870, the six-horse Concord stagecoaches of John Hughes and Company began to transfer freight and passengers to and from Denver from the railhead at Hughes. At the time, Hughes was described as being composed of only a small depot, a section house, a windmill, and a water tank, with herds of cattle and horses scattered over the dry, open prairie.

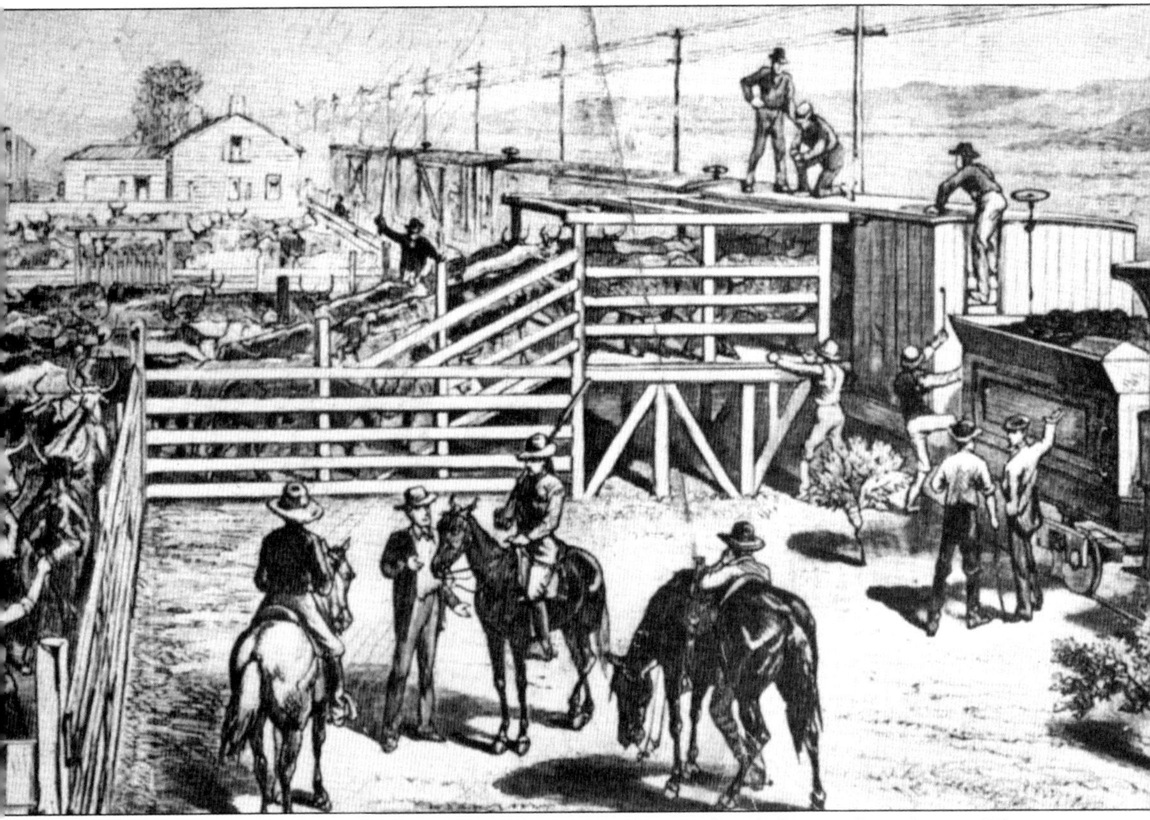

LOADING CATTLE. The completion of the railroads stimulated the cattle industry. The region already had thriving ranches on the open range. Col. John D. ("Jack") Henderson established one of the first major ranching operations just south of present-day Brighton in 1859. Cattle loading is seen in *Frank Leslie's Illustrated Newspaper* in 1877. About that time, the majority of Brighton-area residents were described as being engaged in raising cattle. A similar cattle corral existed north of Long's Peak Street in Brighton.

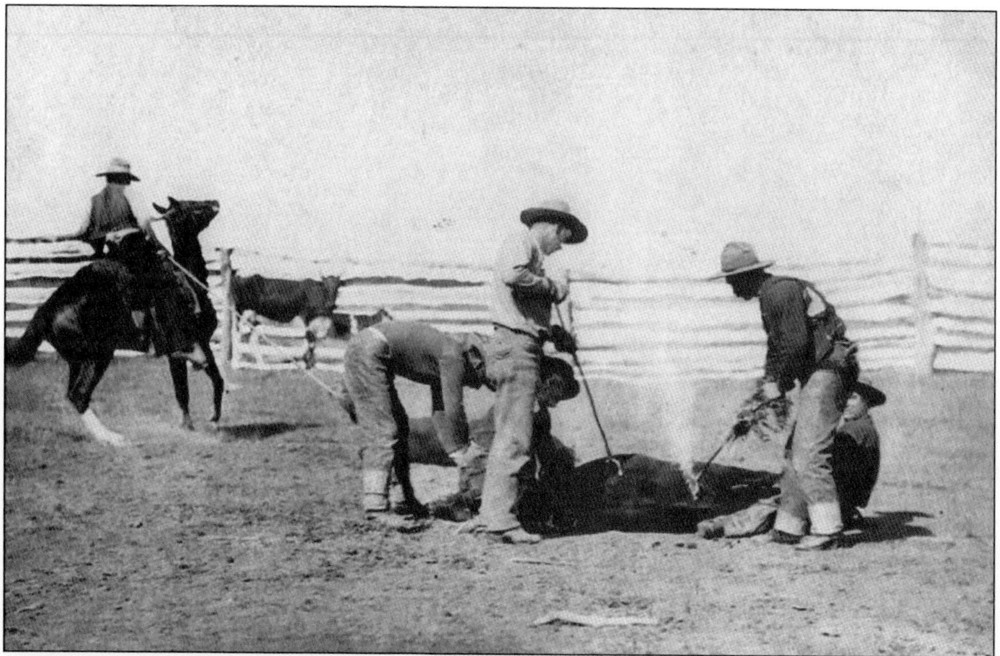

ROUNDUPS. Ranching was a year-round job. In the spring, first came the hunt for horses. Cow ponies running wild during the winter had to be re-broken for the roundup. The roundup was the most important event of the year, finding, identifying, and branding the newborn calves and any unbranded cattle (photographed above in 1888). The first roundups were informal, cooperative affairs among neighbors. From them developed stockmen's associations of the 1870s. Instructions for Roundup I for the year 1888, issued by the Colorado Cattle Growers Association, called for the ranchers of District No. 9 to meet in Brighton. In the fall, the cattle were again rounded up and selected cattle were shipped to market or slaughtered (below in 1907). (Both courtesy of the Library of Congress.)

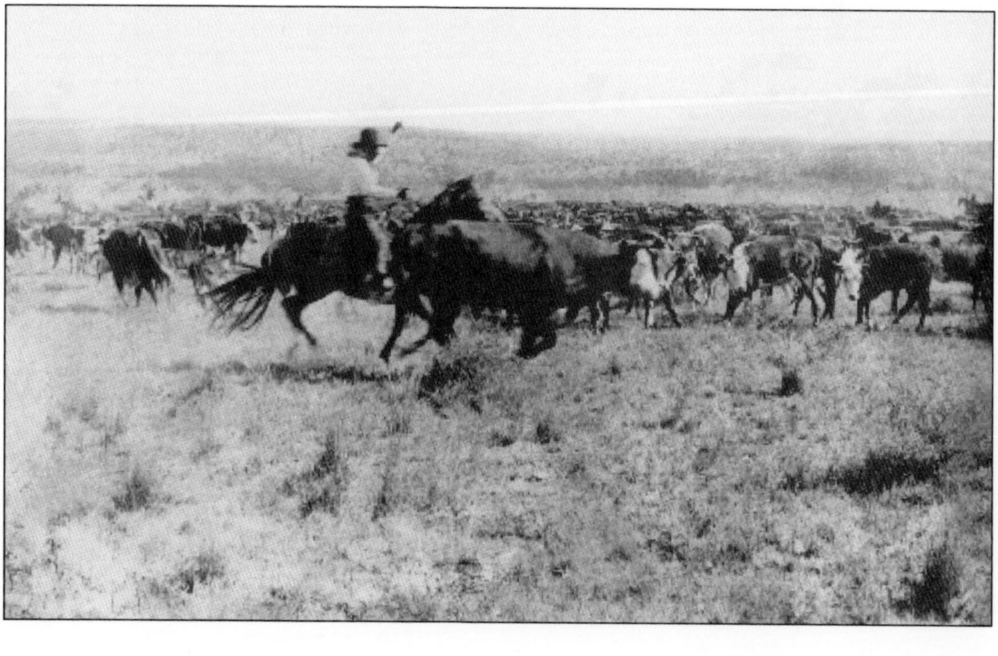

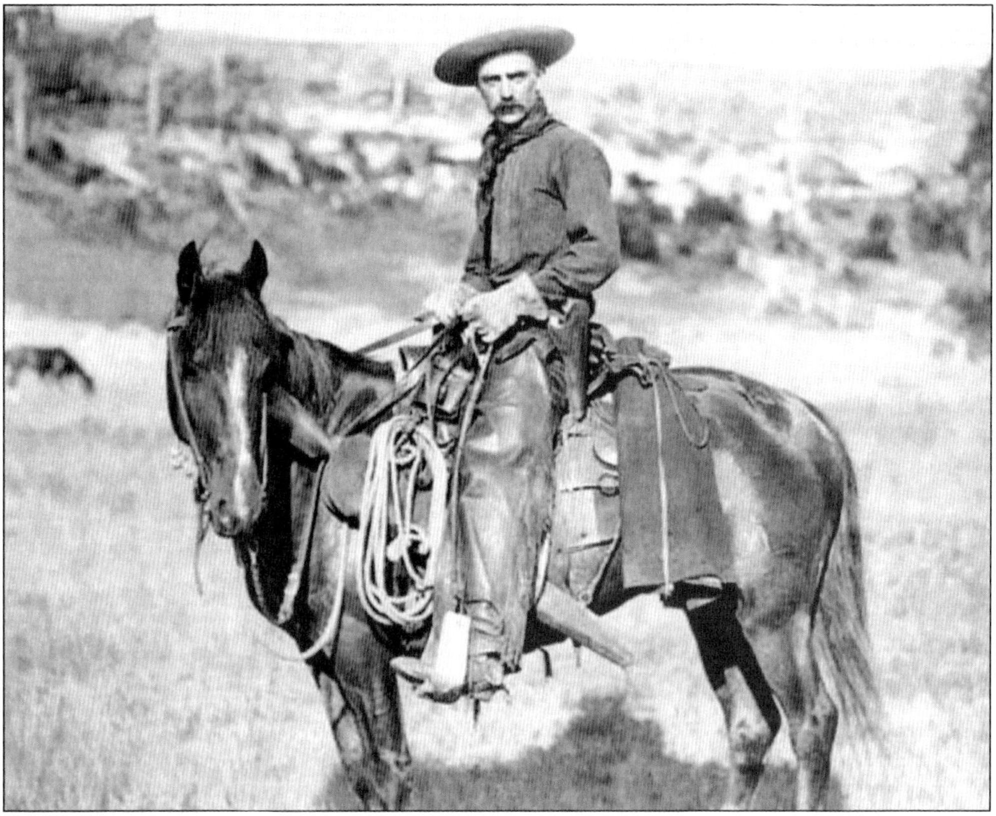

COWBOYS. The Spanish set the style, evolved the equipment and techniques, and even developed most of the vocabulary that became the image of the American cowboy. The braided rawhide rope, known for centuries in Spain as the *reato*, became the American lariat. The heavy leather trousers worn in the chaparral thickets were called *chaparreras*, shortened to chaps. As for the cowhands, from their name *vaqueros* (from the Spanish word *vaca* for cow) came the American term buckaroo. However, the early Spanish raised cattle mostly for hides, not meat. These photographs of cowboys in 1887 (above) and 1905 (below) reflect this Spanish heritage. (Both courtesy of the Library of Congress.)

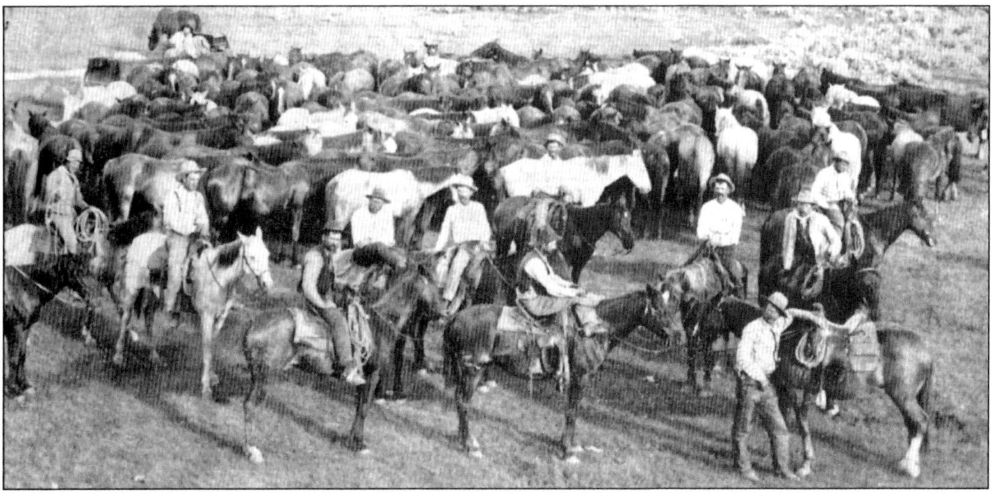

COLORADO BRAND BOOK.

ARAPAHOE COUNTY.

J. W. Adams, Deer Trail. ϑ l. sh., l. s. & l. h. h. b. same l. sh.

Wm. S. Adams, Denver. **WSA** ‖ **Wm. Adams**, Denver. **A**

Levi Ackroyd, Denver. ‖ **Matie Alderdice**, Denver. **Ω**

The Alfalfa Live Stock Co., Littleton. **CE**

David Allen, Woman Creek. **A=**

J. W. Allison, Denver. **R** l s., **JR** l. h., ho. l. e. h. b. **JR** l. sh.

Frank Aichelman, Brighton. **FAA**

The American Cattle Co., Denver. **I—I**, **I** l. sh., **—** l. s., **I** l. h. h. b. 5 l. th., **H 4**, l. s., e. m., o. & u. s., r. & c. l. e.

John P. Anderson, Denver. **JPA**

Arkansas Valley Land and Cattle Co. (ld.), Denver. **—SS** e. m., u. s. r., c. l. **SS** l. s. or l. sh. **◇** l. h. **SS—** l. s. or l. sh. **SS** l. s. **S—S** l. s. **SS** l. s. **S—S** l. s. **OO** l. s. **T** l. s. or l. h. **UP** l. s. or l. h. h. b. **SS**. Other brands, 7, **RS**, **TI**, **LO**, **7C**, **A**, **⊥**, **WB**, **SD**, **T**, **B**, **T⊥**, **—SS**, **C**, **2**, **⌒**, **⌒**, **—⌒—**, **HK**, **7**, **↑**, **S**, **P**, **H-H**, **SS**

John K. Ashley, Denver. **AØ**

John A. Askew, Denver. **JNU** l. s., **TEA** l. s., e. m., c. r. h. b. **♡** l. th.

Mrs. E. A. Autrey, Box Elder. **OJ**

Anna R. C. Ayers, Denver. **ARS** ‖ **Rudolph Baatz**, Denver. **⊙**

C. A. Babcock, Lyman. **4** r. th. h. b. same l. th.

A. S. Babcock, Littleton. **LON** l. s., e. m., c. r., u. ½ c. l.

John S. Babcock, Denver. **BIB** e. m., c. r. s. f. l.

Thos. Bades, Bennett. **TBT**

Clarissa M. Baker, Denver. **CMB**

Sarah Kate Ball, Brighton. **KB**

Wm. W. Ballard, Watkins. **T** h. b., l. sh.

Fred. J. Banks, Watkins. **6+** and **▽**

John W. Banes, Byers. **JU** l. s. & l. h., c. & u. b., l. & u. s., r. e. h. b. same l. sh.

Anselins Banchare, Denver. **D7**

Chas. Bartels, Denver. **K**

Barney & Lamborn, Bennett. **B** l. h. h. b. same l. sh.

F. J. Bancroft, Denver. **O|O** r. s. h. b. same r. sh.

COLORADO STATE BRAND BOOK. When the first Colorado Brand Book was issued by the Colorado Cattle Growers Association in 1884, about half the brands were on horses and cows in what is now Adams County. Many Brighton-area residents were listed, including the Diamond C brand of Daniel F. Carmichael. In 1884, Colorado alone saw 58 new cattle companies formed, many in present-day Adams County. The huge Prairie Cattle Company declared a 42 percent dividend in 1882. Overstocking the ranges led to the Big Die Off during the winter of 1886–1887, when some herds suffered losses of 80 to 90 percent. Many ranchers, even large corporations, went broke. The era of the open range was ending. Barbed wire, invented in 1876, became economical after 1880. The *Brighton Register* in June 1897 reported one of the last large cattle drives on the hills east of Brighton.

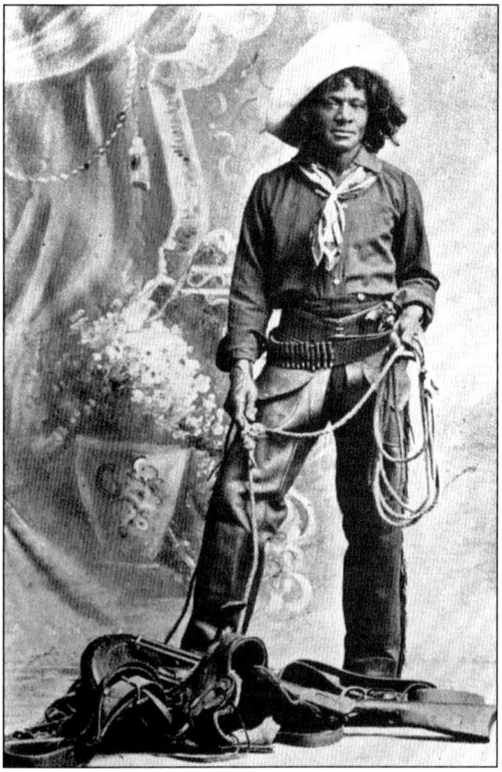

Deadwood Dick. Many of the cowboys were Hispanics or African Americans. Nat Love, known as Deadwood Dick, drove cattle along the Goodnight-Loving Trail across present-day Adams County. He also competed several times in the Adams County Fair and Rodeo in Brighton. This photograph is from the autobiography of Nat Love, which was privately printed in 1907.

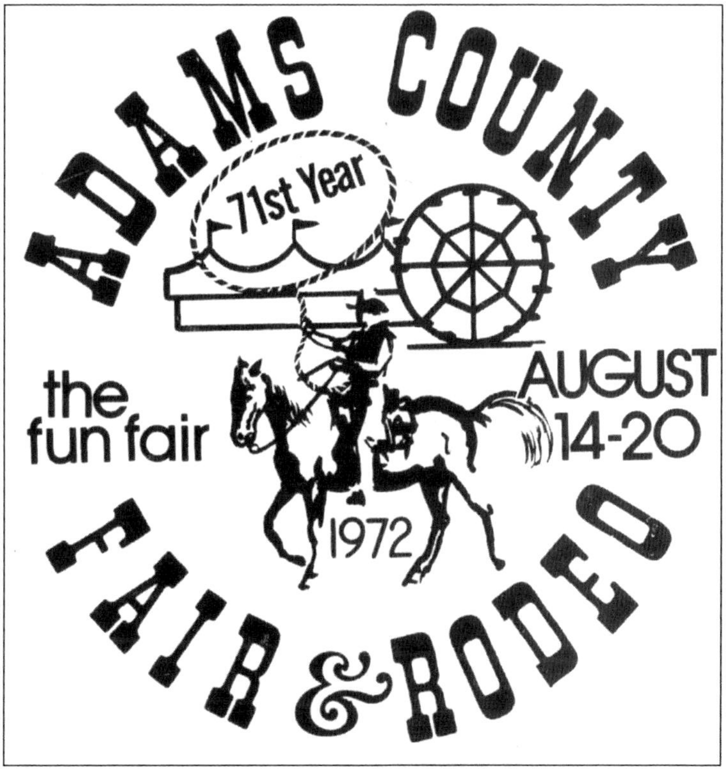

Adams County Rodeo. Adams County has retained its cowboy traditions. The annual Adams County Fair and Rodeo is still part of the official circuit of the Professional Rodeo Cowboys Association (PRCA). The Spanish term for roundup is *el rodeo*, and it is from this that the modern form of entertainment derives its origin. In earlier days, the rodeo was work for the cowboy, not a show.

Four

Founding Fathers

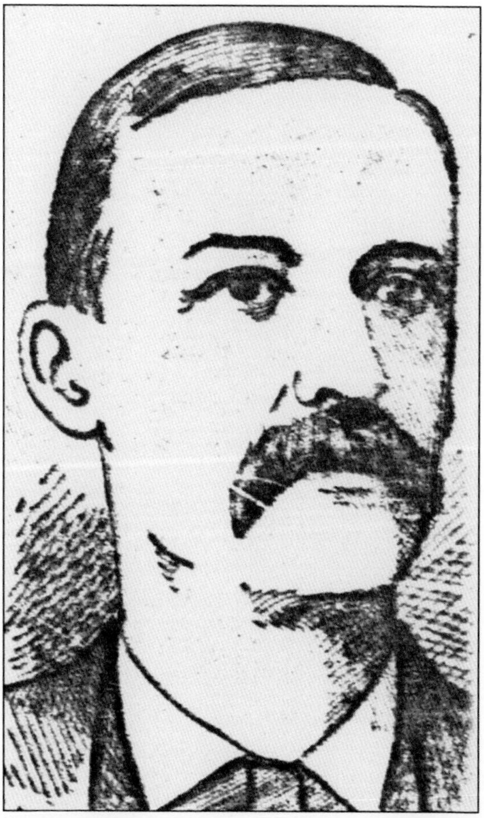

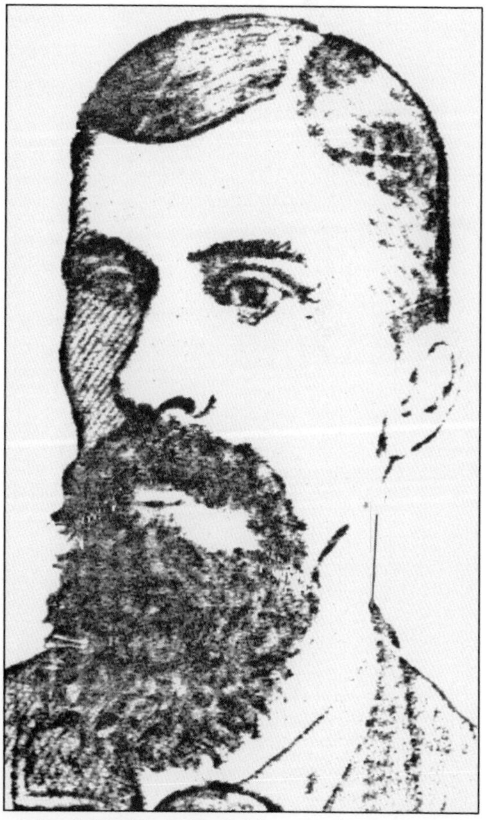

Brighton City Fathers. Daniel Franklin Carmichael (1844–1911, left), a civil engineer for the Union Pacific railroad and real estate developer, was the founder of the city of Brighton. He filed the first plat for Brighton in 1881. Dewey W. Strong (1848–1923, right), a Fort Lupton dairy farmer and merchant, filed the plat for North Brighton in 1882. These early portraits appeared in an article about Brighton in the *Rocky Mountain News*, April 6, 1890.

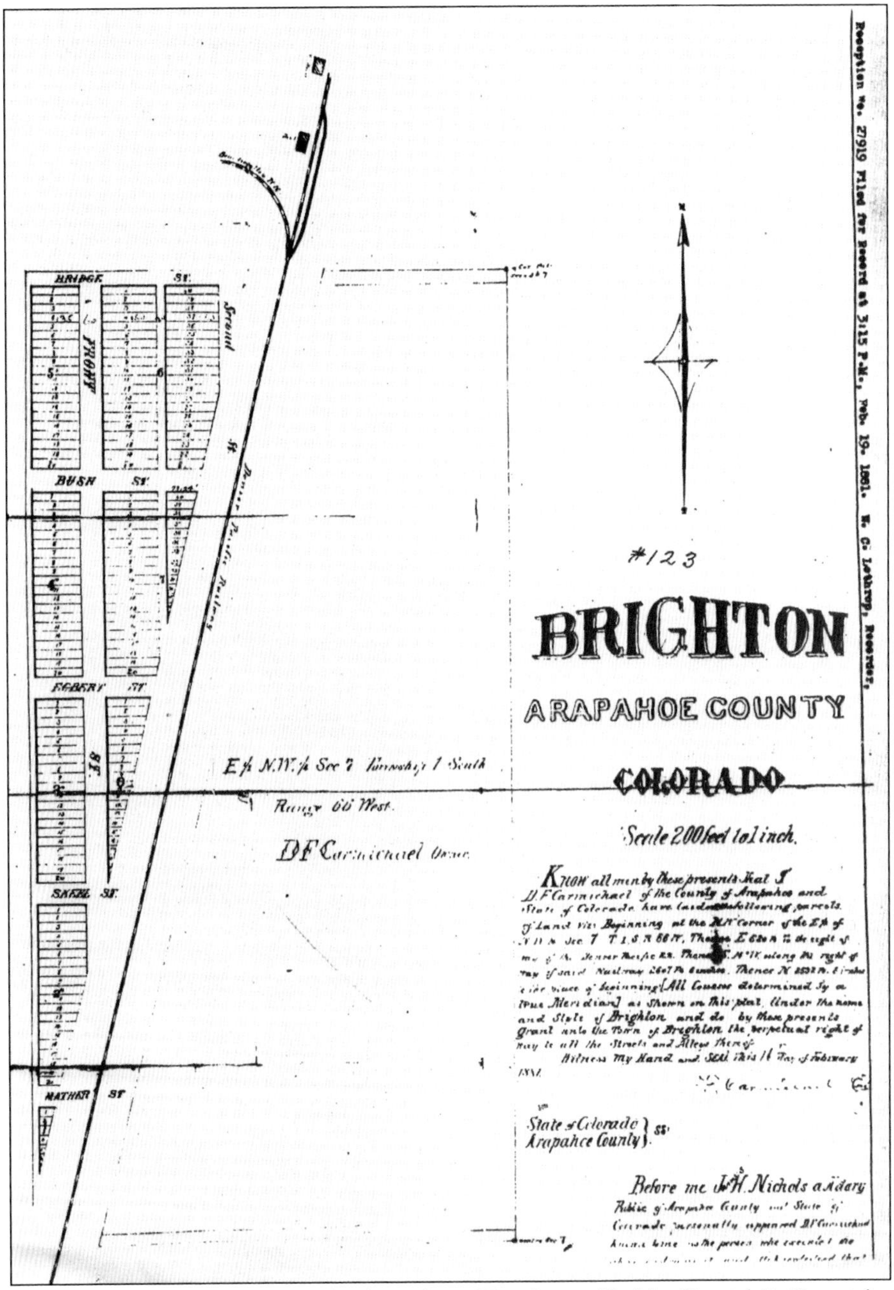

First Plat of Brighton, 1881. The first plat of Brighton, filed by Daniel F. Carmichael on February 16, 1881, was composed of the triangular portion of present-day downtown Brighton south of Bridge Street. The development was bounded on three sides by Bridge Street, Front Street, and the Denver Pacific Railroad tracks. Front Street is now South First Avenue and the Denver Pacific Railroad is now the Union Pacific. The cross streets were named for the Bush family, the first residents of Brighton; the Egbert brothers, engineers with Carmichael during the construction of the Union Pacific; and Almet Skeel, Carmichael's brother-in-law. Second Street, once the County Road along the railroad tracks, is now Cabbage Avenue. (Courtesy of the County Clerk of Adams County.)

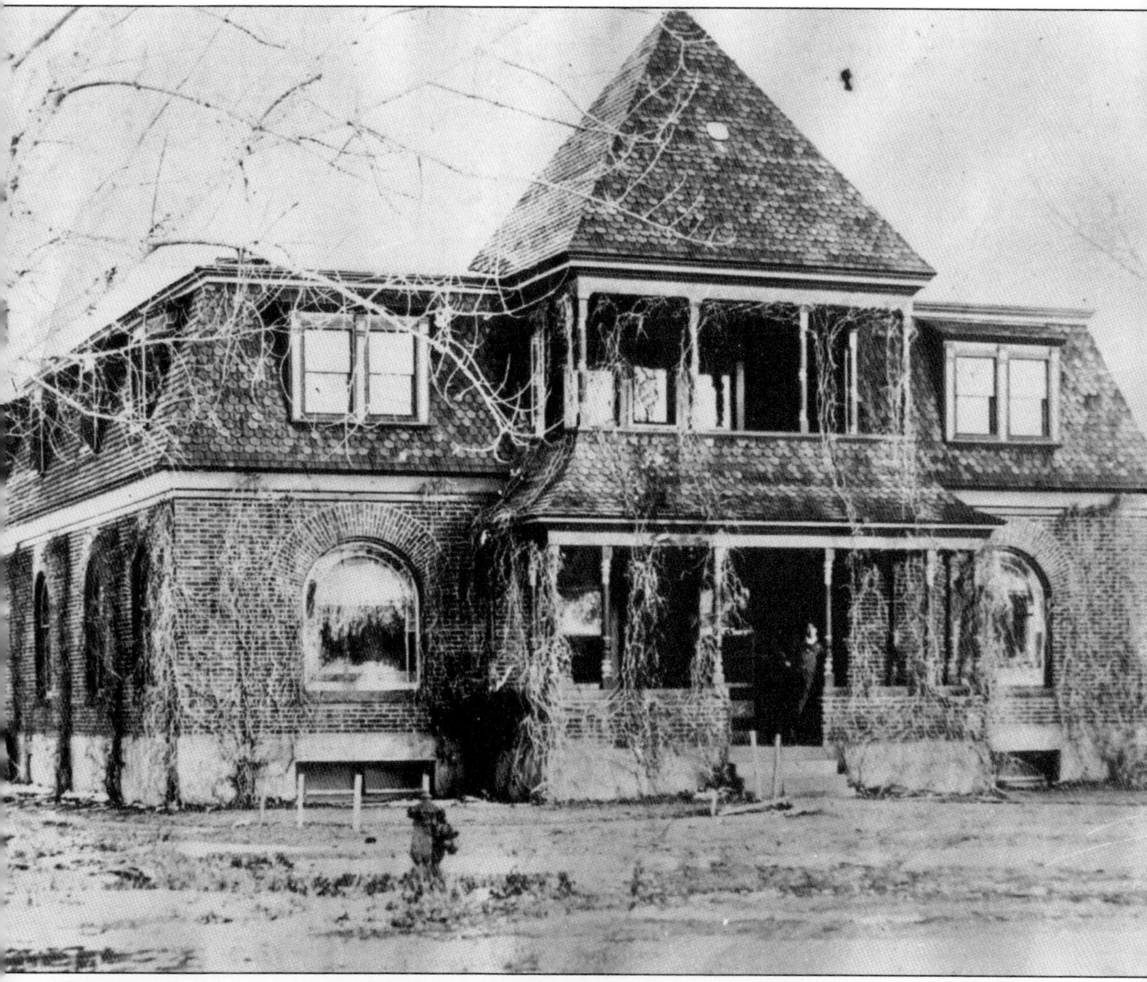

CARMICHAEL MANSION. Daniel F. Carmichael built a home in the new town of Brighton in 1884 and moved from Denver. His wife, Alice Carmichael, was credited in her obituary with naming the new town Brighton. Her obituary lists her birthplace as Brighton Beach, New York. Nearly every state in the United States has one or more municipalities named after Brighton, the popular seaside resort in England popularized by the Prince of Wales (later George IV). The name of the railroad junction, Hughes, was changed to Brighton on *Nell's Map of Colorado* in 1880, one year before Carmichael filed the first plat for the town of Brighton in 1881. The new name for Hughes had been in use for at least two years before. The railroad station changed the name to Brighton in 1879. The name of the post office was officially changed to Brighton on August 4, 1879. (Courtesy of the Brighton Historical Preservation Commission.)

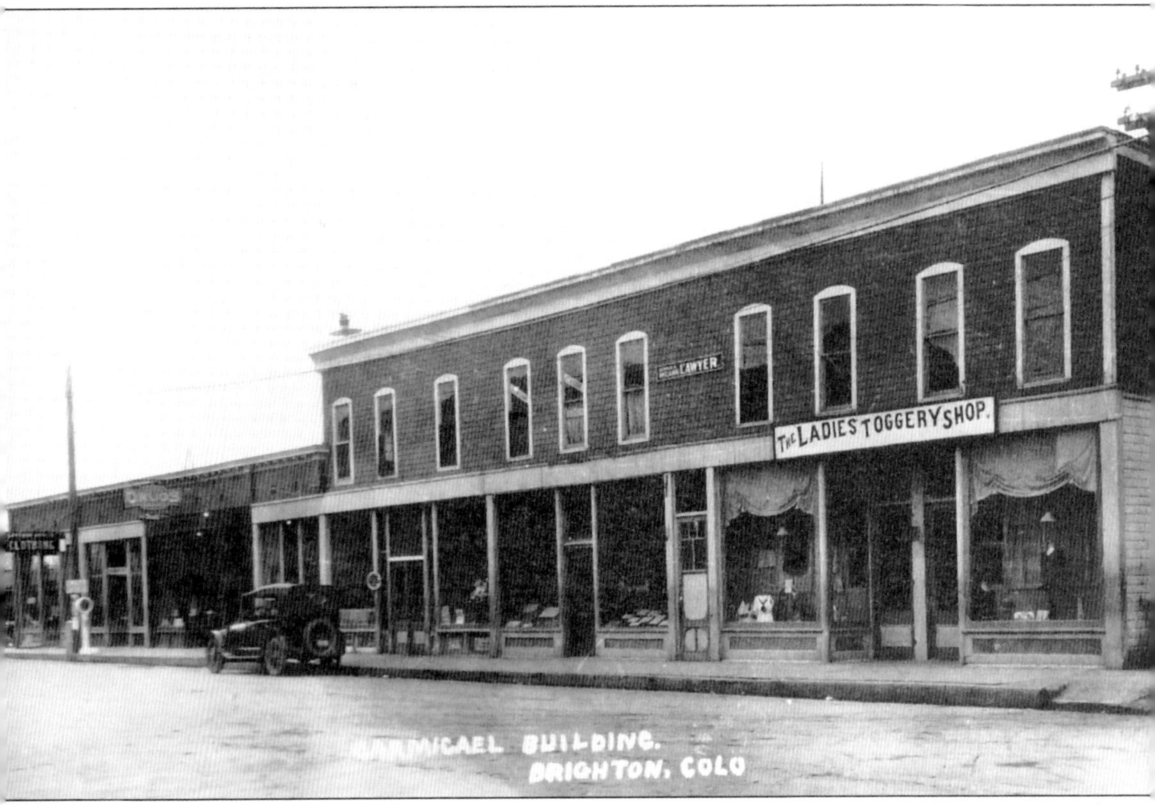

Carmichael Building. Daniel F. Carmichael increased his investment in the new town of Brighton, in 1884, by constructing a business block, the Carmichael Building, on Bridge Street looking down Division (now North Main) Street. Carmichael's offices, the Bank of Brighton, law offices, and a drugstore occupied the building. The Ladies Toggery is a prominent occupant in this postcard. The Ladies Toggery, a longtime local Brighton business, was a name created by the Dalton sisters, Maude and Mabel (Mrs. J. C. Peterson), but used only after their third move to the Carmichael Building. Their first store was on Division Street three stores north of the Swan Livery Stable, the second in the Strong building at Division and Strong Streets. Later the Toggery moved east across the railroad tracks and finally returned to North Main Street when Robert ("Bob") Nitske built his new building on the old site of the Swan Livery Stables. Arthur Nolan owned the Ladies Toggery from 1947 to 1974, when he sold it to Penny Pennock and Mary Samuelson. They finally closed the store in 1987. Samuelson died in 2008. (Courtesy of the Brighton Historical Preservation Commission.)

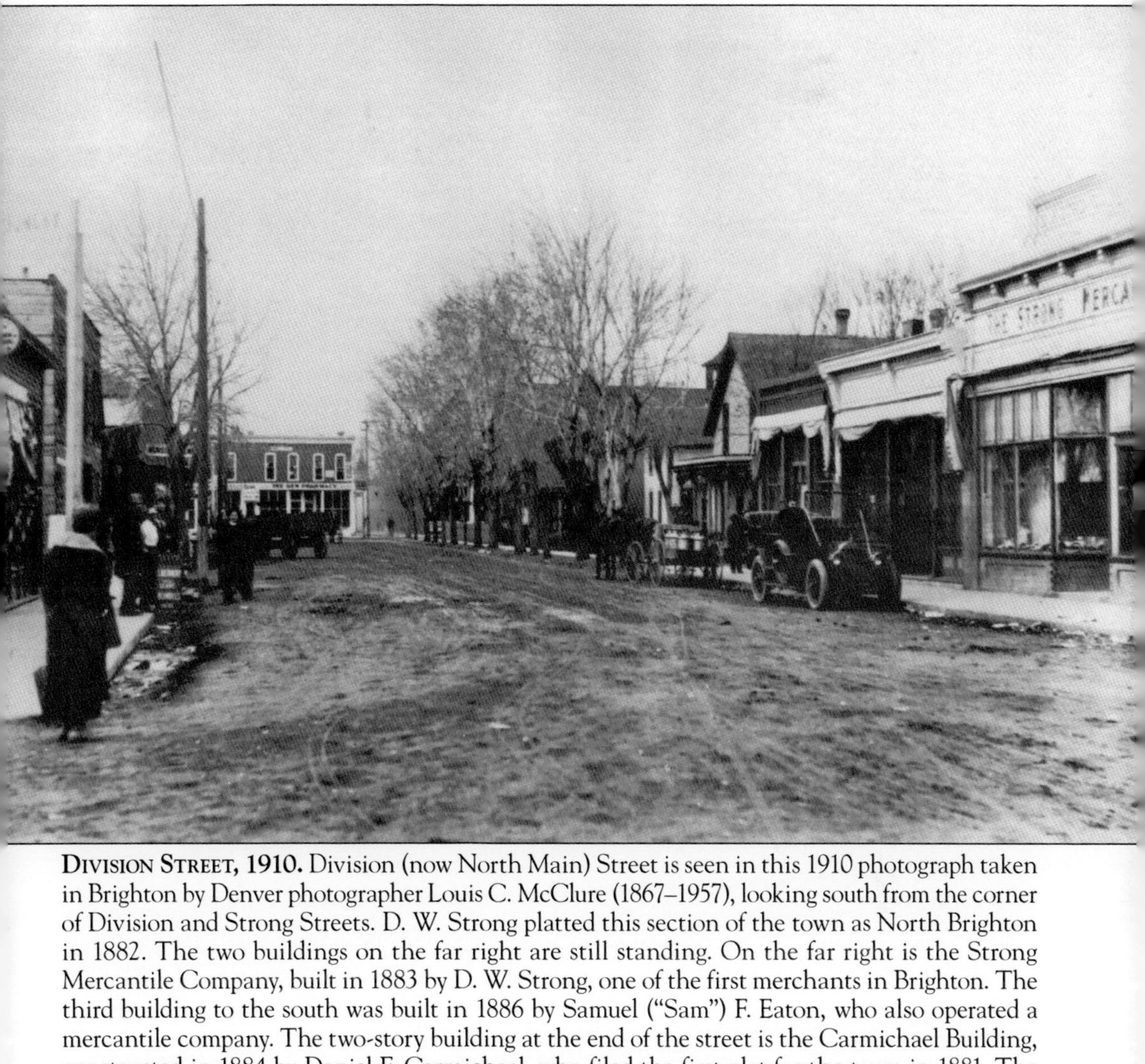

DIVISION STREET, 1910. Division (now North Main) Street is seen in this 1910 photograph taken in Brighton by Denver photographer Louis C. McClure (1867–1957), looking south from the corner of Division and Strong Streets. D. W. Strong platted this section of the town as North Brighton in 1882. The two buildings on the far right are still standing. On the far right is the Strong Mercantile Company, built in 1883 by D. W. Strong, one of the first merchants in Brighton. The third building to the south was built in 1886 by Samuel ("Sam") F. Eaton, who also operated a mercantile company. The two-story building at the end of the street is the Carmichael Building, constructed in 1884 by Daniel F. Carmichael, who filed the first plat for the town in 1881. The Carmichael Building, Brighton's first business block, was torn down in 1937, when Main Street was created and Division Street was extended straight on through that block. (Courtesy of the Denver Public Library Western History and Genealogy Department.)

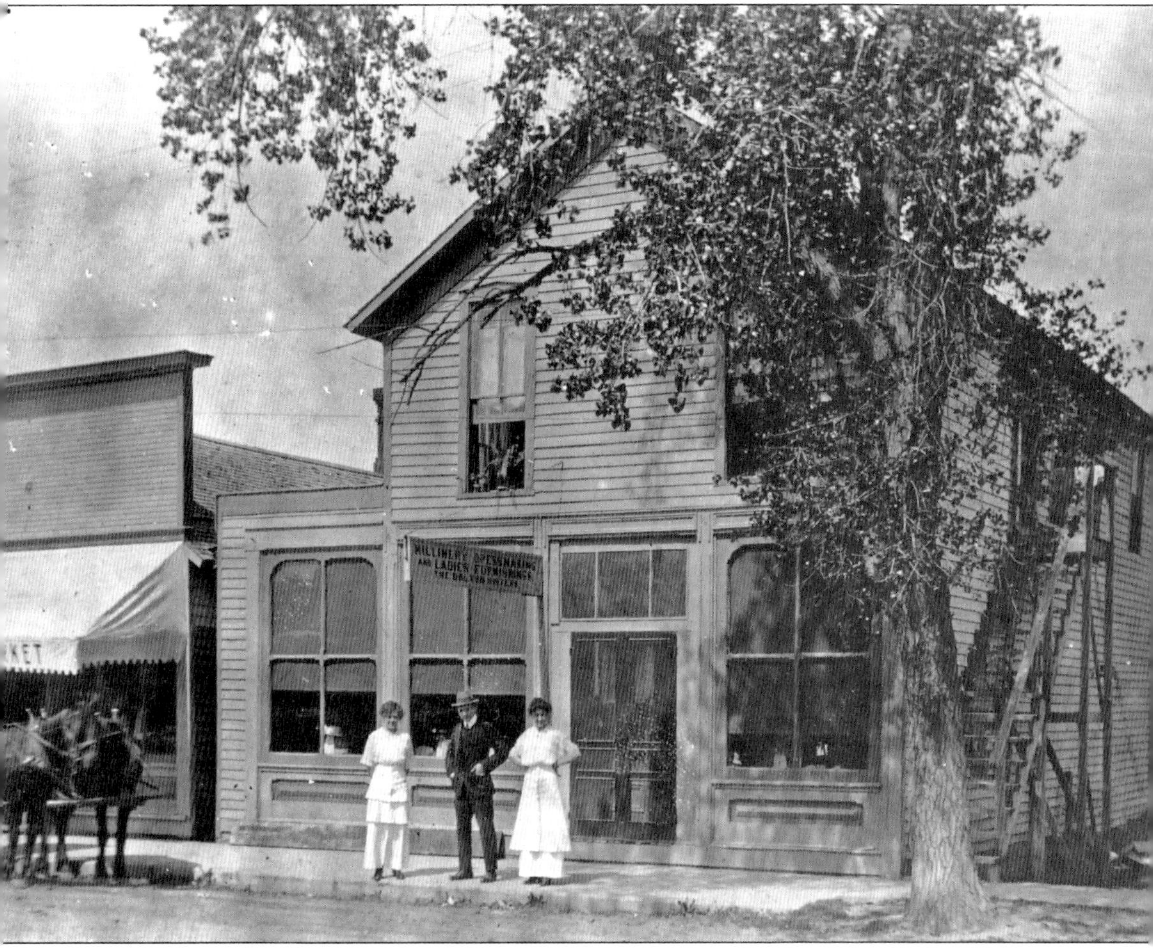

STRONG'S FIRST STORE. The first store D. W. Strong operated on Division Street (now North Main) was one of several the Strong Mercantile Company occupied. After Strong's new store was constructed in 1883 on the southwest corner of Strong and Division Streets (still standing at 45 North Main), this building was rented. At the time this picture was taken about 1916, the Dalton sisters had a store in the building. The Dalton sisters, Mabel (on the left) and Maude (on the right), and a salesman are in front of the store. The building on the left was the first building used by Friedman's Market, which later moved to the corner of Strong Street and Cabbage Avenue. The team and wagon was used by Friedman's for deliveries. Later Strong's first store building was moved farther north to the northwest corner of North Main and Long's Peak Streets, where it served as Red and White chain Eagle Market, with H. H. Bobenhouse as proprietor. It still stands. (Courtesy of the Brighton Historical Preservation Commission.)

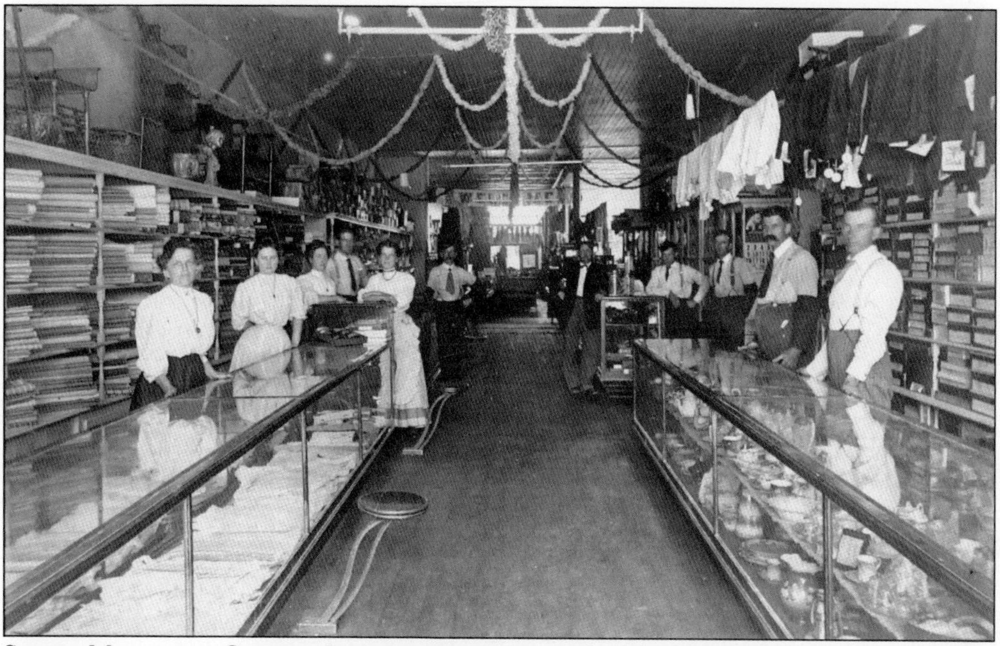

Strong Mercantile Company Interior. This photograph of the interior of the Strong Mercantile Company gives us a glimpse of a typical general store of the period. Notice the segregation of men and women clerks and the display counters for merchandise. There was no self-service. Dewey W. Strong (1848–1923), a Fort Lupton dairy farmer, filed the plat for North Brighton in 1882. Strong's store was constructed in 1883 on the southwest corner of Strong and Division (North Main) Streets. The building later served as the Ben Franklin Store and is still standing at 45 North Main Street. (Courtesy of Beulah Barnard.)

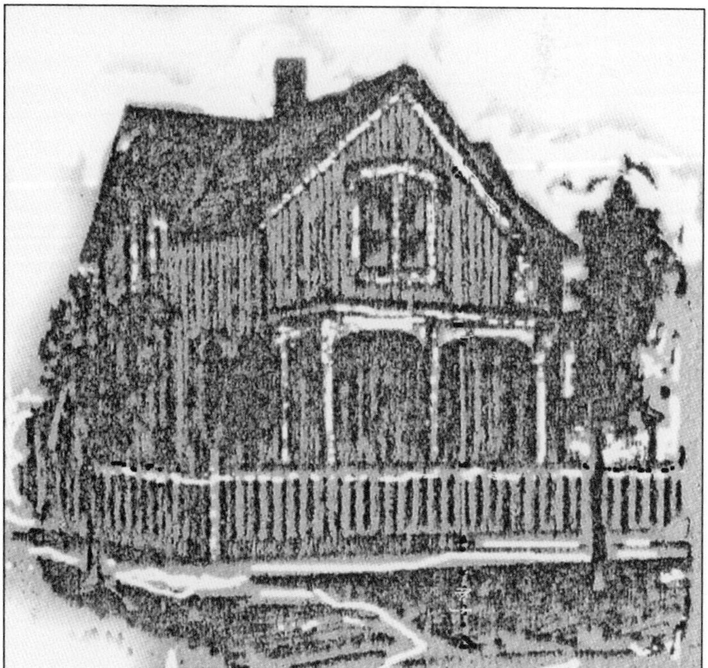

D. W. Strong Residence. Strong built his home at the most prominent location possible, the northwest corner of Division and Bridge Streets. The house was moved west on Bridge Street to the intersection of South First Avenue and Bridge Street when the First National Bank was built on that corner. The house was demolished when the Brighton Professional Building was constructed. The drawing appeared in *Rocky Mountain News* on April 6, 1890.

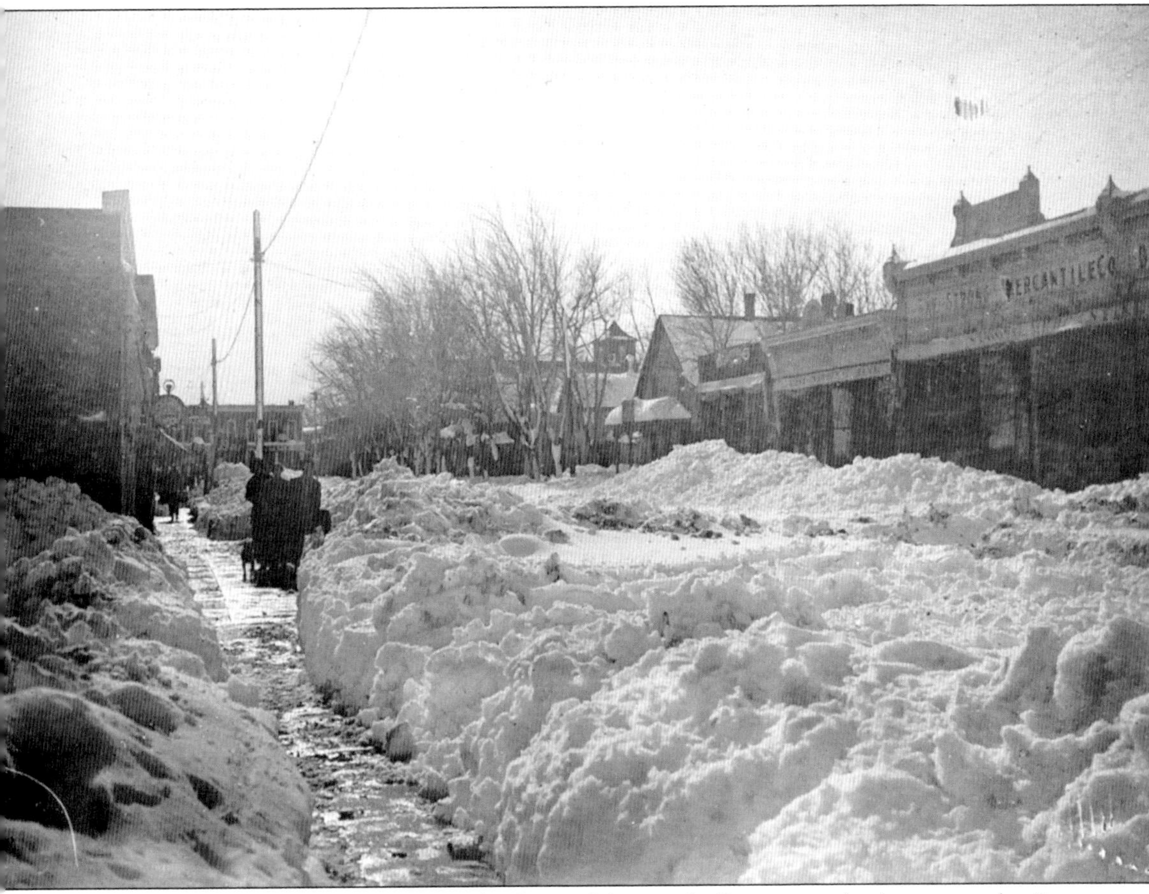

Strong Mercantile Company. The Strong Mercantile Company, also known as the Strong and Twombly Company, is seen here on the right in the snow. John C. Twombly was the business partner of Brighton merchant Dewey W. Strong. The Twombly families were early settlers and prominent members of the Brighton and Fort Lupton communities. Twombly was the leader of the Republican "Twombly Crowd." Twombly built his residence in 1885 or 1886 at the northwest corner of South Fourth Avenue and Bush Street in Brighton. The Twombly home was torn down in 1955 to make way for the new KHIL radio station renamed KBRN in 1960. The Twomblys donated the land behind their house to the Brighton Methodist Church, where their church was built in 1900. The old Methodist church at 76 South Third Avenue was eventually sold to the St. Elizabeth Episcopal Church. The residence of S. F. Eaton, a rival early Brighton merchant, at 107 South Fourth Avenue, still stands on the opposite (southwest) corner of South Fourth Avenue and Bush Street. (Courtesy of the Denver Public Library Western History and Genealogy Department.)

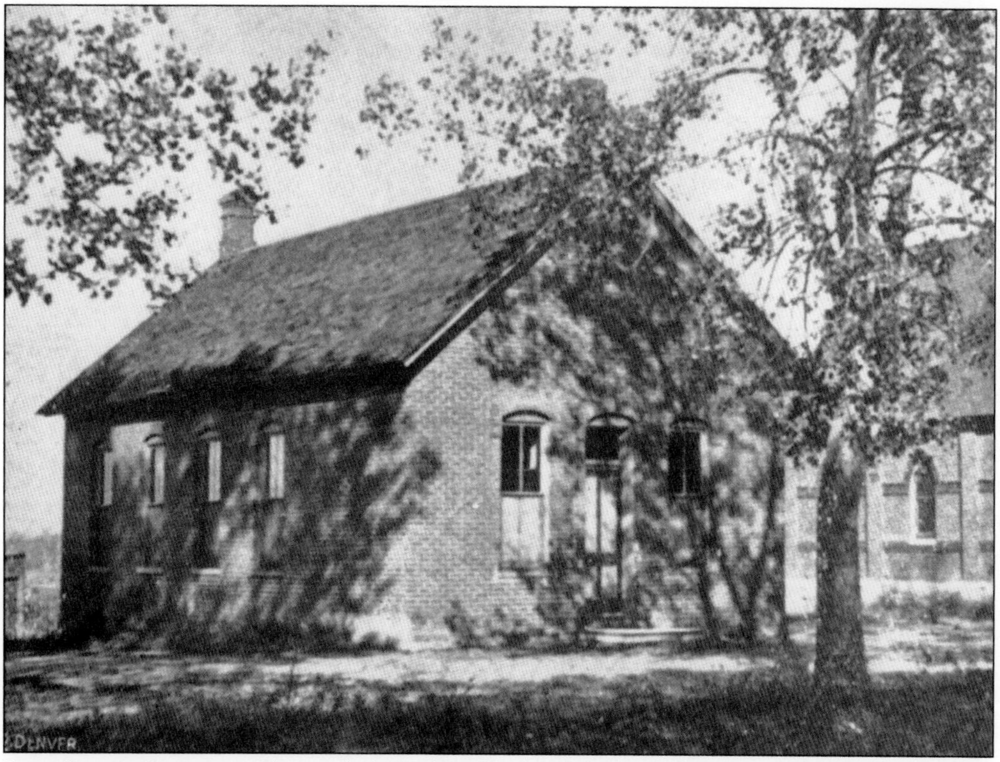

First School Building. The newly formed Brighton School District No. 27 completed construction of a brick schoolhouse on Front Street (South First Avenue) on Valentine's Day, February 14, 1885. It was the first school building in Brighton. A frame grade school building was erected in 1887. The old schoolhouse was torn down to make a parking lot in 1972. (Courtesy of the Brighton Historical Preservation Commission.)

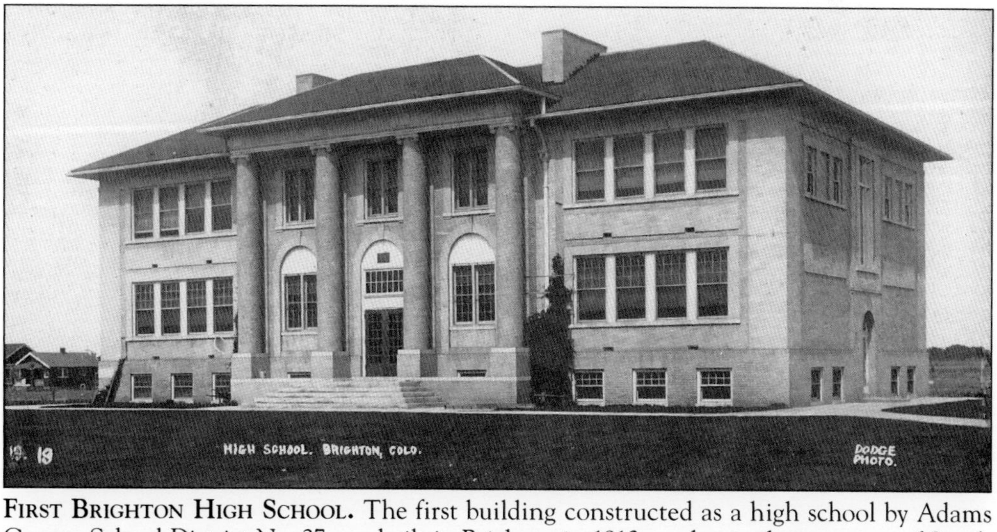

First Brighton High School. The first building constructed as a high school by Adams County School District No. 27 was built in Brighton in 1913 on the southeast corner of South Fourth Avenue and Skeel Street, the present location of South Elementary School. The building originally contained classrooms for 125 students, a gym, and an auditorium. Pictured here in a postcard shortly after it was built, the building was torn down in 1975.

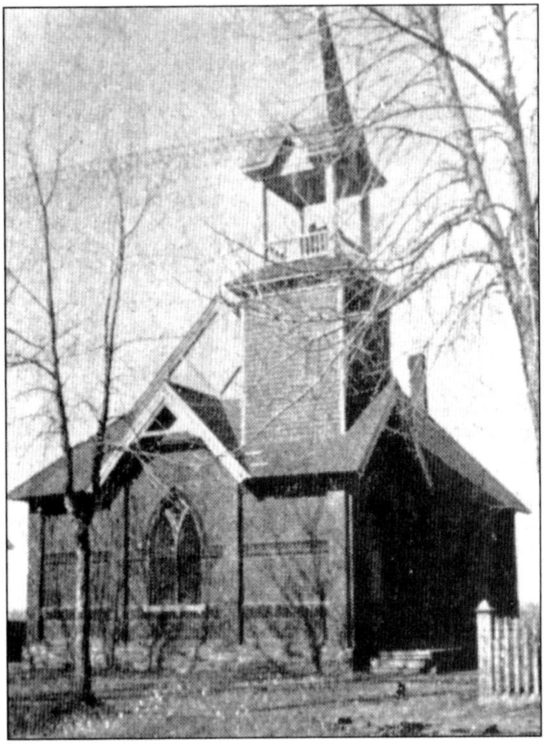

The First Church Building. The drawing (below) of the First Presbyterian Church, the first church building in Brighton, built in 1886, appeared in an article on Brighton in the *Rocky Mountain News* on April 6, 1890, before the familiar steeple was added as seen in the above 1904 photograph. The Presbyterian church was organized in Strong's home in August 1884. He was an elder and trustee of the church and superintendent of the Sunday school. Note the open balcony in the steeple (above), which was later enclosed. Brighton's first school was built in 1884 to the left of the church two years before. Daniel Carmichael donated the land for the church, and the bricks were fired at the Hazzard farm south of Brighton. The Presbyterians used the church until 1917, when they sold it to the Emmaus Lutheran Church. (Both courtesy of the Adams County Historical Society.)

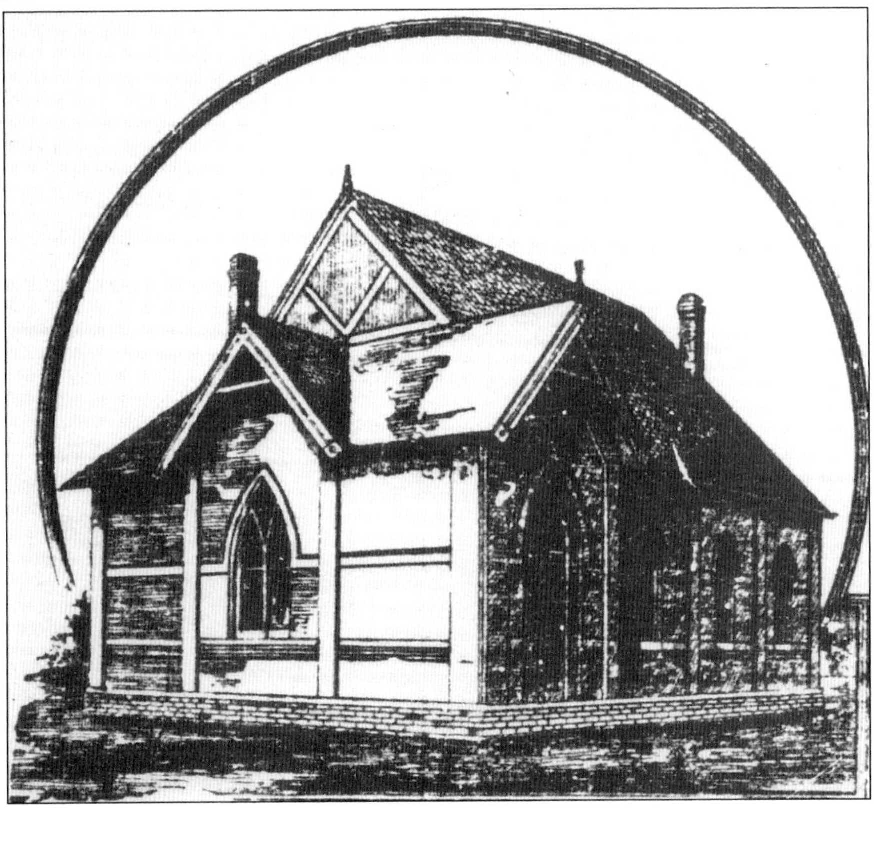

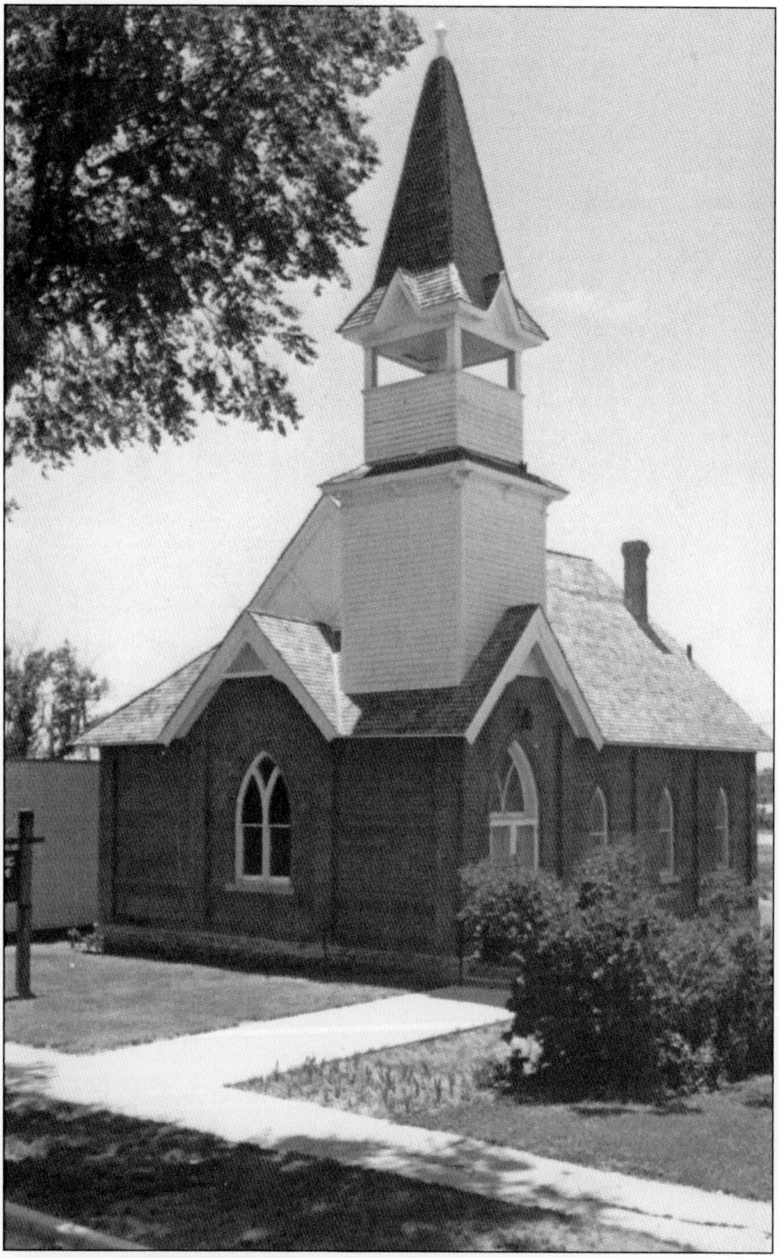

THE 1886 CHURCH. The old First Presbyterian Church at 145 South First Avenue, known as the 1886 Church for the date of its construction, was used by the Presbyterian congregation until 1917, when it was sold to the Emmaus Lutheran Church. When that church dissolved, the Adams County Historical Society held a successful fund drive to purchase the historic building in 1975. The 1886 Church was donated to the City of Brighton by the historical society as part of the Brighton Centennial-Bicentennial Celebration in 1976. The church is now maintained as a historic site by the City of Brighton. The Presbyterian church at 106 South Fourth Avenue weathered years of service, a severe fire in 1936, and extensive remodeling. The congregation moved to a new church at 510 South Twenty-seventh Avenue in 1987. (Courtesy of the Adams County Historical Society.)

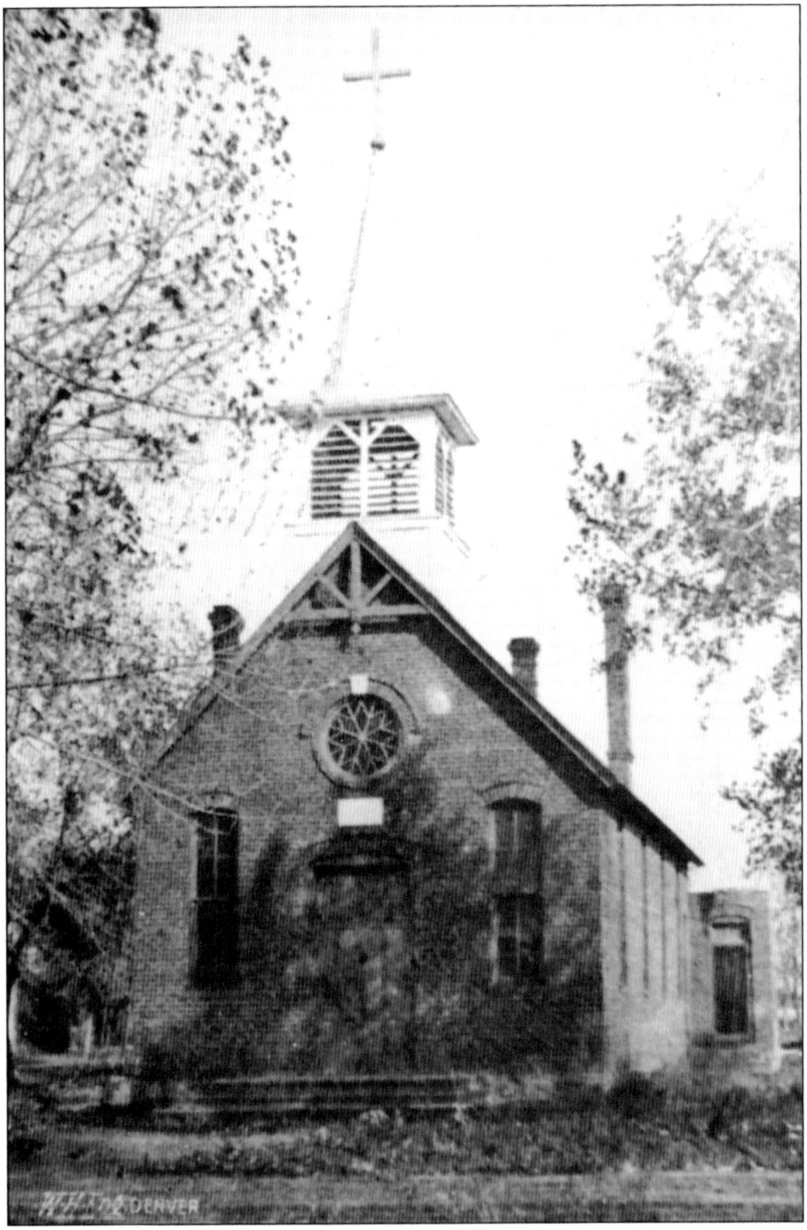

First Catholic Church. Like the Presbyterians, the Catholics in Brighton first met in members' homes, including the home of J. P. Higgins, the sheriff of Adams County. St. Augustine parish was organized in 1887. The original congregation included Frank Aichelman and Andrew and Louis Hagus. The first church was built in 1888 at 139 Division (now North Main) Street, the current site of the *Brighton Standard Blade* newspaper office. The building was later moved to the southeast corner of South Third Avenue and Bush Street, where it later served as the Rice Funeral Chapel. A second church was built in 1930 at South Sixth Avenue and Bush Street. The old church building became the Ricardo Falcon Memorial Community Center after a new church was built at South Sixth Avenue and Egbert Street in 1968 on land Daniel F. Carmichael and William Lovelace donated to the Catholic church in 1906 for a hospital. (Courtesy of the Brighton Historical Preservation Commission.)

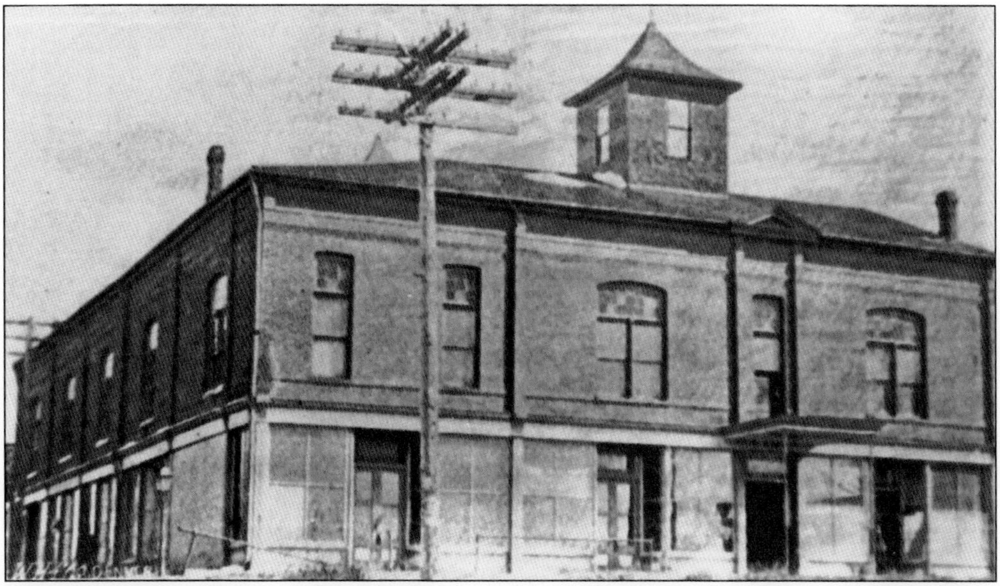

Brighton Opera House, 1904. The Brighton Opera House is seen in this 1904 photograph, published in material prepared to promote Brighton as the permanent county seat of Adams County, founded two years before in 1902. The opera house was constructed by Daniel F. Carmichael in 1888, seven short years after he filed the first plat for the new town. The view is the front of the opera house looking southeast from the opposite corner of Front (now South First Avenue) and Bridge Streets. Notice the telephone poles, a selling point for the Brighton "boosters." (Courtesy of the Brighton Historical Preservation Commission.)

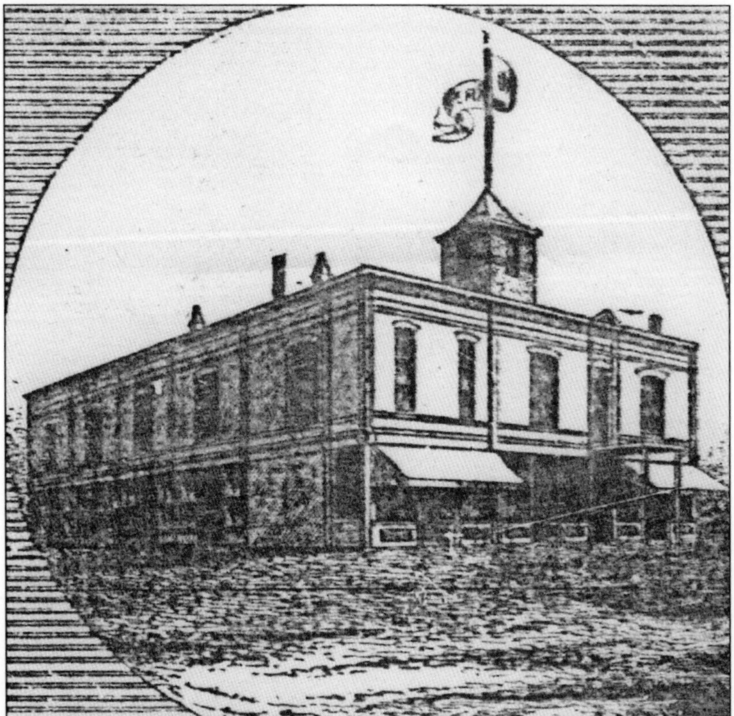

Brighton Opera House, 1890. The Brighton Opera House was depicted in this drawing that appeared in the *Rocky Mountain News* on April 6, 1890, facing Front Street in Brighton, with a banner flying from the tower that topped the imposing three-story brick building.

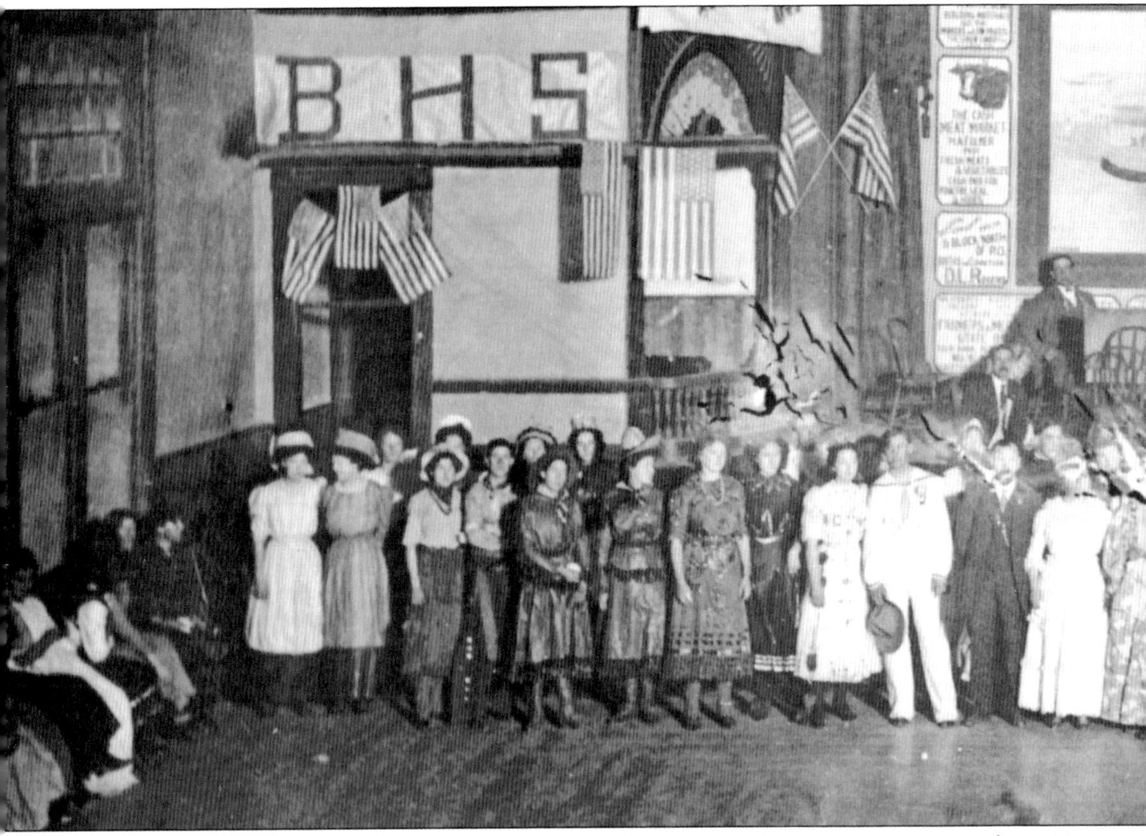

INSIDE THE OPERA HOUSE. The large auditorium in the Brighton Opera House is seen in this c. 1918 photograph. The "BHS" banner on the wall and the costumes seem to suggest the photograph was of a play or pageant in the opera house put on by the Brighton High School. The opera house was

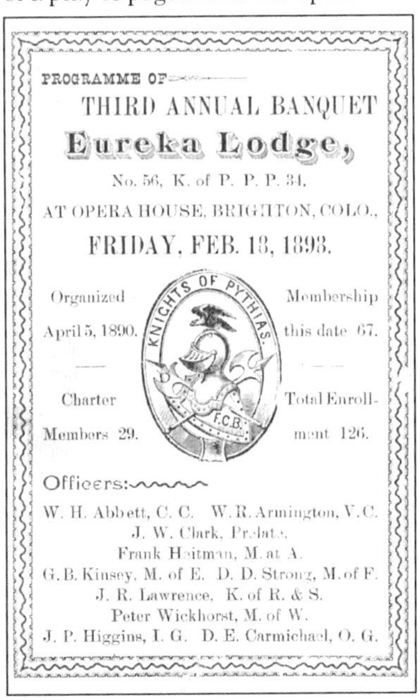

PROGRAMME OF

THIRD ANNUAL BANQUET

Eureka Lodge,

No. 56, K. of P. P. P. 34,

AT OPERA HOUSE, BRIGHTON, COLO.,

FRIDAY, FEB. 18, 1898.

Organized April 5, 1890. — Membership this date 67.

KNIGHTS OF PYTHIAS — F.C.B.

Charter Members 29. — Total Enrollment 126.

Officers:

W. H. Abbett, C. C. W. R. Armington, V. C.
J. W. Clark, Prelate.
Frank Heitman, M. at A.
G. B. Kinsey, M. of E. D. D. Strong, M. of F.
J. R. Lawrence, K. of R. & S.
Peter Wickhorst, M. of W.
J. P. Higgins, I. G. D. E. Carmichael, O. G.

KNIGHTS OF PYTHIAS. The lodge rooms in the Brighton Opera House served as the home for a number of fraternal societies, including the Masons, Eastern Star, Woodmen, Odd Fellows, Knights of Pythias, and Pythian Sisters, as well as a number of social clubs. (Courtesy of Kenneth and Lou Ellen Bromley.)

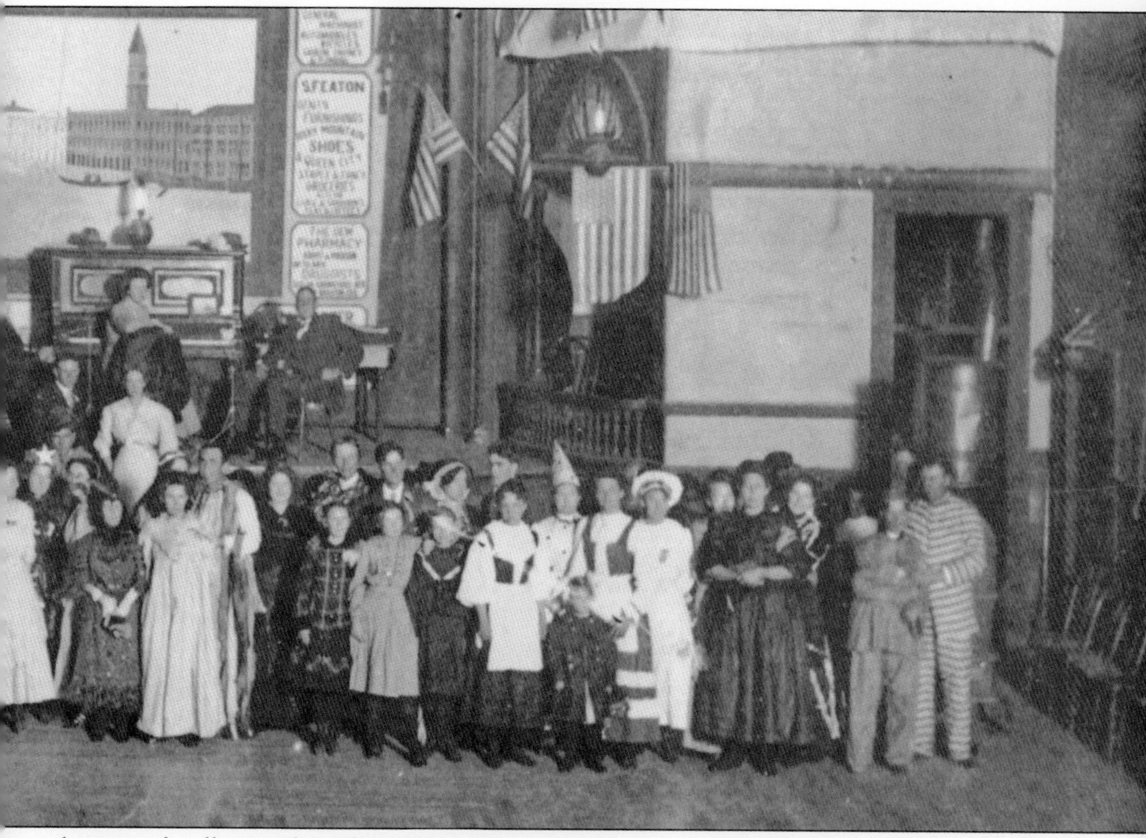

the venue for all sorts of social events, meetings, theatricals, concerts, dances, and other activities for the surrounding area. (Courtesy of the Brighton Historical Preservation Commission.)

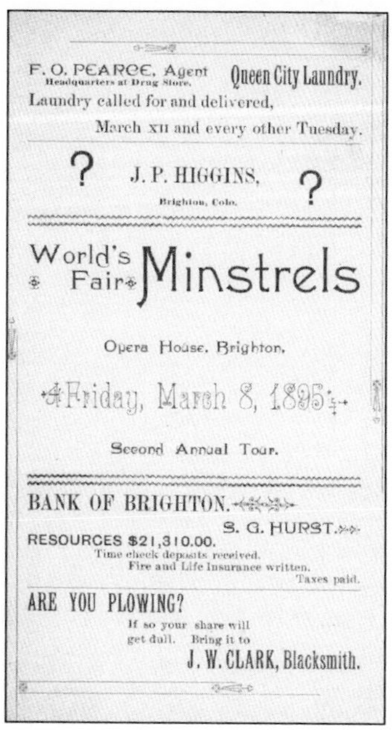

F. O. PEARCE, Agent
Headquarters at Drug Store.
Queen City Laundry.
Laundry called for and delivered,
March XII and every other Tuesday.

? J. P. HIGGINS, ?
Brighton, Colo.

World's Fair Minstrels

Opera House, Brighton,

Friday, March 8, 1895.

Second Annual Tour.

BANK OF BRIGHTON.
S. G. HURST.
RESOURCES $21,310.00.
Time check deposits received.
Fire and Life Insurance written.
Taxes paid.

ARE YOU PLOWING?
If so your share will get dull. Bring it to
J. W. CLARK, Blacksmith.

WORLD'S FAIR MINSTRELS. The Brighton Opera House was on the circuit of a number of theatrical companies. Groups such as the Worlds Fair Minstrels regularly played the opera house on tour between Denver and Cheyenne. (Courtesy of Kenneth and Lou Ellen Bromley.)

ARMINGTON BENEFIT

WON AT LAST

A thrilling Comedy Drama at Armory, to be given by Local Talent,

TUESDAY NIGHT, FEBRUARY 6, 1900.

T. A. McCOOL,
BRIGHTON MEAT MARKET.
Carries a full and fresh stock of groceries, meats and everything good to eat.

Dr. Enos tests eyes for glasses. It costs nothing to find out whether you need glasses or not.

Have your pictures framed at Brighton Pharmacy.

Buy one of those double lots in Malcom's addition, build you a home, and quit paying rent. Low prices, easy terms.
Geo. R. Lee, Agent.

Small but Oh My
BRIGHTON CHEESE FACTORY
Wm. Winbourn, Manager.

W. B. WALKER,
Blacksmith and Horseshoer. I respectfully invite you to give me a trial. I will take my chances of retaining your patronage.

HUBBARD Is in it. Call and see him.

P. HENGER,
Dealer in Boots and Shoes.
I sell the best possible quality and also repair them free. Opposite creamery.

B. H. Swan,
Livery, Feed and Sale Stable.
Good Rigs, and prompt and good attention for transients. Reasonable rates to boarders.

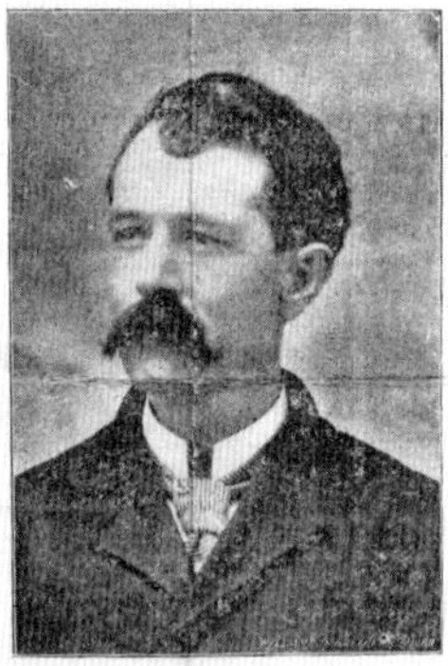

Cast of Characters.

Gen. Warburton	Mr. Geo. Burt
Mrs. Fitzgerald Warburton	Mrs. Dr. Enos
Constance Warburton	Miss Myrtle Metcalf
Lieut. Francis Warburton	Mr. Wm. Winbourn
Ferdinand Fitzsmith	Mr. Fred Wanless
Adolphus Buchanan Esq. (Alias, Wolff & Co.)	Mr. Frank Lytle
Mr. Wolff / Martin	Mr. W. R. Armington
Mary Bounce	Miss Cleora Riggs
Jem Stead (a groom)	Mr. Sam Walter
Servants, officers, etc.	Members of company

Bank of Brighton,
S. G. Hurst, Banker.
Does a general banking business. Insurance.

Geo. L. Munn, Dealer in
HARDWARE,
PUMPS, REPAIRS, PLUMBING.

The Opera House Livery.
New Management. Business carefully attended to. Good, safe, stylish drivers. Good double rigs.
J. A. WIRE, Proprietor.

Dr. JAMES F. ALEXANDER,
BRIGHTON, COLO.
Office adjoining drug store. Residence old Rego house.

CREAMERY MEAT MARKET.
A fine assortment of fresh and salt meat—W. Knecht.

S. F. EATON.
The reliable. Groceries, Dry Goods, Notions, Boots, Shoes.

All kinds of First Class printing at The Register office. We printed this program. We can print anything you want. Try us.

Cottage Home
Board by the day or week.
Convenient. Comfortable.
R. McOuat.

The Elite Saloon,
J. P. Higgins.

F. O. PEARCE,
PAINTER.
Paperhanging, Decorating, Painting. First class, quick, artistic work. References. Satisfaction

W. R. Armington. William R. (W. R.) Armington was the author, director, and producer of many of the theatrical productions that took place in the Brighton Opera House. A multi-talented early resident of Brighton, born in 1861, he came to Brighton in the early 1880s where he worked as a professional photographer and sign painter. A Democrat, he served three terms as the coroner of Adams County from 1902 to 1908. The first military company, the Harvey Light Guards, organized in Brighton in 1888, was commanded by Captain Armington, who headed several other militia companies. They drilled in Armington Hall on the northeast corner of Division (now Main) and Strong Streets and the Brighton Opera House. (Courtesy of Kenneth and Lou Ellen Bromley.)

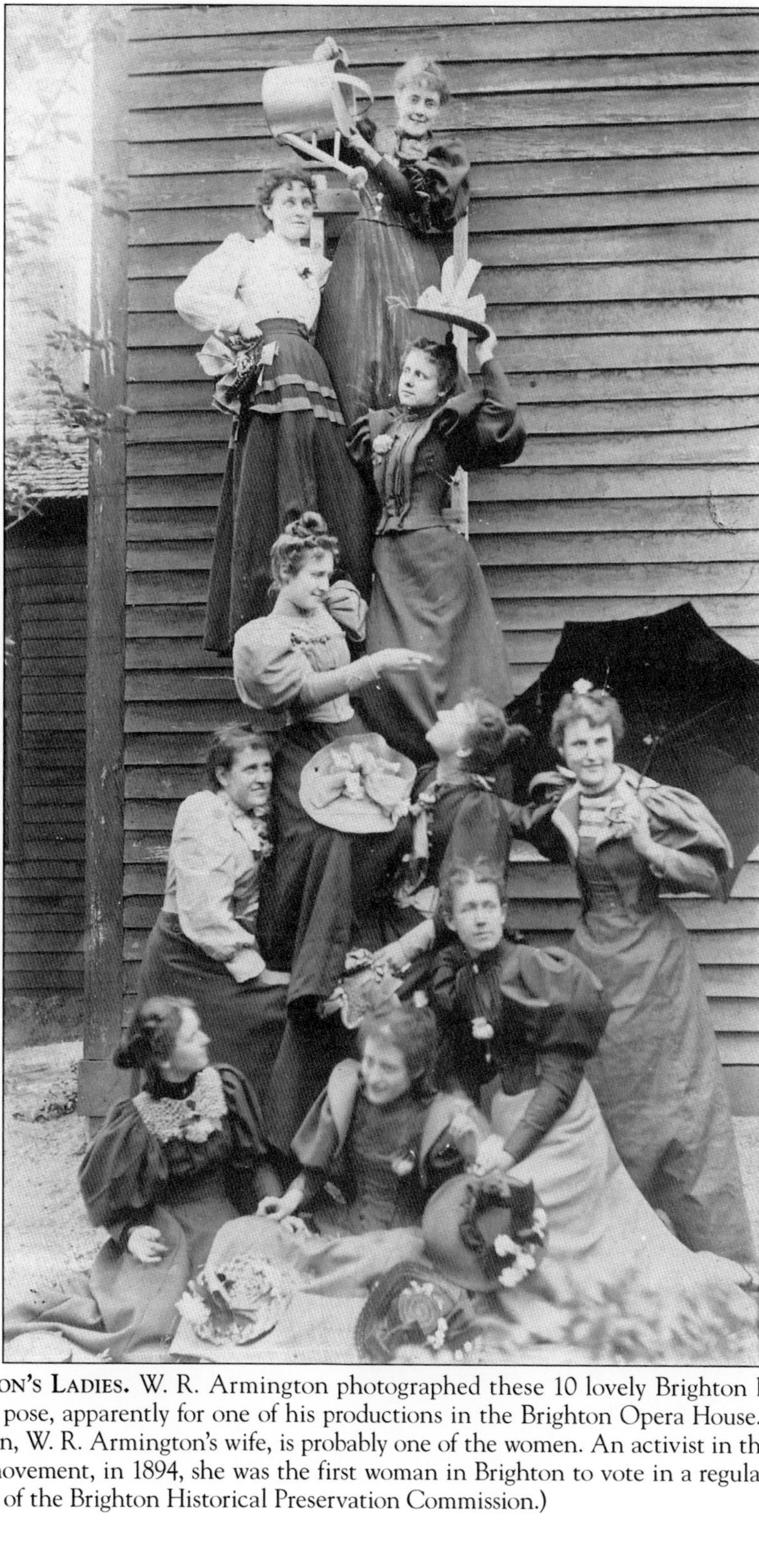

Armington's Ladies. W. R. Armington photographed these 10 lovely Brighton ladies in a theatrical pose, apparently for one of his productions in the Brighton Opera House. Emma B. Armington, W. R. Armington's wife, is probably one of the women. An activist in the women's suffrage movement, in 1894, she was the first woman in Brighton to vote in a regular election. (Courtesy of the Brighton Historical Preservation Commission.)

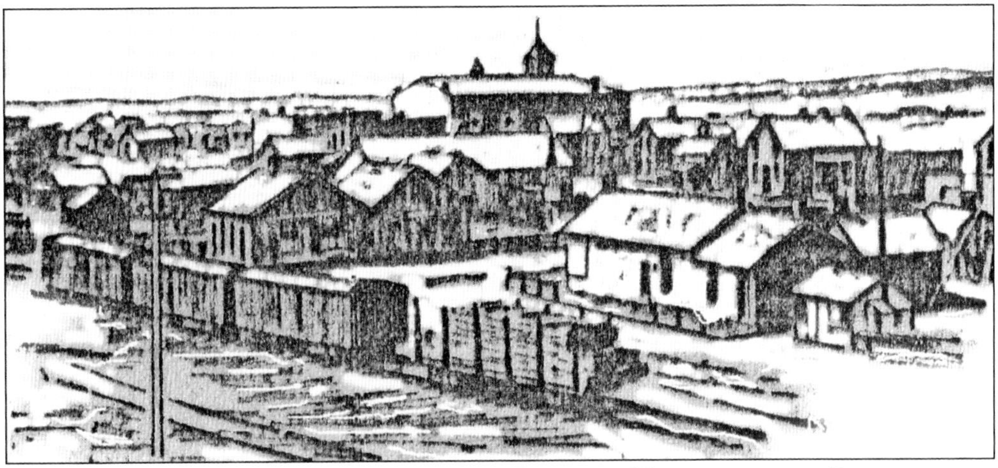

BRIGHTON VIEWED FROM THE DEPOT, 1890. This view of Brighton, looking southwest from the Union Pacific Railroad tracks, appeared in an article in the *Rocky Mountain News*, published April 6, 1890. The Brighton Opera House, the large building with the tower, dominated the town. Note the buildings along Strong Street, the street perpendicular to the railroad, which included the post office and saloons. Strong's Mercantile Company can be seen at the corner of Division (now North Main) and Strong Streets.

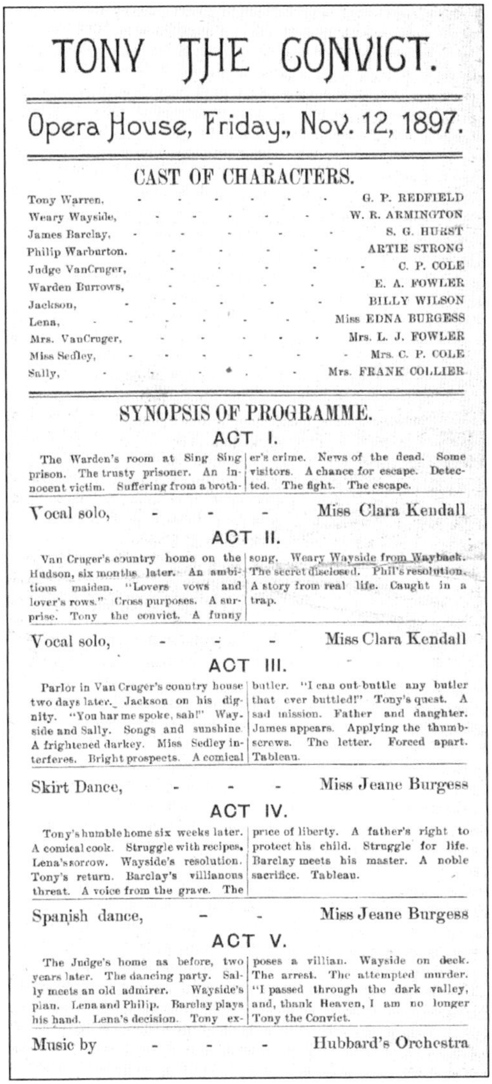

TONY THE CONVICT.

Opera House, Friday., Nov. 12, 1897.

CAST OF CHARACTERS.

Tony Warren,	G. P. REDFIELD
Weary Wayside,	W. R. ARMINGTON
James Barclay,	S. G. HURST
Philip Warburton,	ARTIE STRONG
Judge VanCruger,	C. P. COLE
Warden Burrows,	E. A. FOWLER
Jackson,	BILLY WILSON
Lena,	Miss EDNA BURGESS
Mrs. VanCruger,	Mrs. L. J. FOWLER
Miss Sedley,	Mrs. C. P. COLE
Sally,	Mrs. FRANK COLLIER

SYNOPSIS OF PROGRAMME.

ACT I.

The Warden's room at Sing Sing prison. The trusty prisoner. An innocent victim. Suffering from a brother's crime. News of the dead. Some visitors. A chance for escape. Detected. The fight. The escape.

Vocal solo, - - - Miss Clara Kendall

ACT II.

Van Cruger's country home on the Hudson, six months later. An ambitious maiden. "Lovers vows and lover's rows." Cross purposes. A surprise. Tony the convict. A funny song. Weary Wayside from Wayback. The secret disclosed. Phil's resolution. A story from real life. Caught in a trap.

Vocal solo, - - - Miss Clara Kendall

ACT III.

Parlor in Van Cruger's country house two days later. Jackson on his dignity. "You har me spoke, sah!" Wayside and Sally. Songs and sunshine. A frightened darkey. Miss Sedley interferes. Bright prospects. A comical butler. "I can out-buttle any butler that ever buttled!" Tony's quest. A sad mission. Father and daughter. James appears. Applying the thumbscrews. The letter. Forced apart. Tableau.

Skirt Dance, - - - Miss Jeane Burgess

ACT IV.

Tony's humble home six weeks later. A comical cook. Struggle with recipes. Lena's sorrow. Wayside's resolution. Tony's return. Barclay's villianous threat. A voice from the grave. The price of liberty. A father's right to protect his child. Struggle for life. Barclay meets his master. A noble sacrifice. Tableau.

Spanish dance, - - - Miss Jeane Burgess

ACT V.

The Judge's home as before, two years later. The dancing party. Sally meets an old admirer. Wayside's plan. Lena and Philip. Barclay plays his hand. Lena's decision. Tony exposes a villian. Wayside on deck. The arrest. The attempted murder. "I passed through the dark valley, and, thank Heaven, I am no longer Tony the Convict.

Music by - - - Hubbard's Orchestra

***TONY THE CONVICT*, 1897.** Local productions, such as the play *Tony the Convict*, staring G. P. Redfield, W. R. Armington, and S. G. Hurst in 1897, were regular events at the opera house. (Courtesy of Keeth and Lou Ellen Bromley.)

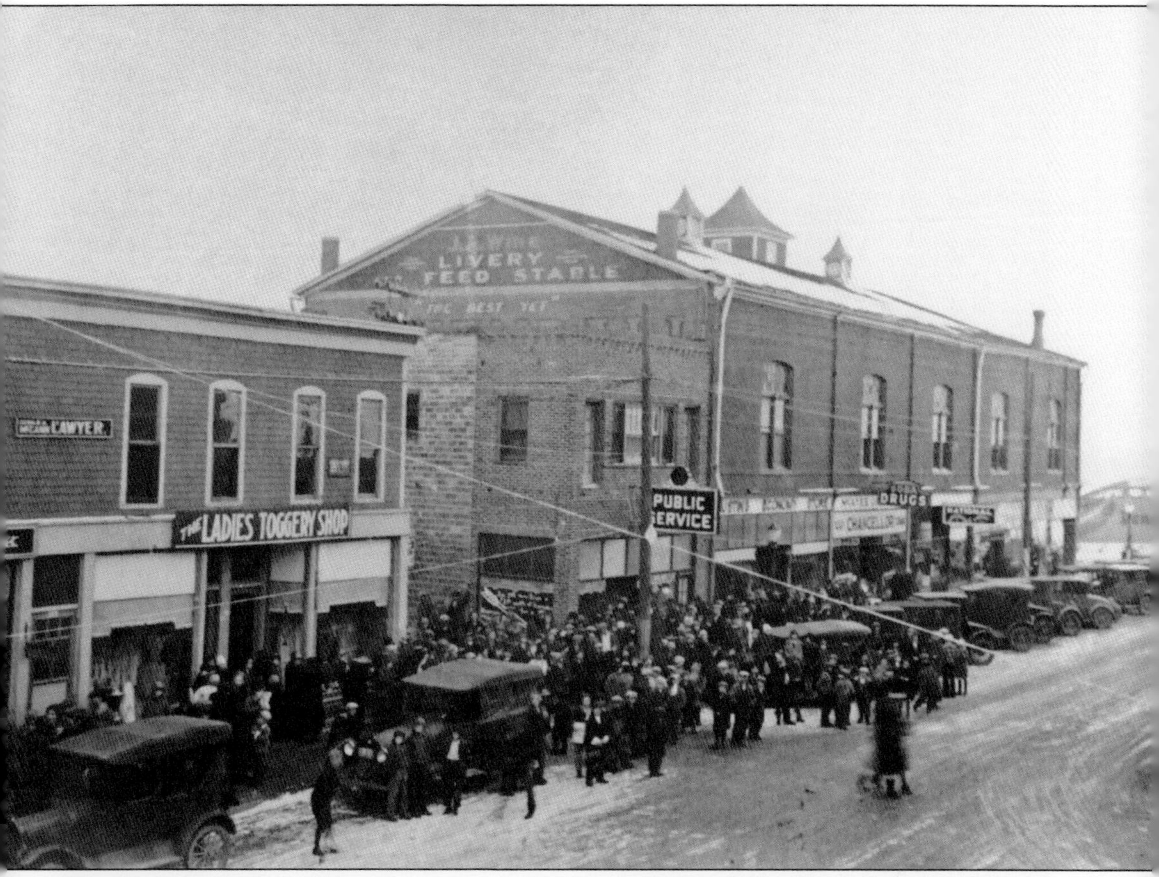

Wire Building, 1926. Although the ownership of the building changed hands several times, the Brighton Opera House (seen here in this 1926 photograph looking southwest from the corner of Bridge and Main Streets) continued to be referred to as the Wire Building in later years. James A. Wire owned the livery stable and eventually the whole business block when Daniel F. Carmichael sold the building after his finances were hard hit by the Panic of 1893. The northwest corner of the building was once the Brighton Post Office. At least one movie theater was located in the building, and its auditorium was the cultural center of Brighton. The first high school classes and a number of the town's churches began there. It was there that the clubs and associations promoting the social and industrial growth of Brighton met. When the old Wire Building burned down on the morning of July 25, 1955, 13 businesses and professional establishments and 12 second- and third-story apartments were destroyed. An important past of the history of Brighton vanished in the flames. (Courtesy of the Brighton Historical Preservation Commission.)

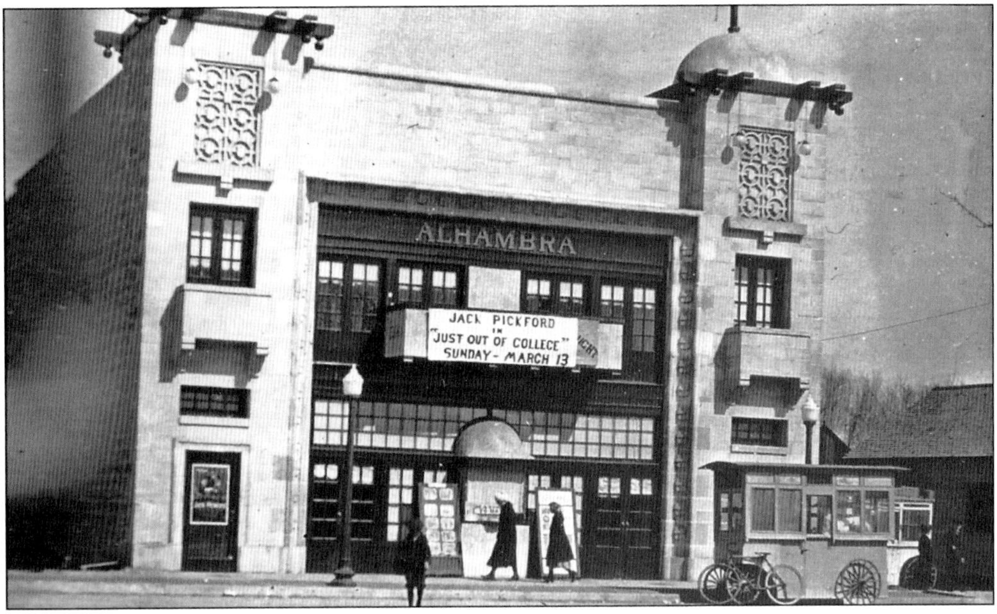

ALHAMBRA THEATRE. The Alhambra Theatre, built by J. N. Counter and his partner, Horace James, manager, opened October 19, 1920. It seated over 600 people. The marquee advertises the current movie, Jack Pickford in *Just Out of College*, Sunday, March 13. Jack Pickford (1896–1933), author, director, and producer, was Mary Pickford's brother. The movie was released in 1920, so this photograph was undoubtedly taken in 1921. The Alhambra was remodeled and reopened as the Rialto Theatre on March 29, 1923, with a new Wurlitzer organ and an electric sign out front. (Courtesy of the Brighton Historical Preservation Commission.)

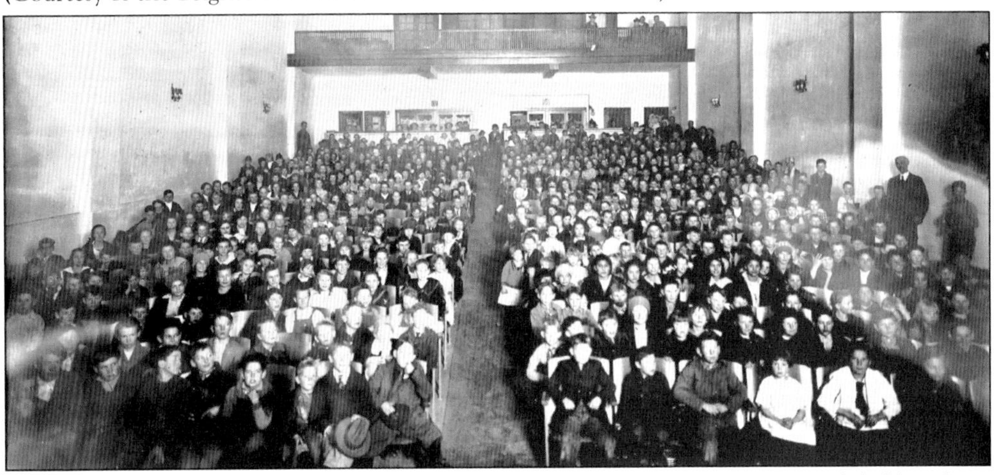

REX THEATER. The Rialto Theatre—formerly the Alhambra Theatre—was remodeled by Glenn W. Miller, manager, and reopened as the Rex Theater on December 21, 1935. The Saturday matinee at the Rex was a weekly event for the children of Brighton (seen in this photograph). In the early 1950s, ten cents paid the ticket to two feature movies, cartoons, newsreels, a weekly episode of a serial, and often a contest or some special give-away. The Rex Theater burned down in 1954. United Lumber Company built its store and offices on the same foundations. When their building was demolished in 2008 to make way for the construction of the new Brighton Branch of the Rangeview Library, the tunnels that had been under the theaters was exposed, revealing the long history of the site. (Courtesy of the Brighton Historical Preservation Commission.)

Five

Gem of the Valley

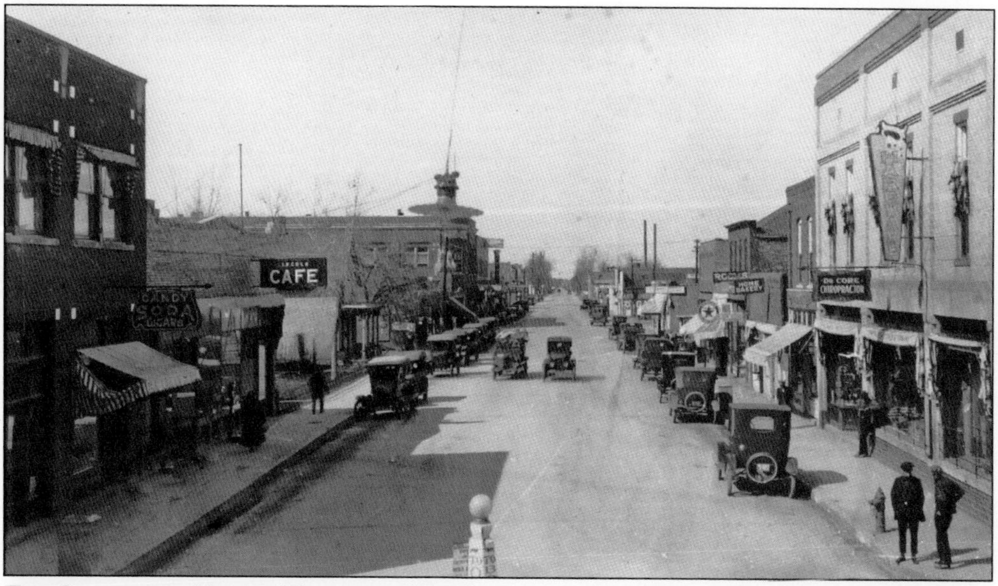

The Gem of the Valley. The town of Brighton was called "The Gem of the Valley" in local newspapers. The rapid growth of Brighton is reflected in this postcard of downtown Brighton viewed from in front of the Carmichael Building on Bridge Street looking north, down Division (North Main) Street. Note the similarity with downtown Brighton today. (Courtesy of the Colorado State Archives.)

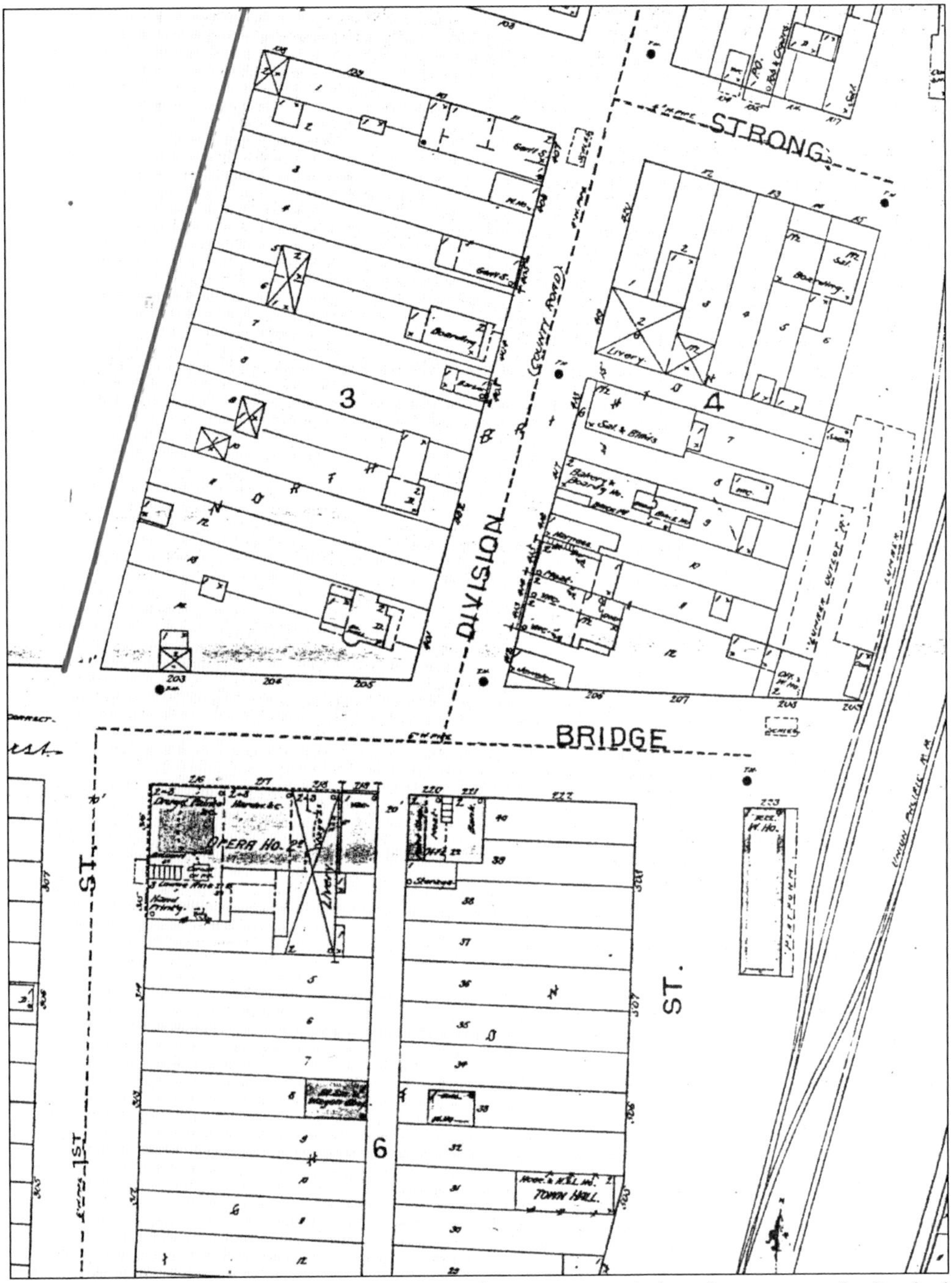

Downtown Brighton, 1893. Downtown Brighton was recorded in this portion of a Sanford Insurance Company map of the community prepared in 1893. Note the location of the Brighton Opera House and Livery Stable, Carmichael Business Block (220–221 Bridge Street), Brighton Town Hall and Fire Department (505 Second Street), D. W. Strong Residence (401 Division Street), Strong Mercantile Company (407 Division Street), Swan Livery Stable (419 Division Street), and Counter Lumber Company (208 Bridge Street). The addresses do not coincide with current address numbers. (Courtesy of the Brighton Historical Preservation Commission.)

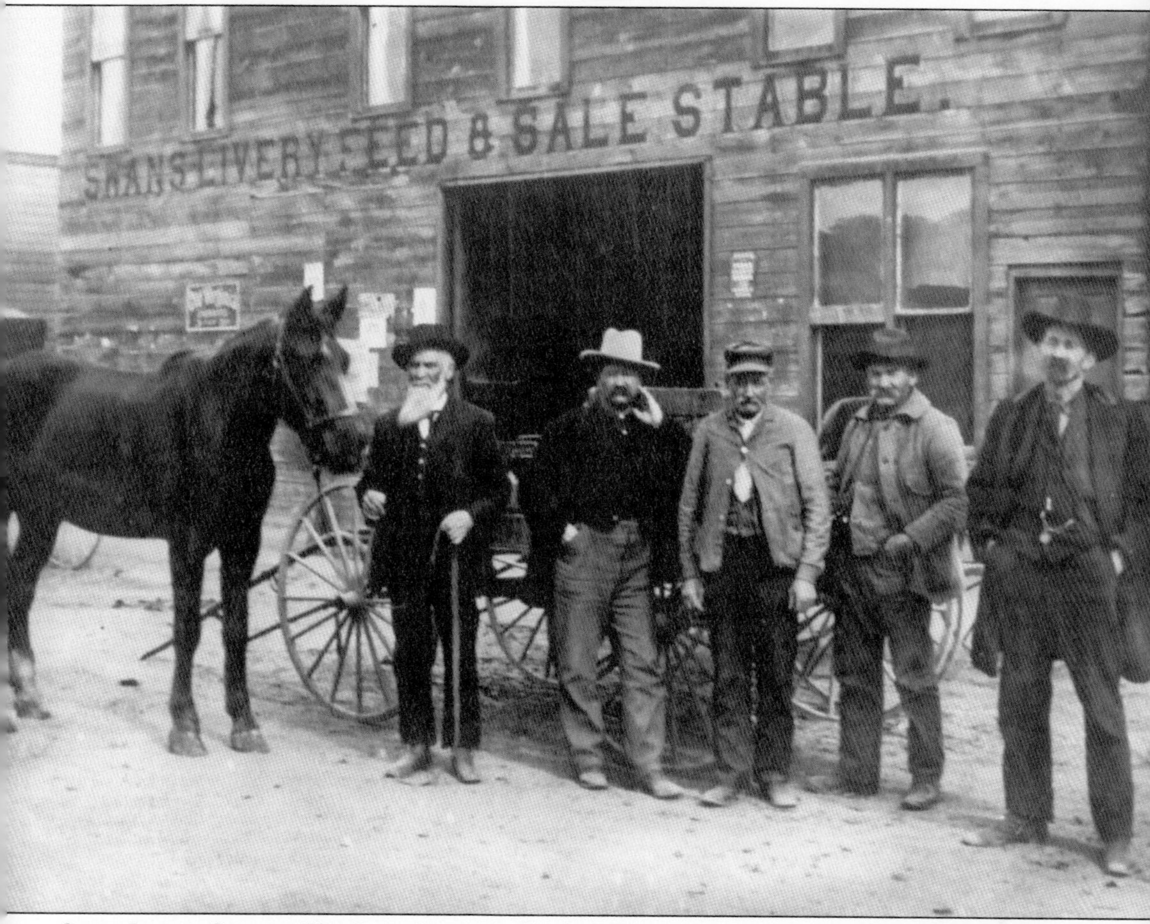

Swan Livery Stable. The Swan Livery Stable (419 Division Street) was built in 1887 by B. F. Swan, the man on the far left with a white beard. Also pictured are members of the Blyler family, John Blyler (third from left), Fred Pierce (fourth from left), and ? Milhien (fifth from left). The building was located on the east side of Division Street in the center of the block between Bridge and Strong Streets. It burned down in 1921 in a fire that also razed two other buildings. (Courtesy of the Adams County Historical Society.)

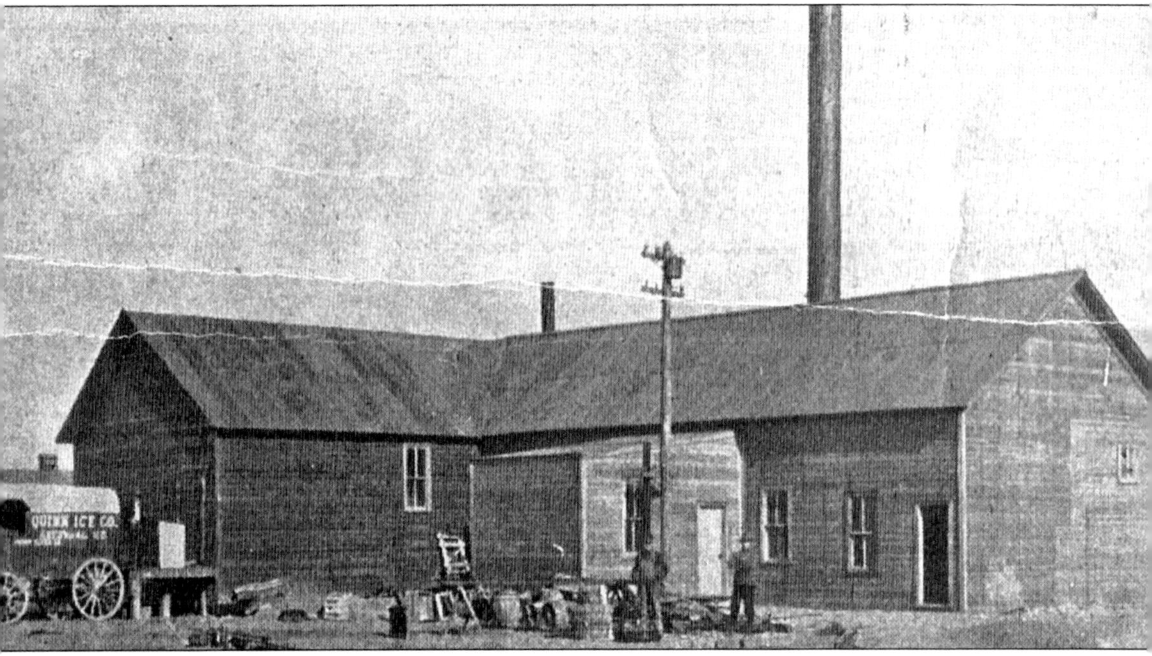

Brighton Fuel and Ice Company. The Brighton Fuel and Ice Plant was established by a group of Brighton merchants to service the growing population. Note the sign on the wagon, Quinn Ice Company. When the electricity failed in downtown Brighton, as it often did in the early days, the joke was that Quinn was asleep at the switch. In 1928, the *Brighton Directory* listed the Brighton Fuel and Ice Company offices at 65 South Second Avenue and their plant at 215 North Fifth Avenue. Later Benjamin ("Ben") Fischer operated the Brighton Ice Company at 210 North Fifth Avenue. (Courtesy of the Brighton Historical Preservation Commission.)

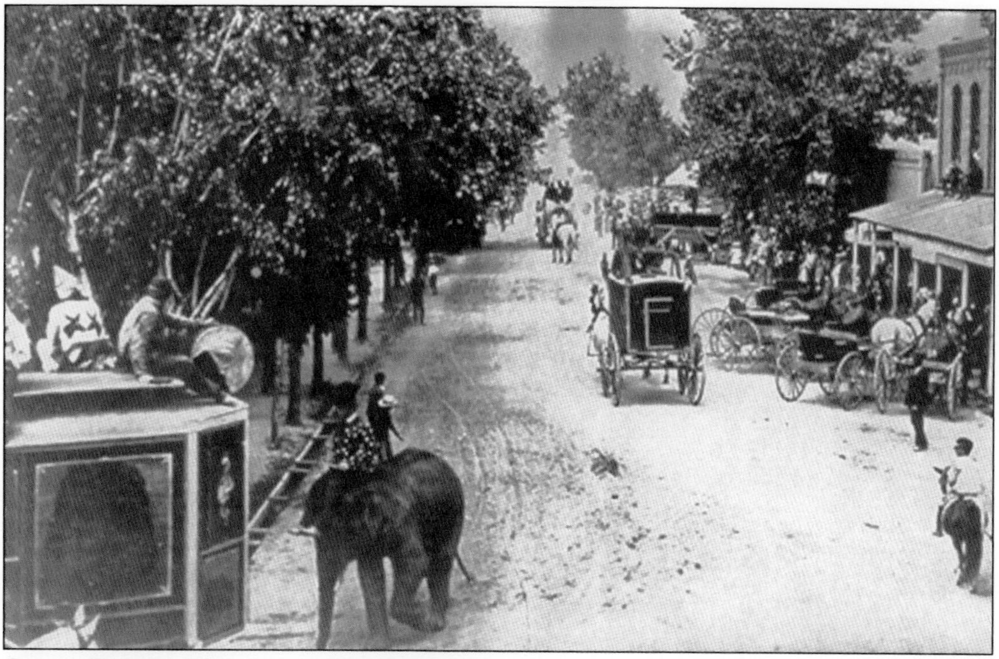

Circus Parade. This circus company may have been the one from the Chicago World's Fair that visited Brighton in 1894. The circus parade (above), complete with elephants, is seen on Division (North Main) Street looking north. The buildings on the right housed the Leffingwell Mercantile Company. The trees on the northwest corner on the left surrounded the home of Dewey W. Strong. The house was later moved to the present site of the Brighton Professional Building across from the intersection of South First Avenue and Bridge Street. Note the dirt streets and the open irrigation ditch along the left side of the street. Water was brought from the Brighton Lateral of the Fulton Ditch one block east to water the lawns of houses along Division Street. (Both courtesy of the Brighton Historical Preservation Commission.)

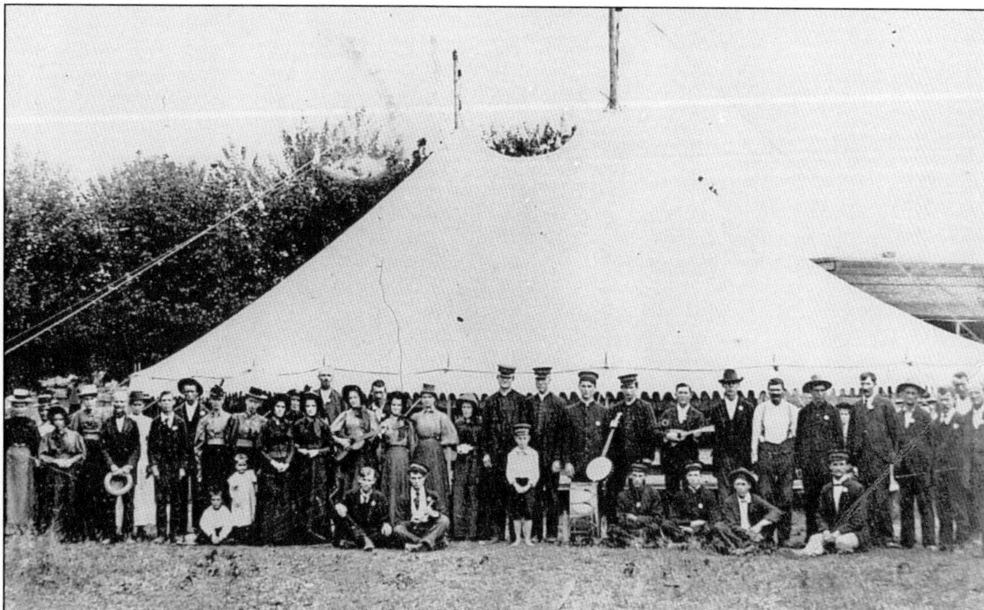

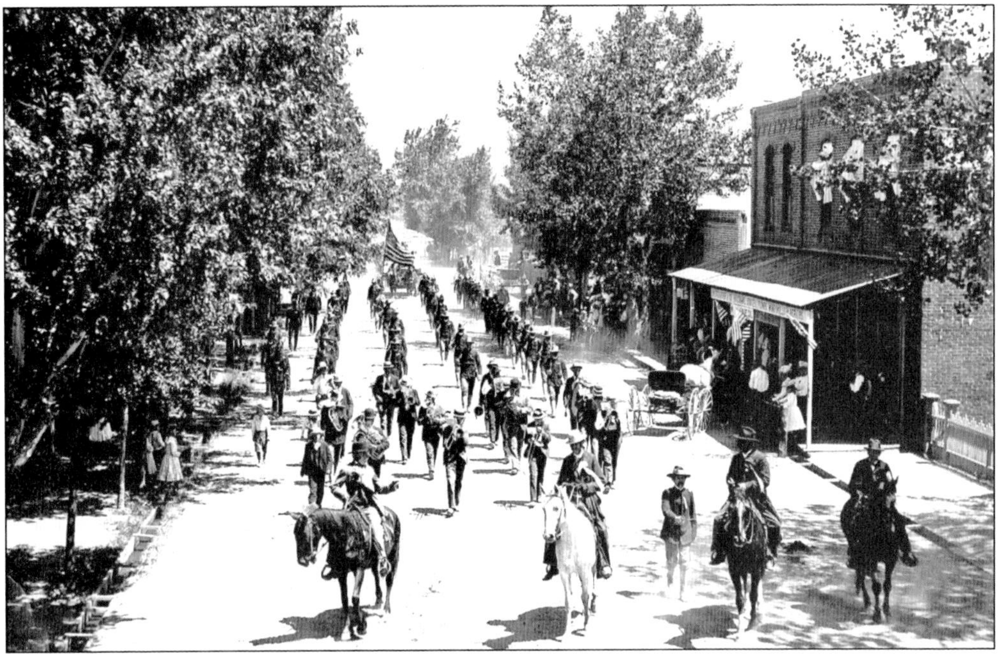

Leffingwell Hardware Company. The Leffingwell Hardware Company occupied the first two buildings on the right at the intersection of Bridge and Division (now Main) Streets in the photograph above. These two buildings were demolished in 1916 and the bricks reused in the construction of the business block that now occupies that site. Photographer Louis C. McClure (1867–1957) captured the view of downtown Brighton (shown below) in 1910 from in front of the Carmichael Building looking north, down Division Street. D. W. Strong's house occupied the opposite corner to the left of the intersection, behind the trees. A. S. Leffingwell's home, 601 Walnut Street, on the northeast corner of Walnut and North Sixth Avenue, overlooked the Town Park, the proposed site of the first Adams County Courthouse, now the location of the new North Elementary School. (Both courtesy of the Denver Public Library Western History and Genealogy Department.)

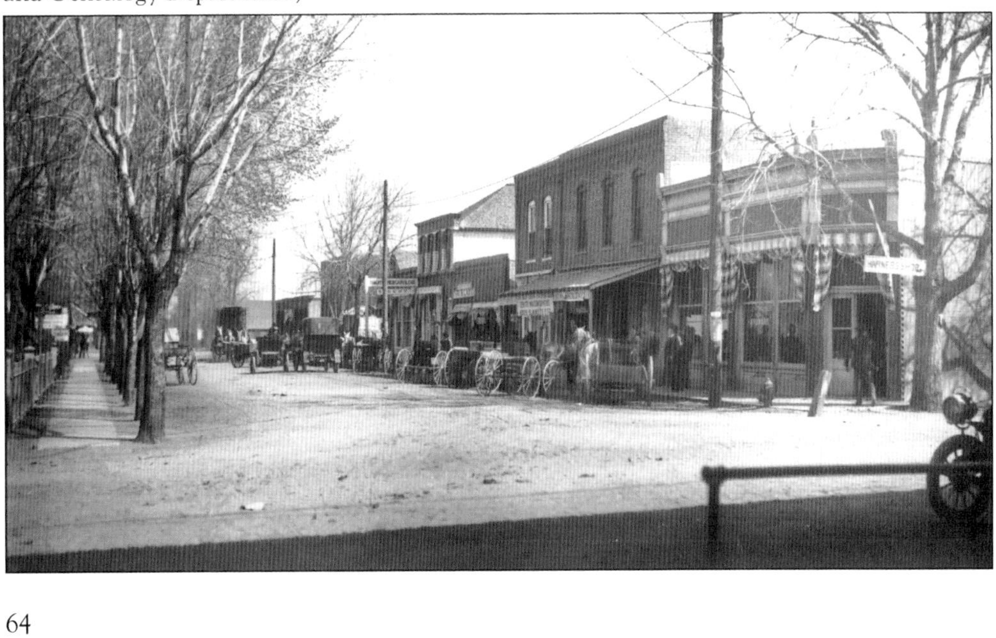

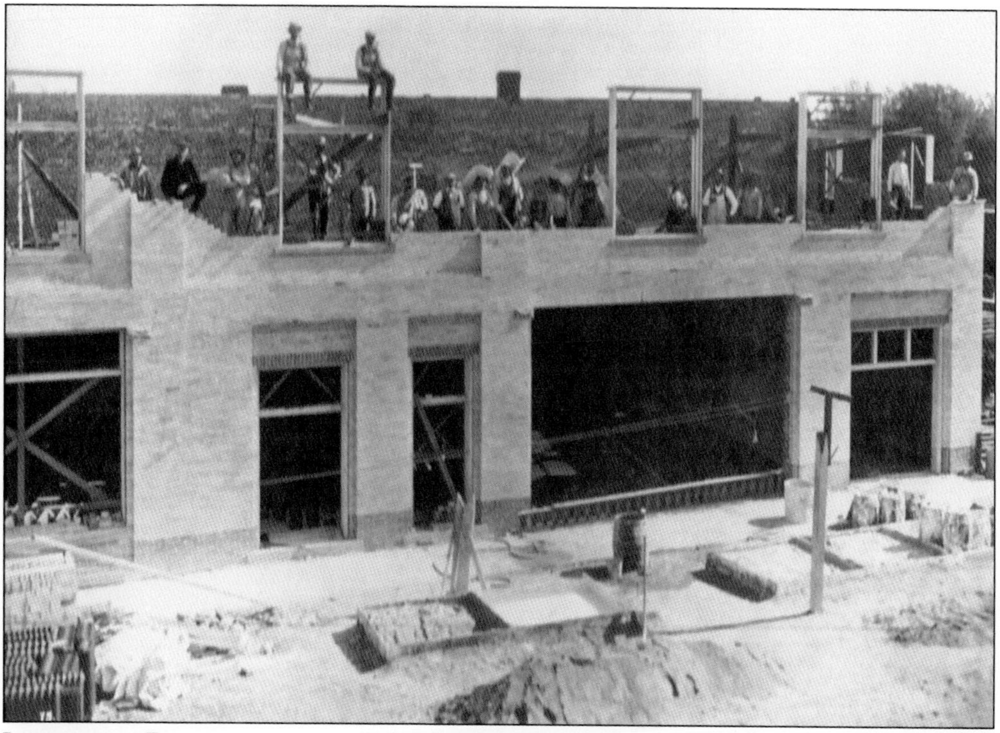

Leffingwell Building, 1916. A. S. (Archie Scott) Leffingwell built this business block on the northeast corner of Bridge and Main Streets in Brighton in 1916. The building still dominates the intersection. Two of the other three corners were occupied by the old Brighton Opera House (later called the Wire Building) on the southwest corner that burned down in 1955 and the Brighton State Bank on the northwest corner. The Leffingwell family sold the Leffingwell Hardware Store building in 1961. (Above courtesy of the Brighton Historical Preservation Commission; below courtesy of Beuhlah Barnard.)

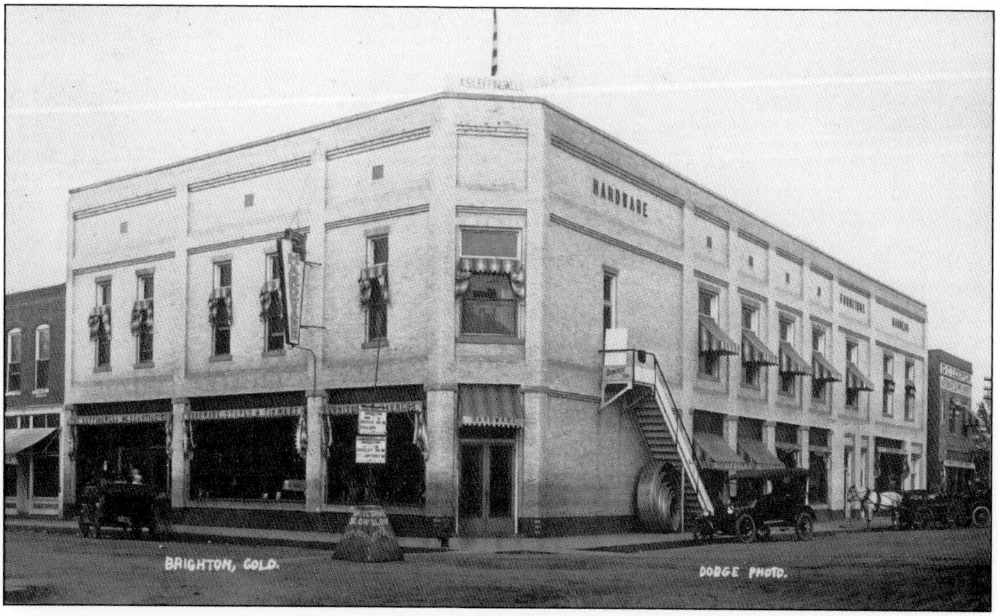

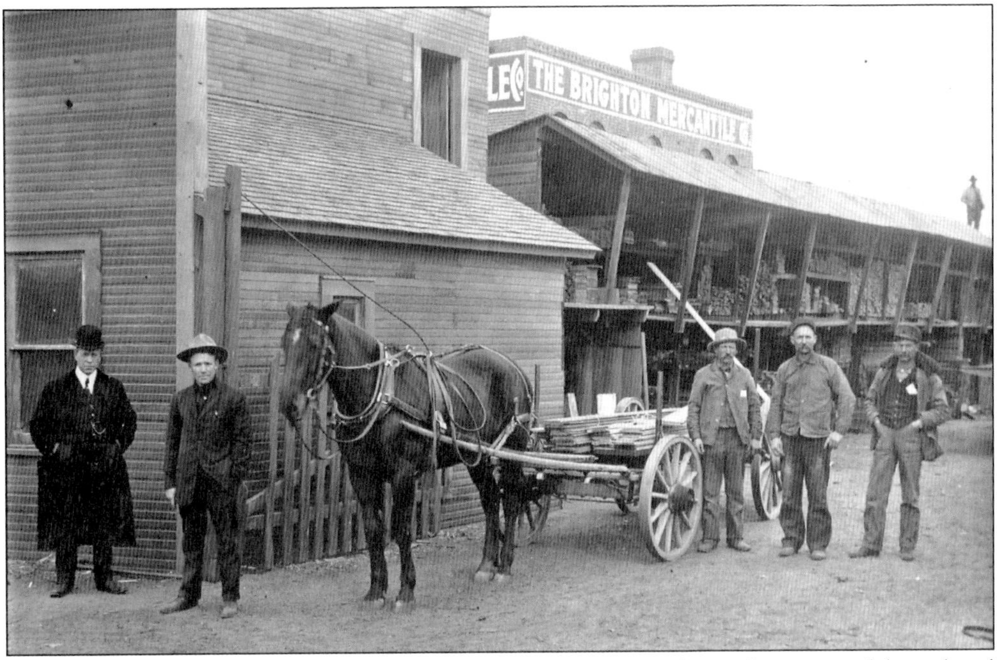

Counter Lumber Company. The Counter Lumber Company was located just west of the railroad track at 170 Bridge Street in Brighton, later the location of Hunter Hardware. The company, owned by J. N. Counter, supplied lumber and other supplies for the construction of many major buildings in Brighton, including the Adams County Courthouse. Counter Lumber Company later became United Lumber Company at the new site of the Brighton Public Library. J. N. Counter lived in Brighton from 1903 until his death in 1923. He served in the state legislature (1914–1916) and owned a number of businesses, including the Gordon Hotel and the *Brighton Blade*. His son, James C. Counter, was also a prominent member of the community. (Both courtesy of the Brighton Historical Preservation Commission.)

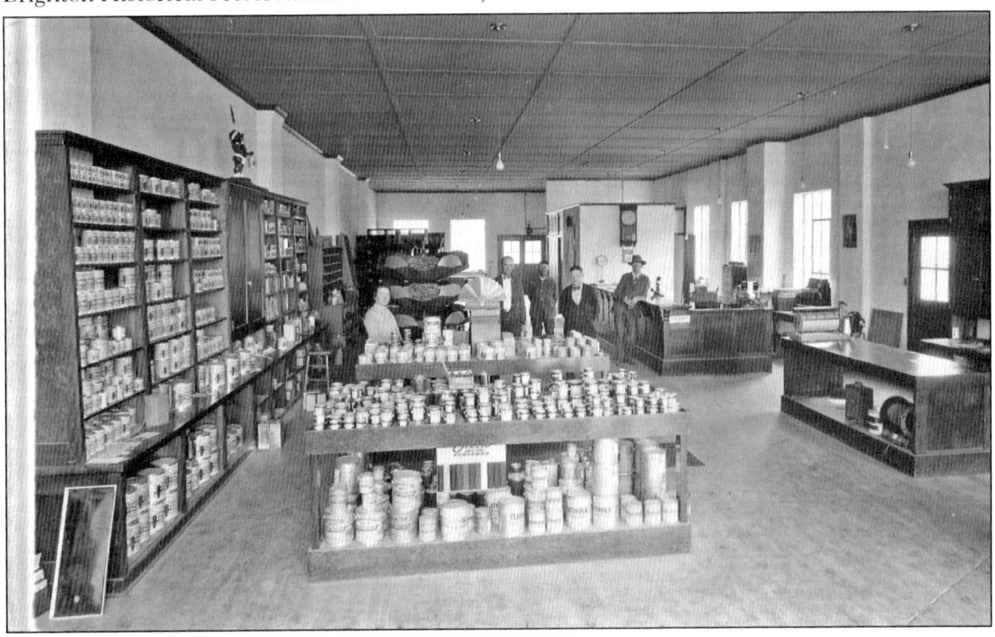

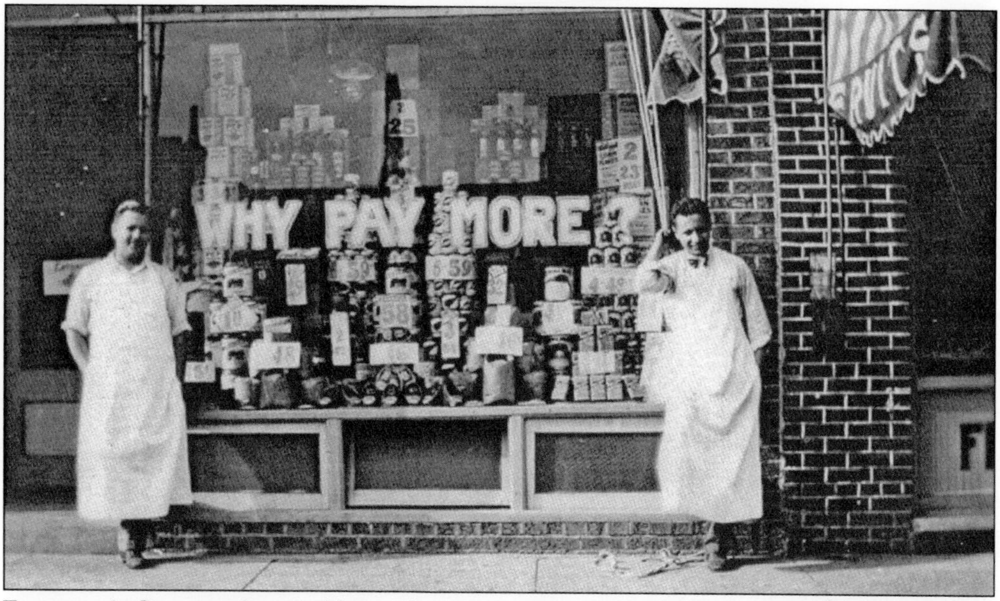

FRIEDMAN'S GROCERY STORE. Above, the owners of Friedman's Grocery Store, Samuel ("Sam," left) and Myer Friedman (right), wearing their familiar long white aprons, were photographed in the 1930s standing in front of their store in Brighton. The window displays a sign that reads, "Why Pay More?" The interior of the store (below) shows the variety of goods available. The business began in 1912 with Hyman Friedman, a Russian immigrant, who began peddling fruits and vegetables in Brighton. He opened the first grocery store on Main Street and in 1922 moved to the familiar location at 115 Strong Street. The store expanded in 1935 when a new brick building was constructed on the site. The store was open for business downtown for three generations. Jerry Friedman acquired the business from his father, Myer Friedman, in 1977. A number of grocery stores occupied the building after he retired. (Both courtesy of the University of Denver Penrose Library, Images of Jewish Families Material Culture Collection.)

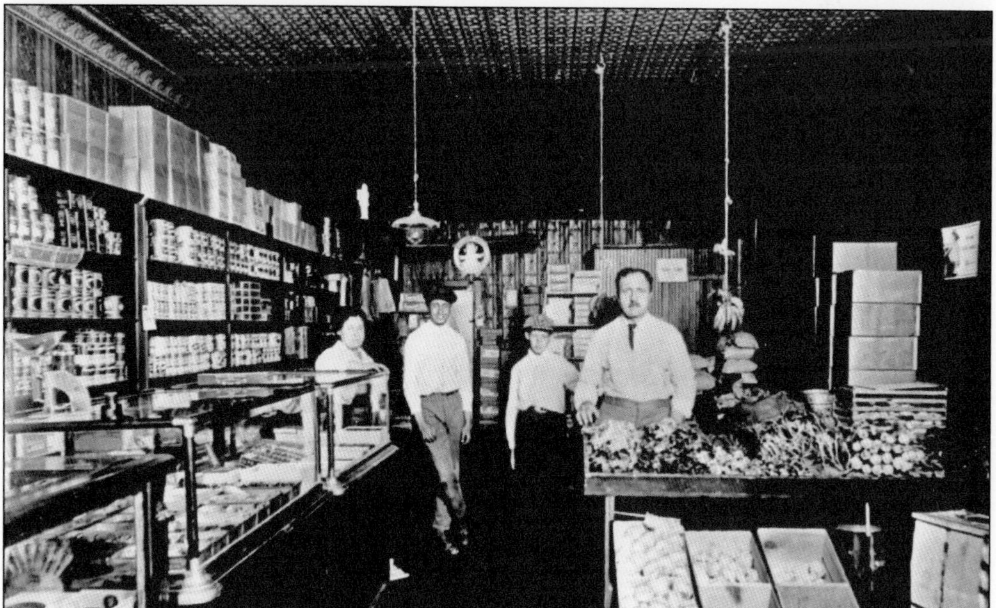

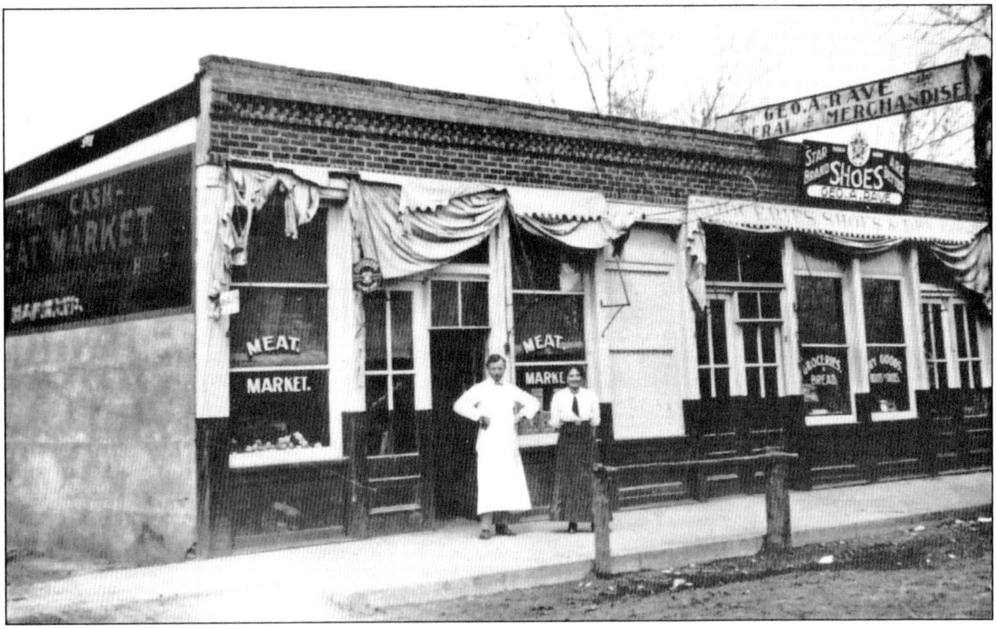

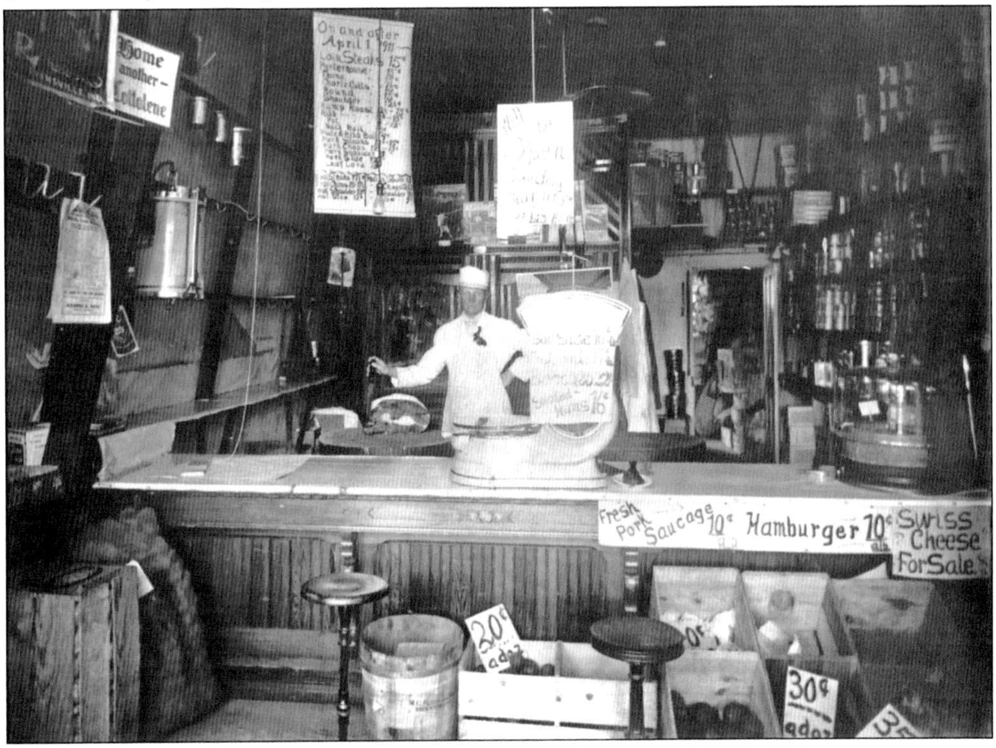

George A. Rave Mercantile Company. The George A. Rave Meat Market and Mercantile Company occupied buildings at 137–139 North Main Street, the present location of the *Brighton Standard Blade* newspaper office. Their advertisement in the 1928 *Brighton Directory* proclaimed, "When you want good home-cured hams, bacon, smoked and fresh sausage, corn-fed beef and pork, staple and fancy groceries, shoes and dry goods at the right prices see George A. Rave." (Both courtesy of the Brighton Historical Preservation Commission.)

Six

THE COUNTY SEAT

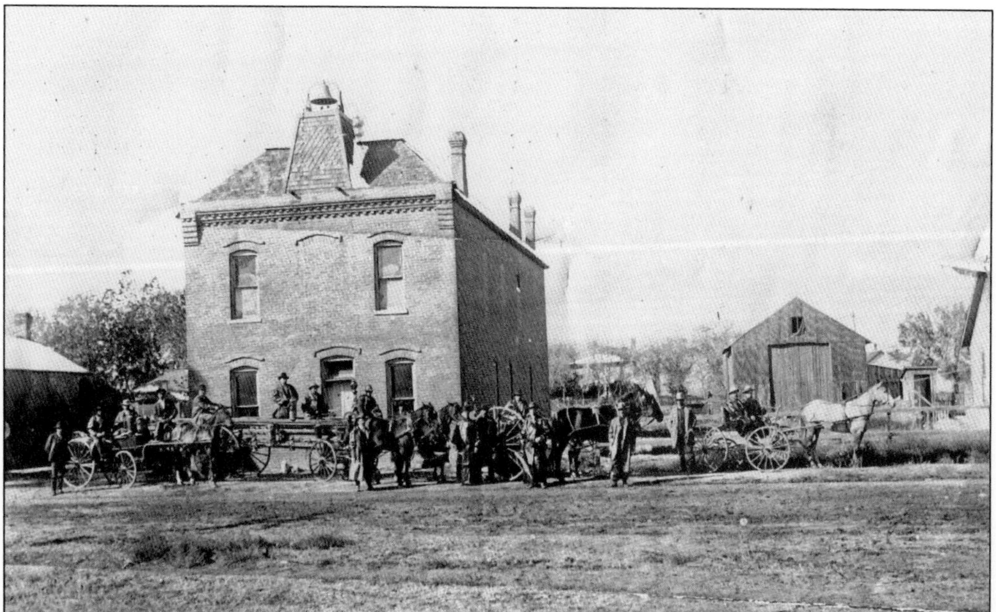

BRIGHTON TOWN HALL AND FIRE STATION. The Brighton Town Hall and Fire Station, built in 1887, the same year the town was incorporated, was the site of the first meeting of the Board of County Commissioners of Adams County on December 4, 1902. Note the fire bell and the horse-drawn fire equipment. The building faced the railroad tracks and what is now Cabbage Avenue. (Courtesy of the Brighton Historical Preservation Commission.)

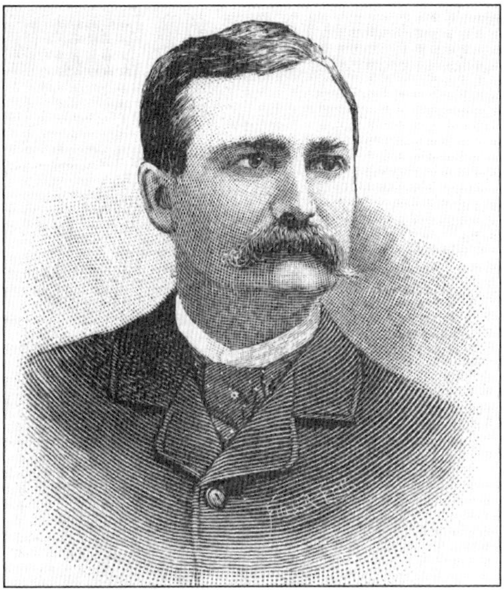

Alva Adams. Adams County was named after Alva A. Adams (1850–1922). Although Adams served three terms as governor during the stormiest period in Colorado politics, he was one of the state's most popular governors. Born in Wisconsin, his family moved to Greeley when his brother contracted tuberculosis. Beginning by hauling ties for the Denver and Rio Grande Railroad building south from Denver, he became a lumber and hardware dealer in the new towns of Colorado Springs and South Pueblo. A Democrat, he was elected to the state legislature in 1876 and as governor in 1886 and again in 1896 and 1904.

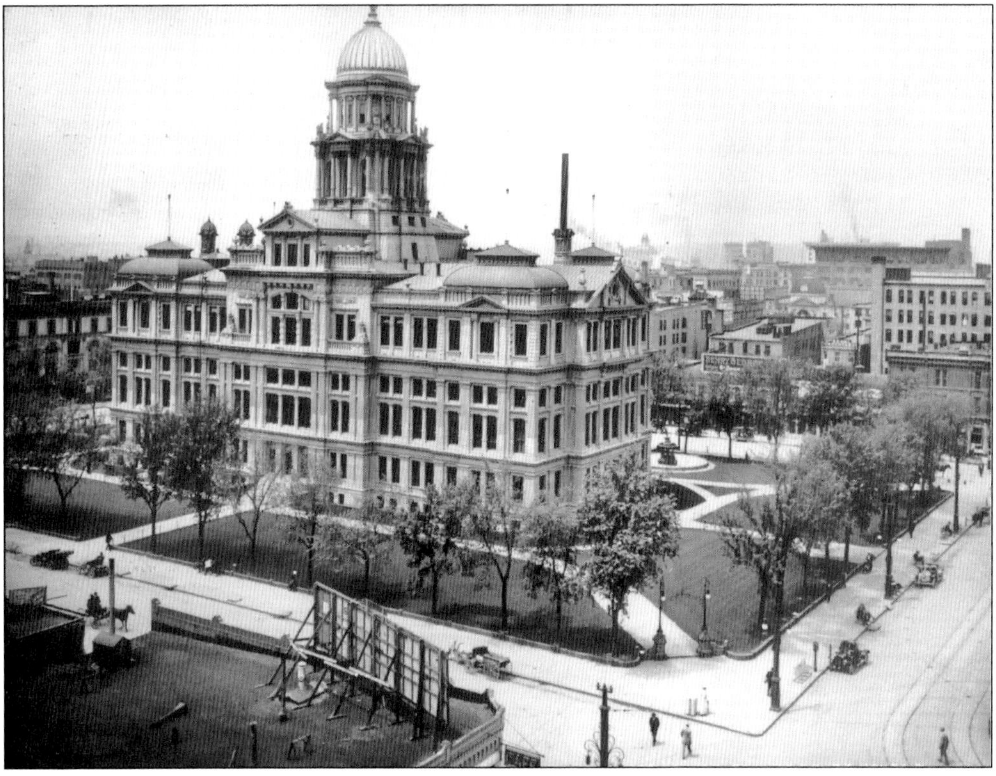

Arapahoe County Courthouse. Adams County was formed out of old Arapahoe County, which was originally formed by Kansas Territory in 1855. When Colorado became a territory, Denver continued as the county seat. The county extended east all the way to Kansas. The Arapahoe County Courthouse in Denver, seen here, was built in 1883 and demolished in 1934. When the city and county of Denver was formed in 1902, old Arapahoe County was divided up into the city and county of Denver, South Arapahoe (now Arapahoe) County, and Adams County. (Courtesy of the Denver Public Library Western History and Genealogy Department.)

EMMETT A. BROMLEY. Emmett Bromley (1858–1922), state legislator from Brighton, has been called the "Father of Adams County." Both he and real estate developer and fellow member of the legislature Daniel F. Carmichael campaigned for years for the formation of Adams County before the state legislature created the county in 1902. Bromley Lane in Brighton is named after him. Emmett Bromley was a Brighton farmer, rancher, dairyman, and banker. He owned 200 acres at what is now South Fifteenth Avenue and Bromley Lane. Bromley was born in Peru, New York, on February 14, 1858, and came to Denver in 1877. He was married in Golden, Colorado, in 1877. His record of public service includes deputy sheriff and assessor in old Arapahoe County, two terms in the Colorado House of Representatives, two terms in the state senate, and clerk of the District Court in Adams County for 12 years. (Courtesy of Kenneth and Lou Ellen Bromley.)

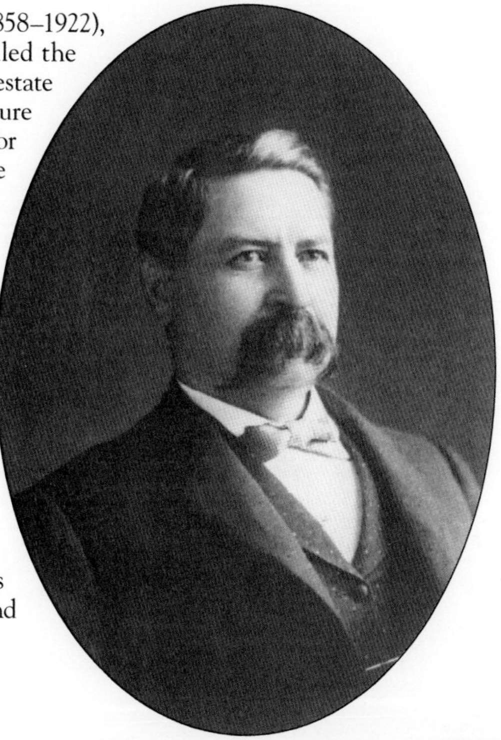

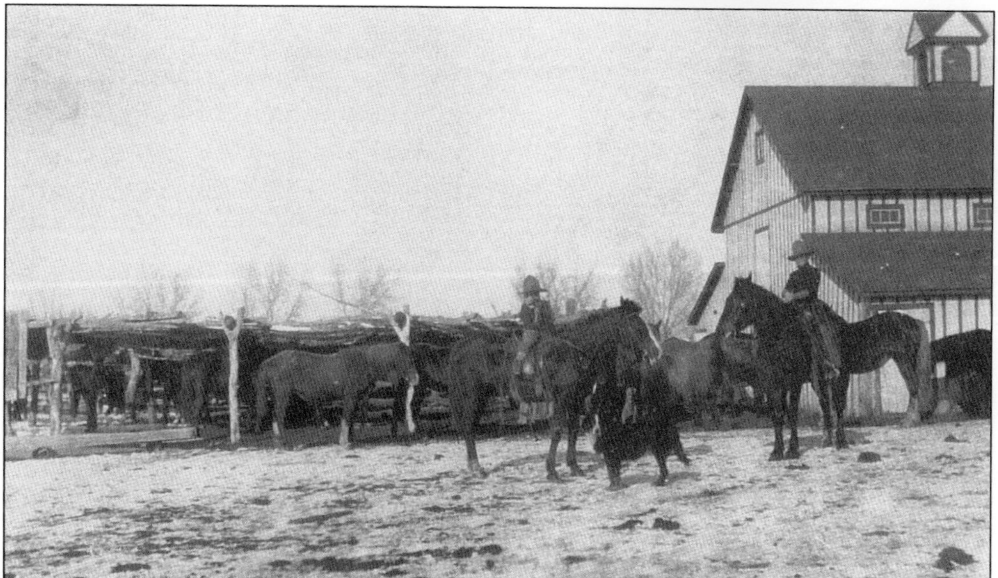

BROMLEY FARM ON BROMLEY LANE. Bromley Lane, now a major thoroughfare in Brighton, was named after Emmet Bromley. The Bromley family farm was located just off of Bromley Lane near Fifteenth Avenue. The house and barn were recently designated as a historic site. The boys on the horses in front of the Bromley barn are John Bromley (left) and Emmett Bromley Jr. (right). The Bromleys raised the Cleveland bay horses and purebred dogs. Later the Kolzuma and Hishinuma families occupied the farm. (Courtesy of the Brighton Historical Preservation Commission.)

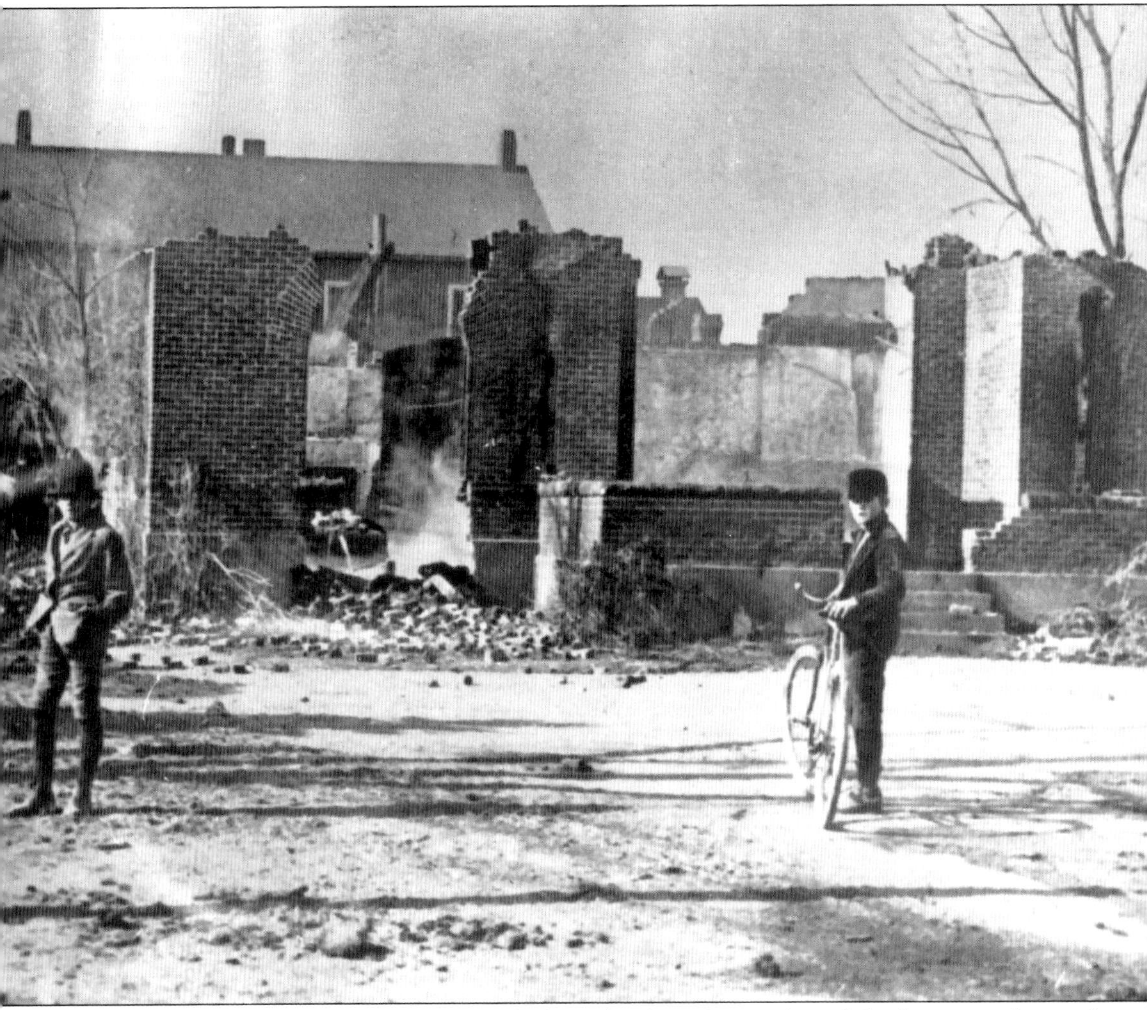

The First County Courthouse. Newly formed Adams County leased the former residence of Daniel F. Carmichael, the founder of Brighton, as its first courthouse for $100 a month in 1902. Carmichael built the handsome two-story brick structure in 1890 at what is now the end of Court Street at 34 South Third Avenue. The county assessor and county superintendent of schools were housed on the second story. All the other county officials had offices on the first floor. The county jail was in the basement. The Carmichael Mansion burned down on January 19, 1904, along with $20,000 and all the county records. The house was rebuilt and used for many years as the manse (or parsonage) for First Presbyterian Church. The Herman Reuter residence at South Fifth Avenue and Bridge Street in Brighton served as the Adams County Courthouse from 1904 to 1906. The house was later moved to 1010 Bridge Street, where it was known as the Llewellyn Nursing Home and the Doolan Hospital. In 1960, it was moved again to Base Line Road, where it was remodeled into apartments. (Courtesy of the Brighton Historical Preservation Commission.)

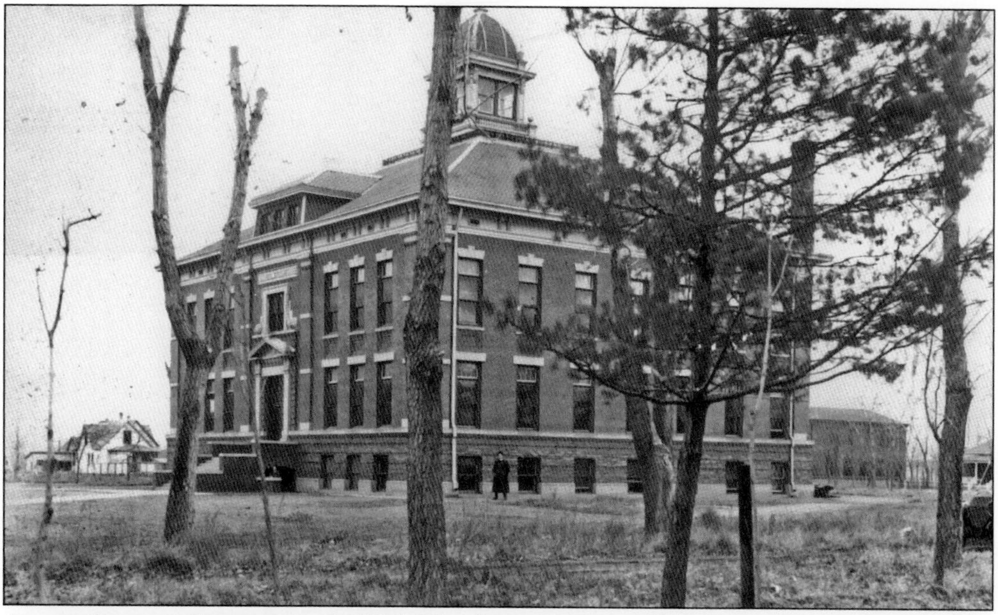

ADAMS COUNTY COURTHOUSE, 1906. The first permanent Adams County Courthouse was completed in 1906 on what was known as Skeel Corner, a half block on the southeast corner of South Fourth Avenue and Bridge Street. The building is now the eastern half of the present Brighton City Hall. Note the cupola and third floor (attic) that were removed when the building was expanded in 1939 by the Public Works Administration (PWA). Looking to the northeast from South Fourth Avenue and Court Place, the two-story Brighton District No. 27 school building (later the North Elementary School) can be seen in the background on the right. The school once housed classrooms for all 12 grades from first grade to high school. (Courtesy of the Denver Public Library Western History and Genealogy Department.)

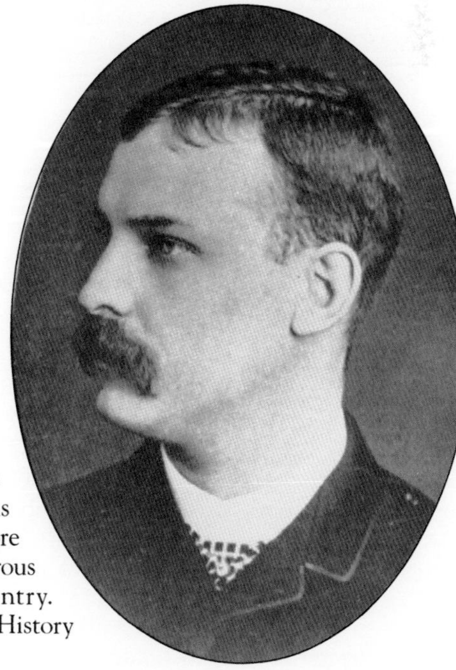

JOHN JAMES HUDDART, ARCHITECT. The first permanent Adams County Courthouse was designed by Denver architect John James Huddart (1856–1930). Huddart was born in England and educated at Alston College. He worked in Ireland and Brazil before coming to Denver. Huddart designed a large number of notable buildings in Denver, including the Charles Boettcher residence at Twelfth and Grant Streets, and he drew the plans for several additions to the old Albany Hotel. Before his death in Denver at 72, Huddart designed numerous schools and courthouses throughout the country. (Courtesy of the Denver Public Library Western History and Genealogy Department.)

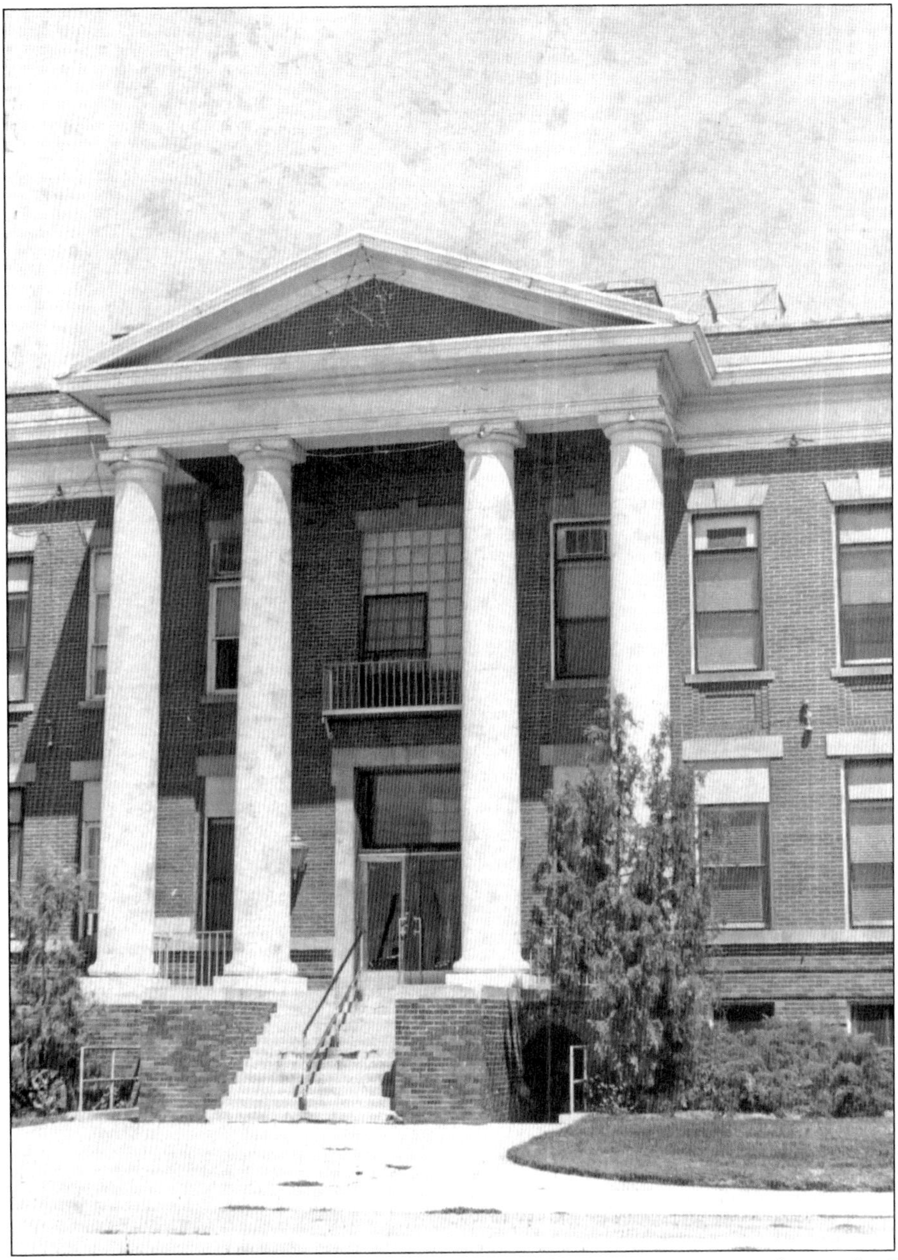

ADAMS COUNTY COURTHOUSE, 1939. A Public Works Administration project during the Great Depression almost doubled the size of the courthouse. The construction project under R. H. Woodmansee, engineer inspector for the PWA, added to the west side of the building. The architects for the project, Richard O. Perry and Lester James of Denver, did an excellent job of duplicating Huddart's original design in the new addition, but they removed the Spanish tiled roof, really a fourth story containing the jury rooms, replacing it with a flat roof and added a portico with four Doric columns to the new west entrance, changing the style of the building from Victorian to classical architecture. In 1975, Adams County sold the old courthouse to Frank Mann in exchange for land at Adams County Regional Park in Henderson. Mann, in turn, sold the building to the City of Brighton for use as the city hall.

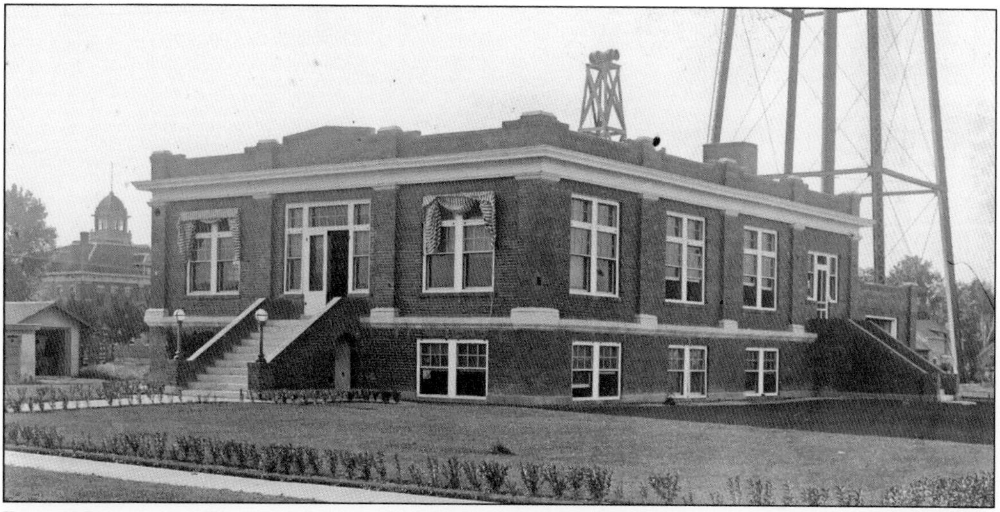

Pump House and Public Library. In 1904, when the Adams County officials purchased the land at Skeel Corner, the southeast corner of South Fourth Avenue and Bridge Streets, from Carmichael Investment Company for the new Adams County Courthouse, they also purchased the water works and electric company that Daniel F. Carmichael had developed, located just behind his home on South Fifth Avenue. The town created a modern water system with the familiar water tower and pump house (seen on the postcard above). The upper floor of the building housed the Brighton Public Library (seen below) at 675 Bush Street for many years before a new library building was constructed on South Eighth Avenue on the former Adams County Fairgrounds. The building has been extensively remodeled as the Brighton Senior Center. The library, now part of the county Rangeview Library system, is building a new building on the former site of United Lumber Company at 307 Bridge Street. (Above courtesy of the Colorado State Archives; below courtesy of the Brighton Historical Preservation Commission.)

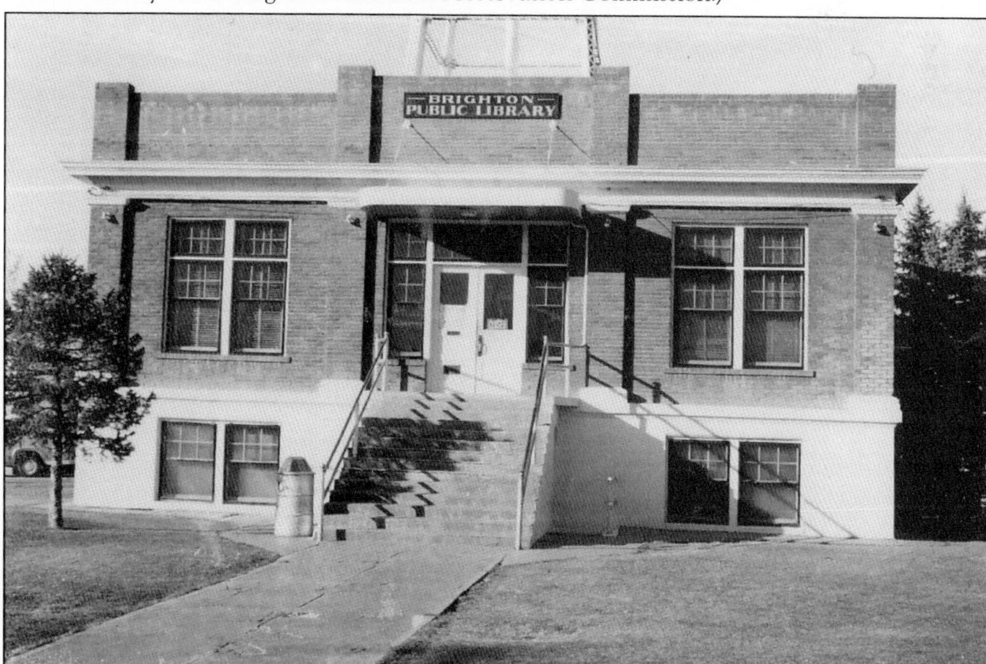

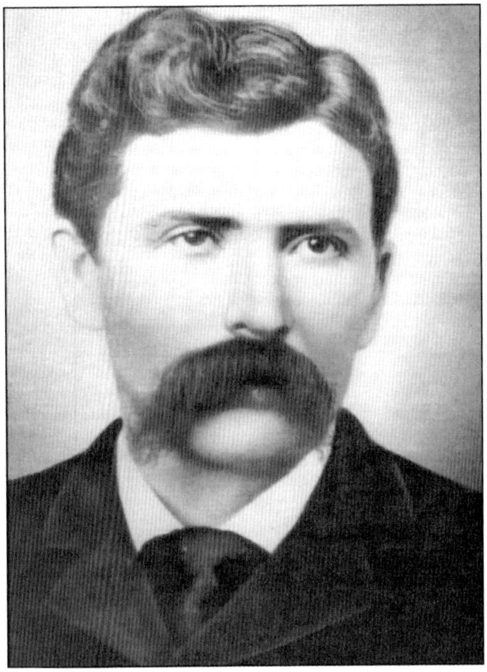

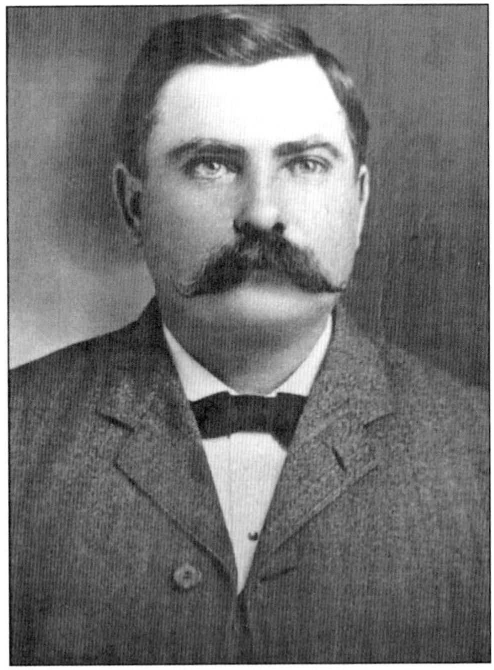

Martin R. Bromley and J. P. Higgins. Martin R. Bromley, Emmett Bromley's brother, was the first sheriff of Adams County (1902–1904). James P. Higgins, the popular second sheriff of Adams County, served two terms from 1904 to 1908. (Above left courtesy of Kenneth and Lou Ellen Bromley; above right courtesy of the Brighton Historical Commission.)

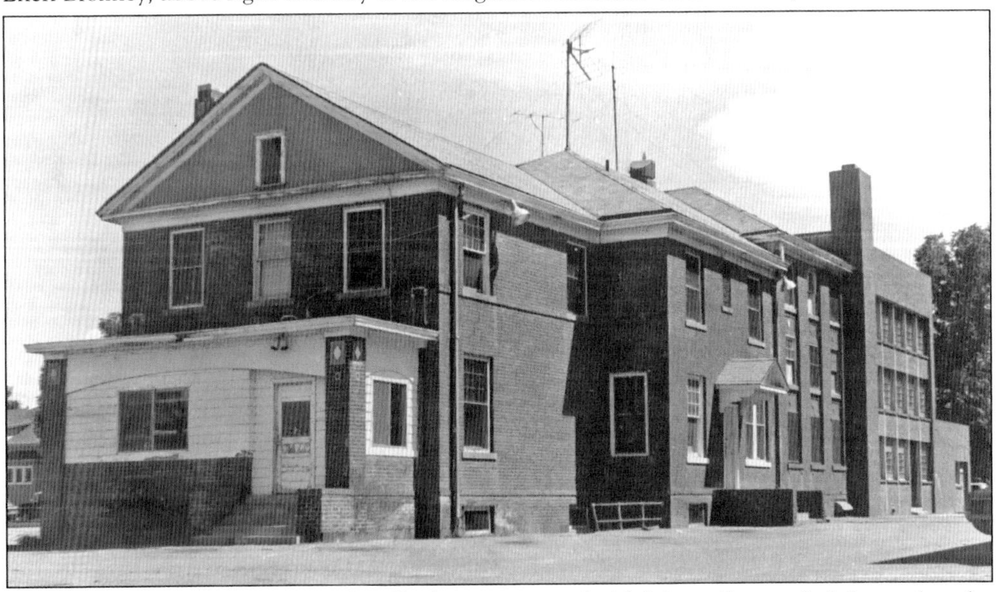

Old Adams County Jail. The sheriff's department and old Adams County Jail, located to the rear (east) of the old county courthouse on the southwest corner of Bridge Street and South Fifth Avenue, also served as the residence of the sheriff of Adams County. The sheriff's wife cooked the meals for the prisoners. The building, which faced Bridge Street, was emptied when a modern sheriff's office and county jail was built on East Bridge Street in 1977. It was torn down by the City of Brighton in 1977 to create a parking lot.

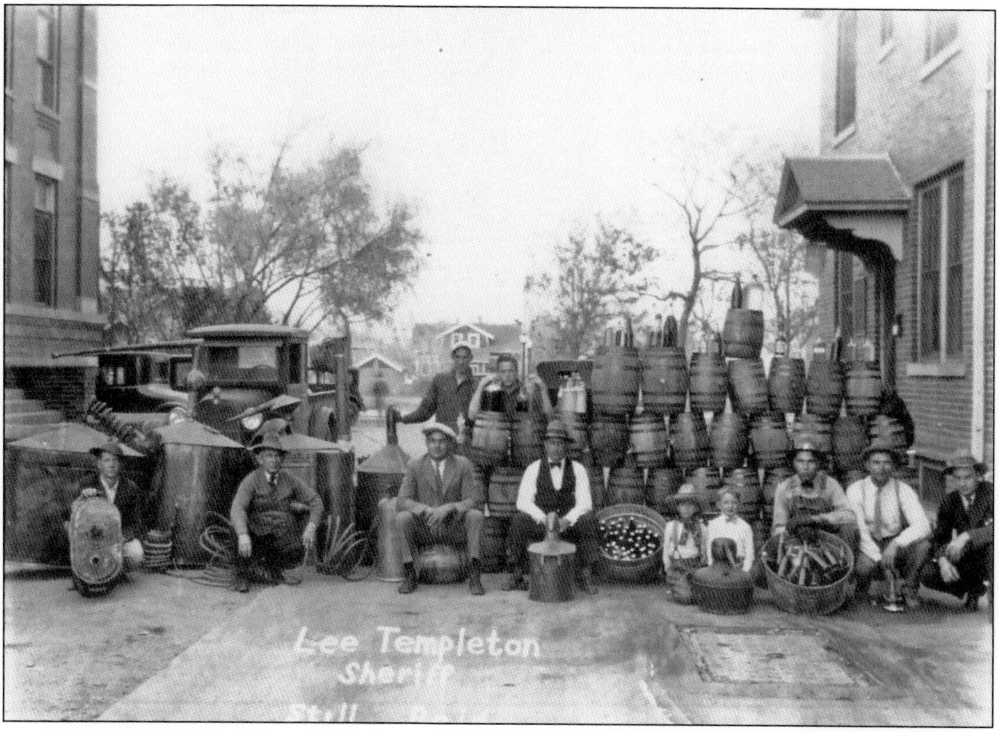

Sheriff Lee Templeton. Lee Templeton and members of the Adams County Sheriff's Office posed for these photographs between the Adams County Courthouse and the old Adams County Jail. Templeton served as sheriff of Adams County from 1926 to 1934, during Prohibition. Adams County, situated between Denver and Cheyenne, experienced a lot of illegal activity during that period, as evidenced by these photographs of confiscated stills, kegs of alcoholic beverages, and gambling equipment. (Both courtesy of the Brighton Historical Preservation Commission.)

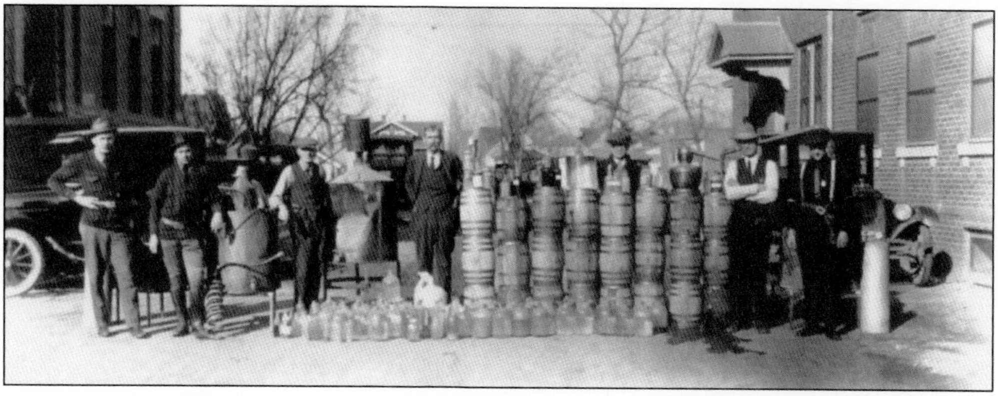

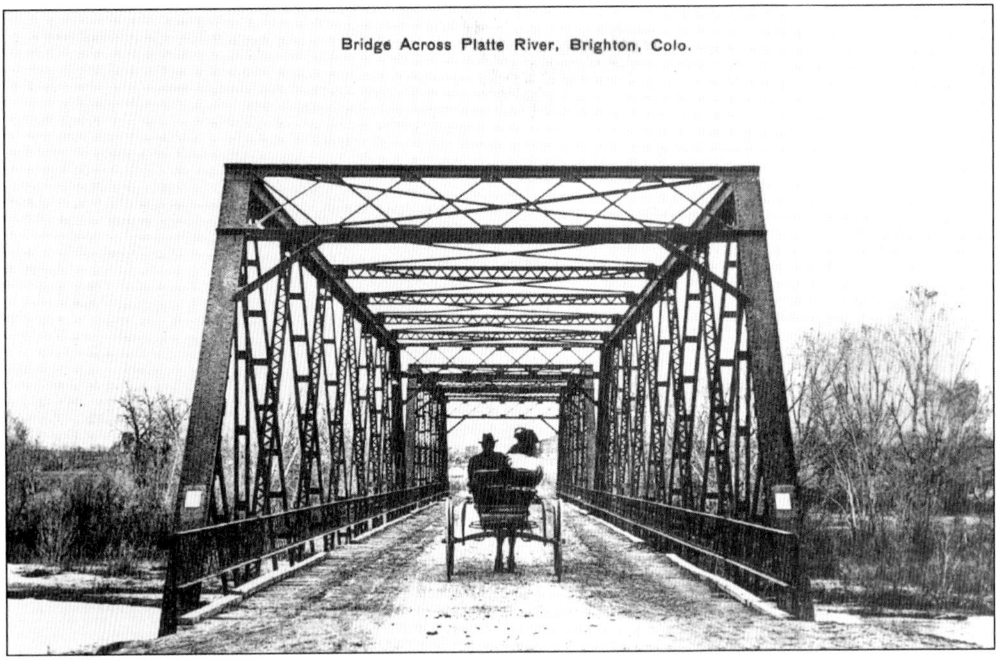

WATTS BRIDGE. The bridge over the South Platte River on Bridge Street (now Highway 7) was featured on this popular postcard (above). When the bridge was constructed (as seen below), it was named the Watts Bridge for Fred P. Watts, the head of the first Board of County Commissioners of Adams County (1902–1904) when the county was formed in 1902. The bridge, composed of two identical spans, was considered an engineering marvel in its time. (Both courtesy of the Brighton Historical Preservation Commission.)

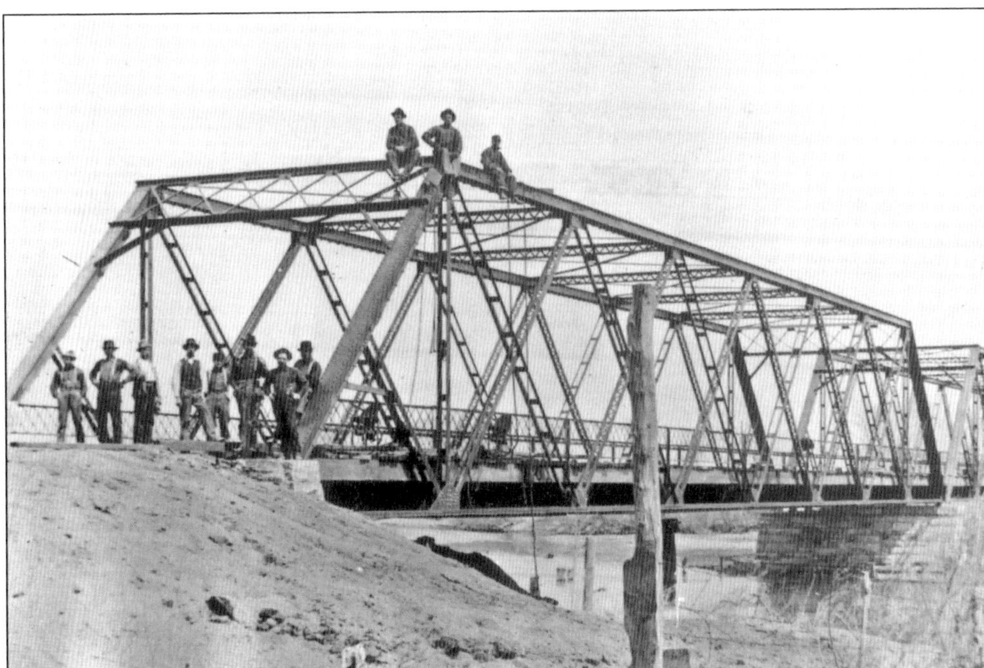

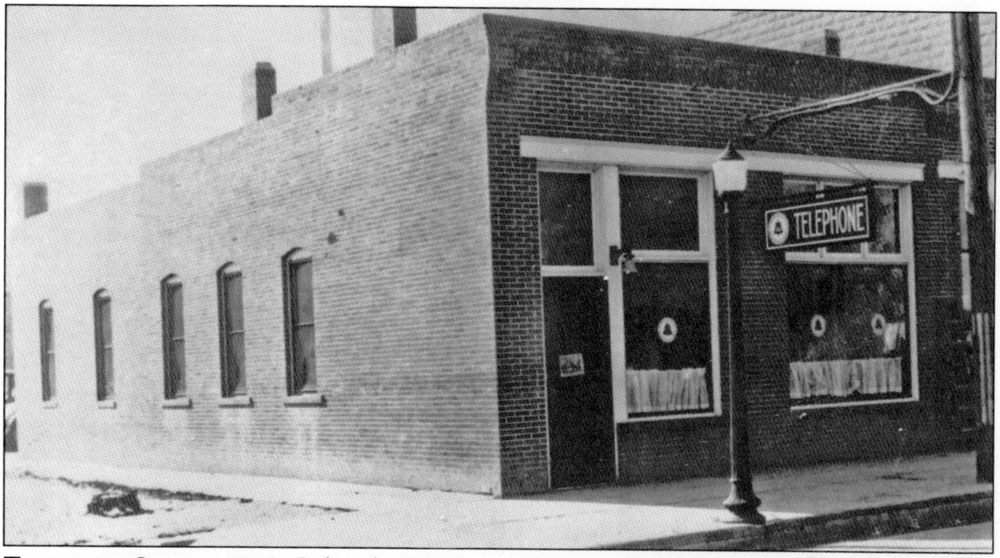

Telephone Office, 1916. Colorado Telephone Company building (later the Mountain Bell Telephone Company office in Brighton) was built by J. N. Counter just west of the Herman Reuter residence, which served for a time as the temporary Adams County Courthouse. The Colorado building became the new main office of the telephone company in August 1916, when the company discontinued two existing central offices and moved into the new building. Daniel Carmichael installed the first "Edison" telephone in Brighton to connect his home on South Fifth Avenue with his offices at the Brighton Opera House. The first long-distance call was possible in 1895 when telephone lines were strung between Denver and Greeley by the Colorado Telephone Company, which received a 25-year franchise from Brighton. Local phones and burglar alarms were installed by W. R. Armington, the Adams County coroner from 1904 to 1908. The first telephone office was in James MacKeon's Furniture Store. Herman Kramer is seen (below) on the telephone in his office in the Farmers State Bank (now the Elks building). (Above courtesy of the Colorado Historical Society; below courtesy of Evelyn Tepe.)

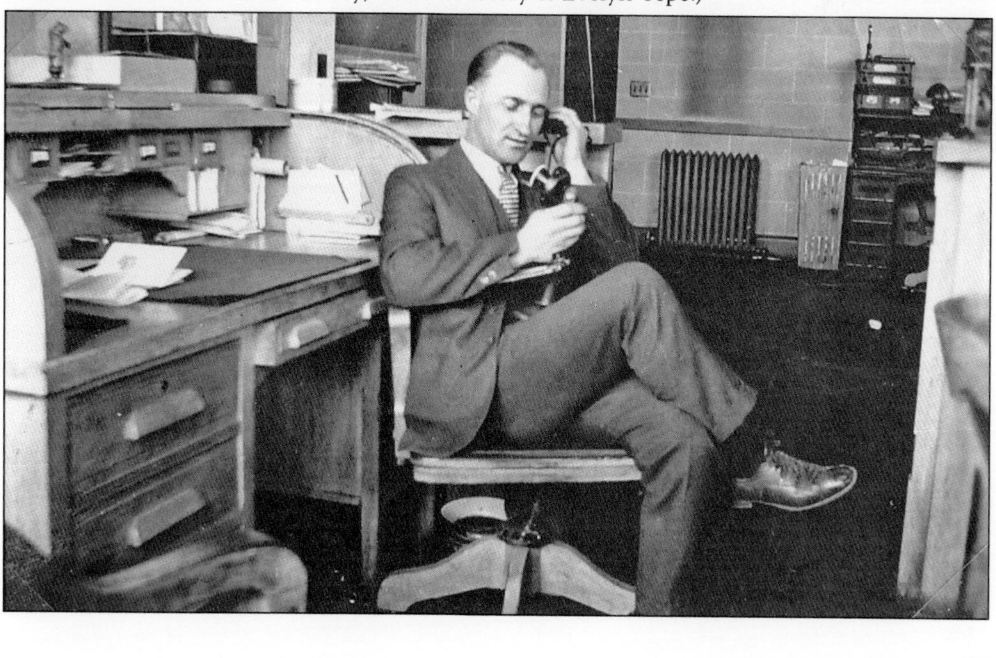

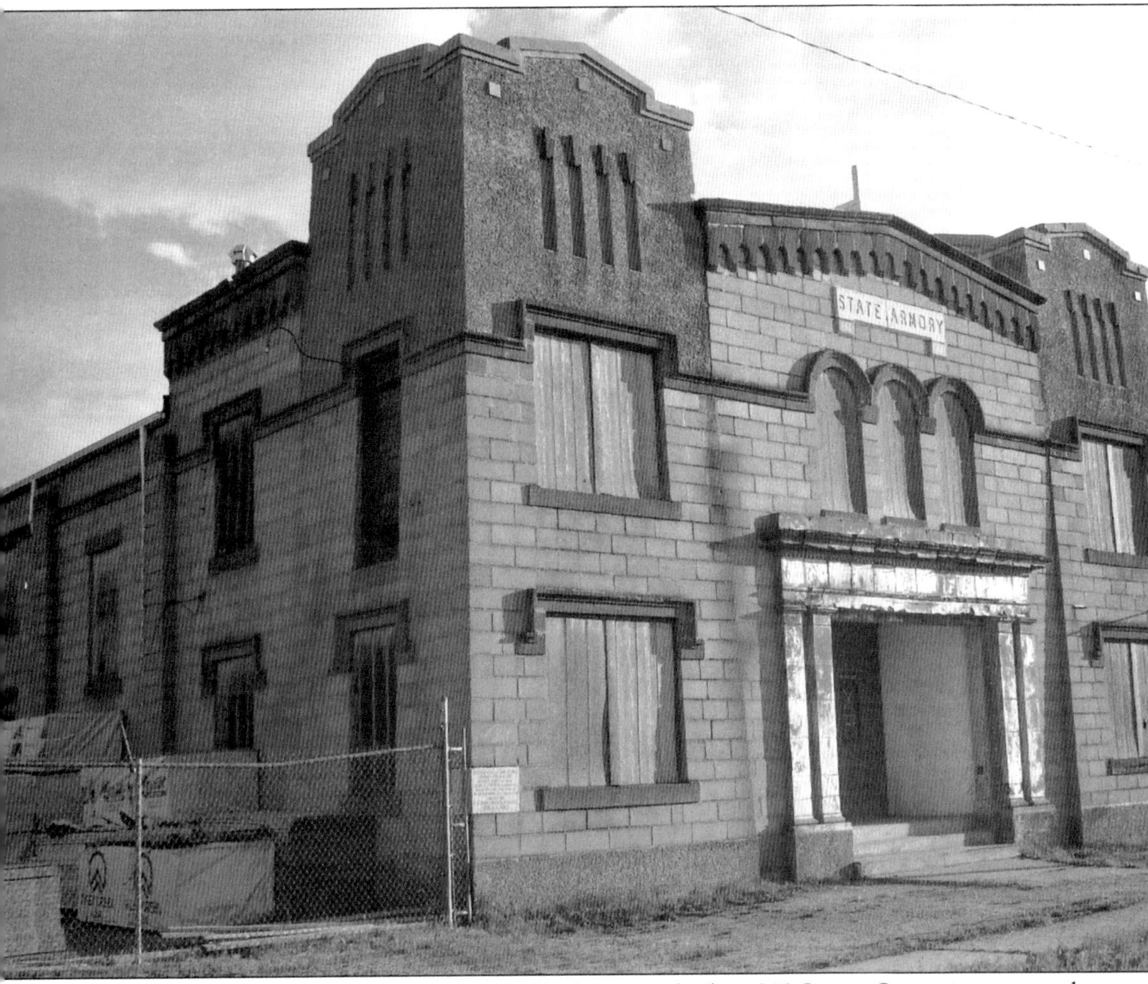

Brighton Armory. The state armory in Brighton was built at 300 Strong Street, just across the railroad tracks from the Union Pacific railroad station, in 1921 for Company K, 157th Infantry, Colorado National Guard, when they were moved to Adams County. Headquarters Company, Third Battalion, used the armory in Brighton from 1928 until September 16, 1940, when the battalion was mobilized as part of the 45th Infantry Division and stationed at Fort Sill, Oklahoma, in World War II. The American Legion Philip Wade Post No. 46 bought the armory in 1946. The Legion post sold the armory to the United Lumber Company. United Lumber used the old armory building as a warehouse until the company closed in 2007. In September 2008, groundbreaking ceremonies were held for a new library and cultural center that included the restored armory. (Courtesy of the Brighton Historical Preservation Commission.)

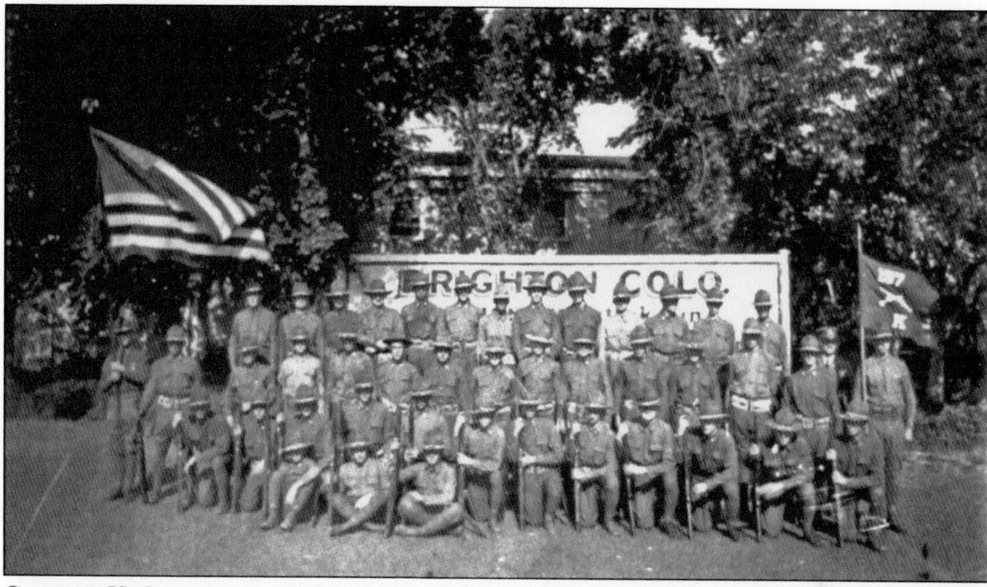

Company K. Company K, 157th Infantry, Colorado National Guard, posed for their portrait when they were moved to Adams County in 1921, clearly identifying their location in Brighton. Note the Company K flag. (Courtesy of the Brighton Historical Preservation Commission.)

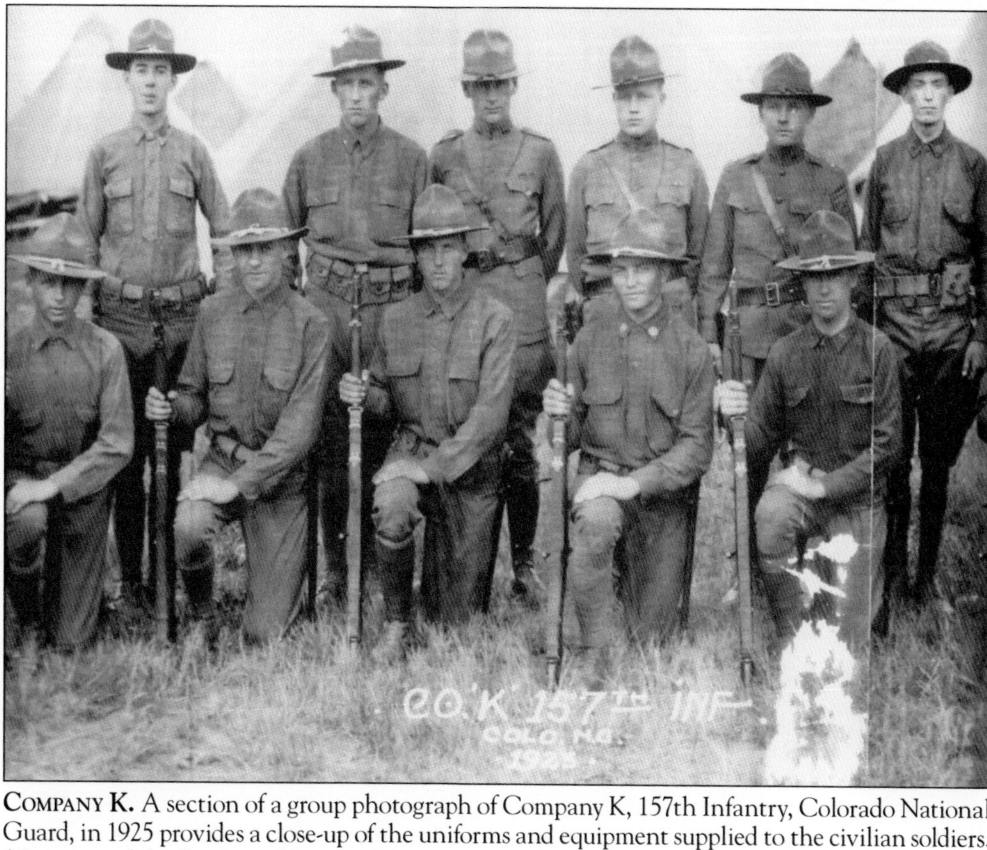

Company K. A section of a group photograph of Company K, 157th Infantry, Colorado National Guard, in 1925 provides a close-up of the uniforms and equipment supplied to the civilian soldiers. (Courtesy of the Brighton Historical Preservation Commission.)

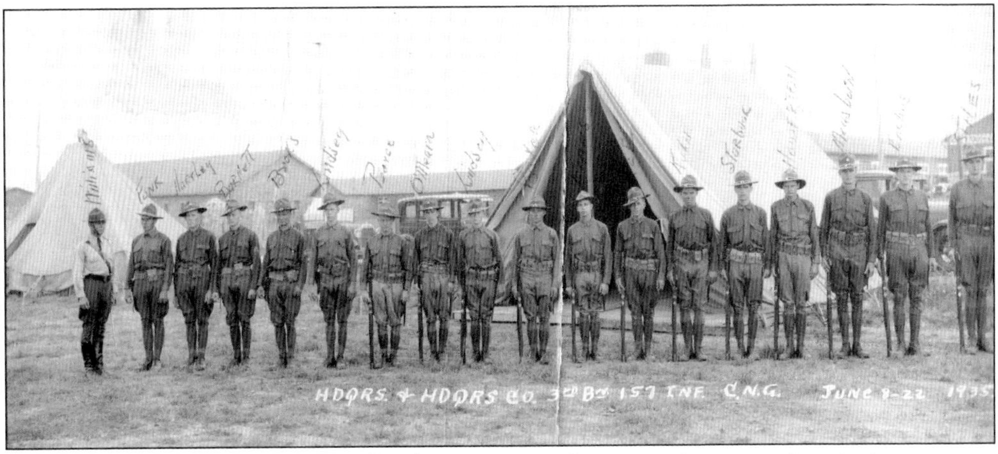

HEADQUARTERS COMPANY, 1935. Brighton-area residents stood at attention during summer training to be photographed in June 1935. The photograph is identified as Headquarters Company, Third Battalion, 157th Infantry, Colorado National Guard. (Courtesy of the Brighton Historical Preservation Commission.)

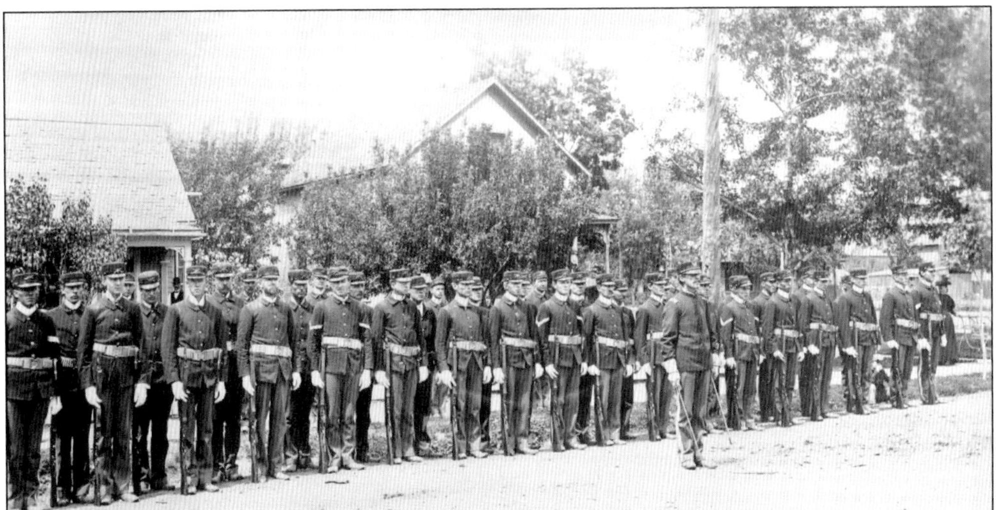

COMPANY K, 1926. Company K, 157th Infantry, Colorado National Guard, is seen in this photograph drilling on the street in Brighton in 1926. Company K, composed largely of Adams County residents, used the state armory in Brighton until 1928, when the company was moved to Fort Morgan. (Courtesy of the Denver Public Library Western History and Genealogy Department.)

Seven

Agriculture and Industry

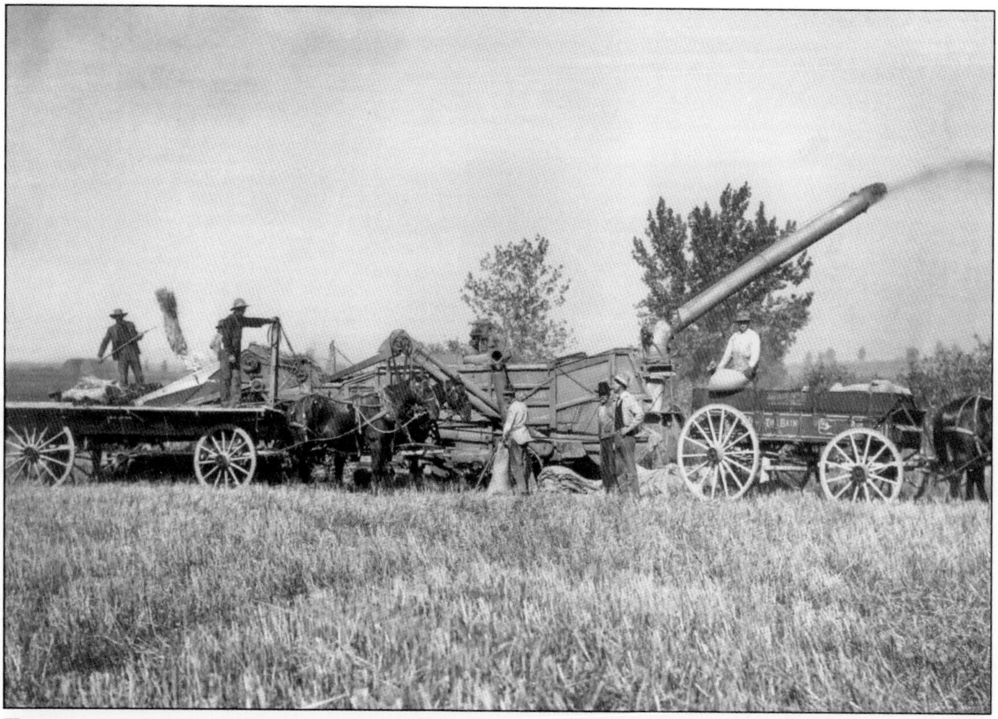

Threshing Machine. The construction of large irrigation systems along the South Platte created a thriving farming economy and the industries related to it. The threshing machine is an example of changing technology. The threshing machine (seen here) was powered by a steam tractor and moved from farm to farm during the wheat harvest, along with an attending crew. The system was replaced by highly mobile combines that now combine all this equipment into one unit. (Courtesy of the Brighton Historical Preservation Commission.)

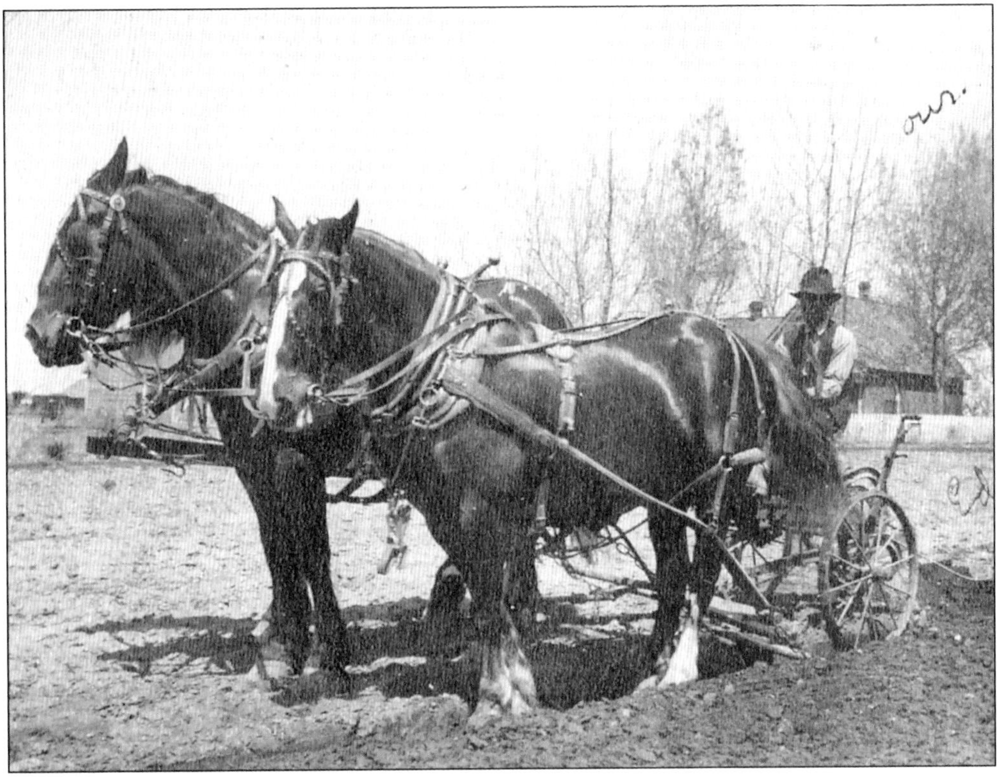

Replacing the Horse. Edward ("Ed") Kramer, who farmed north of Brighton, is seen in these two photographs. First Kramer can be seen in the 1919 photograph above plowing with a handsome team of horses, and then Kramer was photographed later (below) plowing with a steam tractor. (Both courtesy of Evelyn Tepe.)

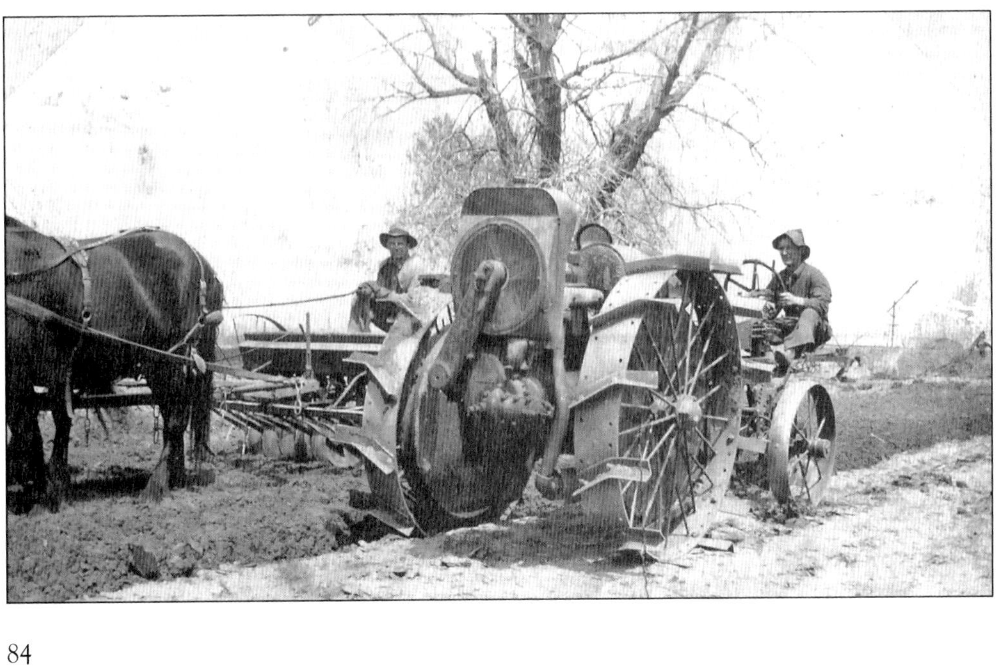

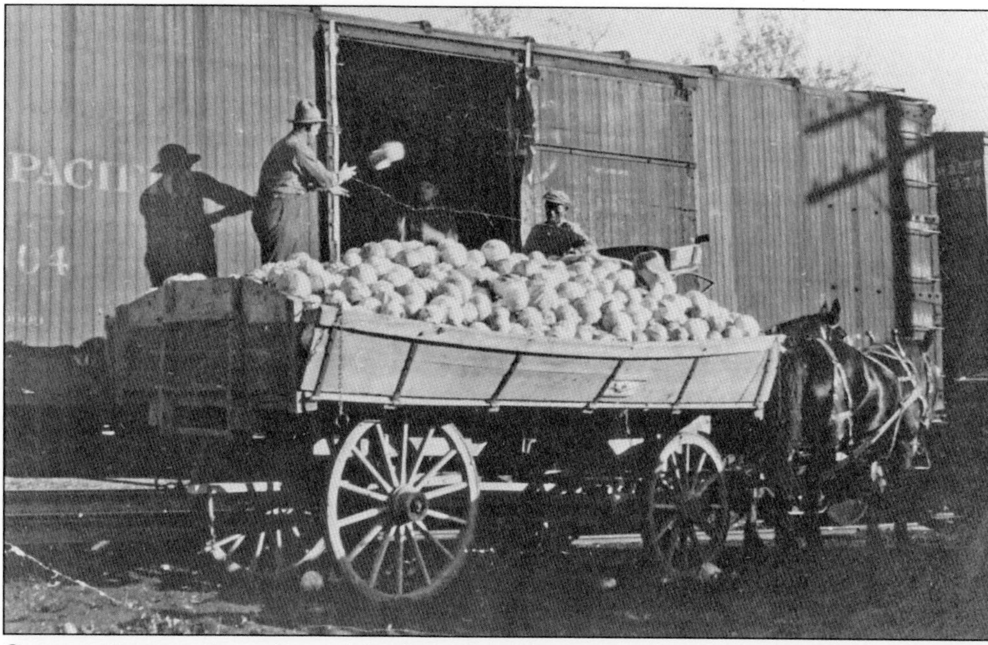

Cabbage Avenue. According to Maude Lindstom Fransen in her book *All the Way*, an account of the history of the Methodist Church and the City of Brighton, it was John C. Twombly, the business partner of Brighton merchant Dewey W. Strong, who circulated a petition to change the name of South Second Avenue along the railroad tracks to Cabbage Avenue. The Schloo and Bender families are credited with raising the first cabbage in the area.

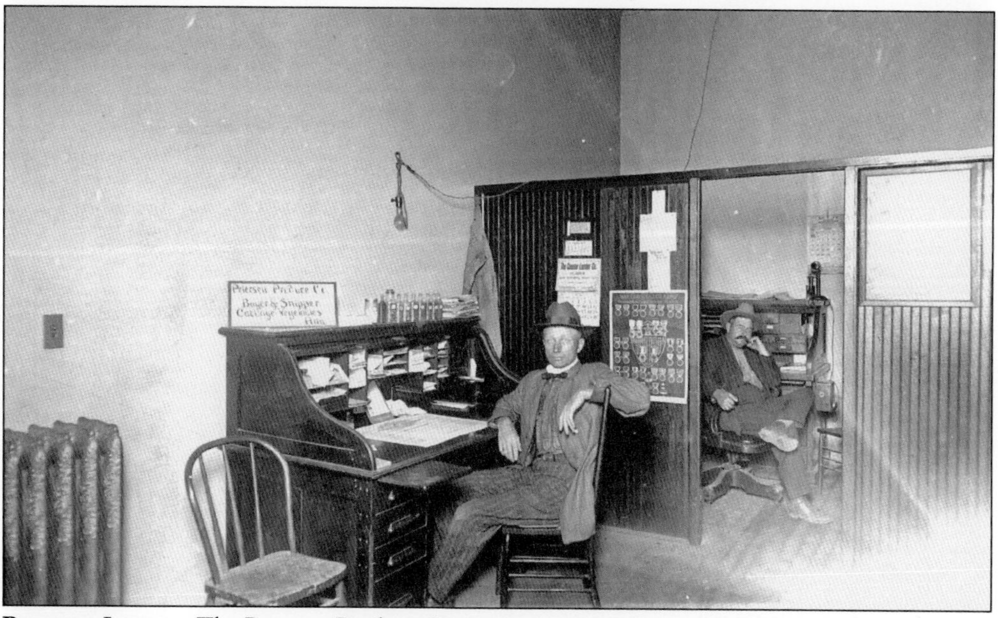

Produce Jobbers. The Petersen Produce Company was one of several such firms in Brighton that bought and shipped produce from Cabbage Avenue. The sign in the photograph says "Petersen Produce Company, Buyer and Shipper, Cabbage, Vegetables, Hay." A calendar from the Counter Lumber Company is on the wall, along with a U.S. Army poster. (Courtesy of the Brighton Historical Preservation Commission.)

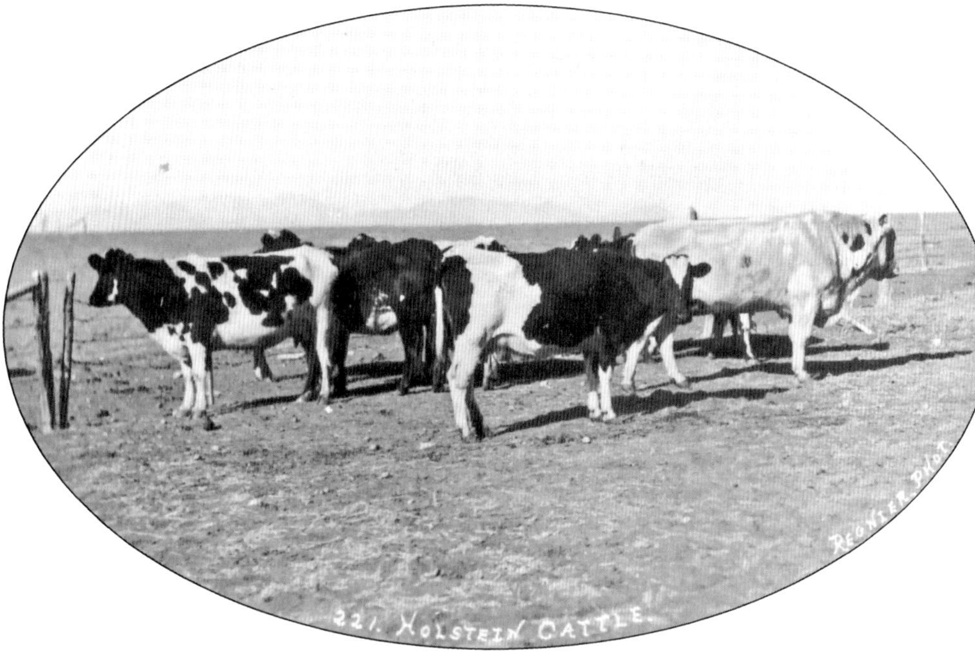

Dairy Cows. The pasture lands along the South Platte and the proximity to Denver created a thriving dairy industry in Brighton and the surrounding area. Holstein and Jersey milk cows (seen here) were imported by area dairy farmers to improve the herds. (Courtesy of the Brighton Historical Preservation Commission.)

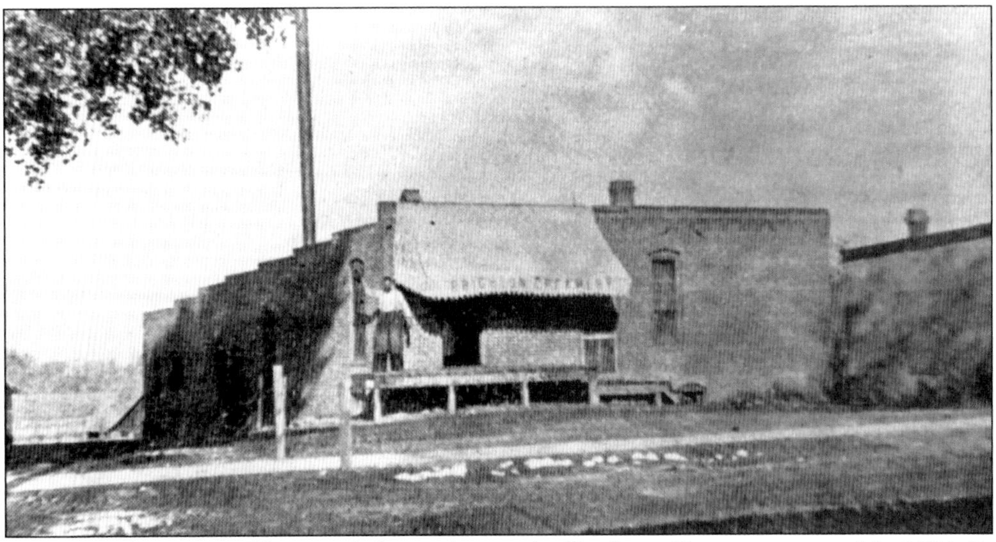

Brighton Creamery. The town's first industry, the Brighton Creamery, opened in 1884. D. W. Strong and 15 other men, all farmers in the area, joined resources in March 1883 to build the creamery. Sixteen of the stockholders sold their shares to two men, Thomas Hodge and H. H. Houghton, in 1884. Hodge operated the creamery, which made butter and cheese, for many years, while Houghton operated the Brighton Creamery Store in Denver. Hodge built his house just south of the plant. In 1894, the creamery was destroyed by fire. The 28-by-57-foot building was rebuilt in 1894 and back in business in 1895. (Courtesy of the Brighton Historical Preservation Commission.)

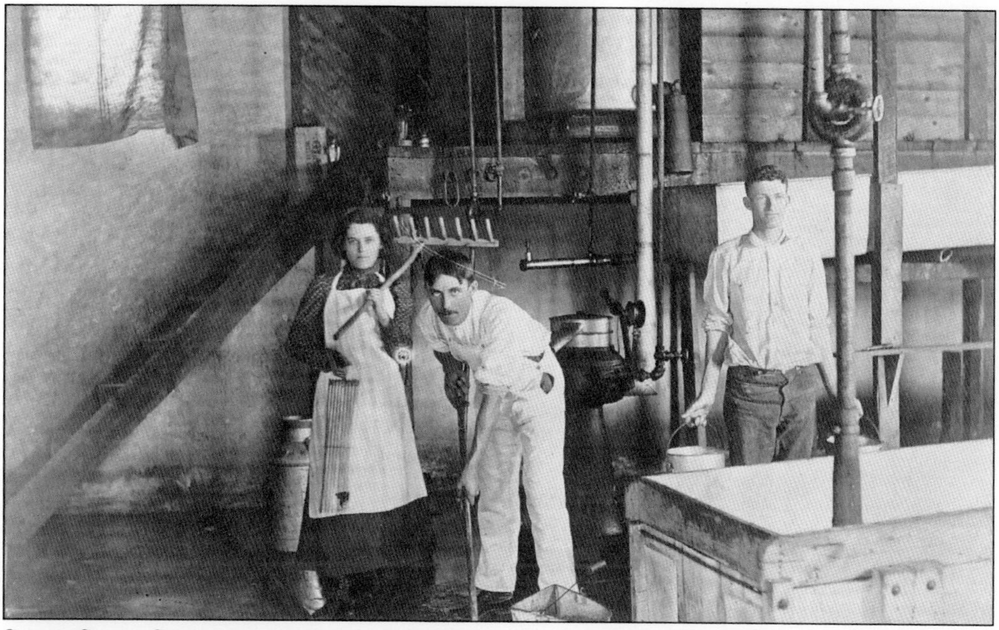

Silver State Creamery, 1906. The Silver State Creamery in Brighton, also known as the Frink Cheese factory, managed by O. E. Frink, was owned by the Silver State Creamery and Produce Company, which also owned other creameries in Brighton and Fort Lupton. Frink moved his family from Denver to Fort Lupton in 1895. He had a wholesale commission house, two meat markets in Denver, and several small creameries in outlying towns. He bought the Bendell Creamery in Fort Lupton in 1897 and started the Frink Cheese Factory on North Main Street in 1899. In 1904, he organized the Silver State Canning Company (later known as the Fort Lupton or Blayney Canning Company). After Frink died in 1916, his daughter, Daisy Frink Counter (seen in the 1906 photograph with Walter Fink, on the left, and George Kelsey, on the right) became first the secretary-treasurer and then president of the company. (Both courtesy of the Historical Preservation Commission.)

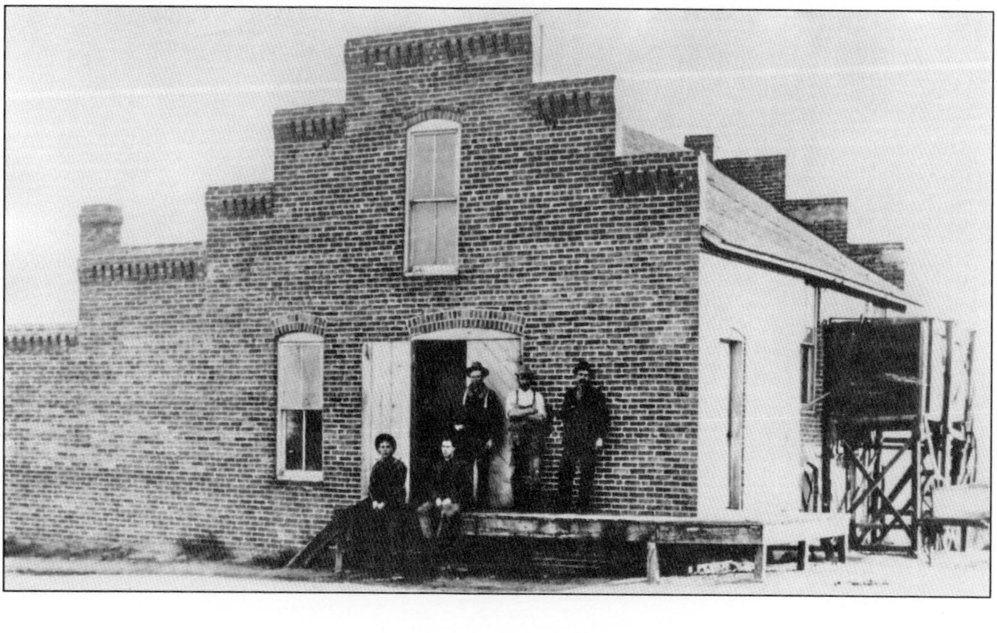

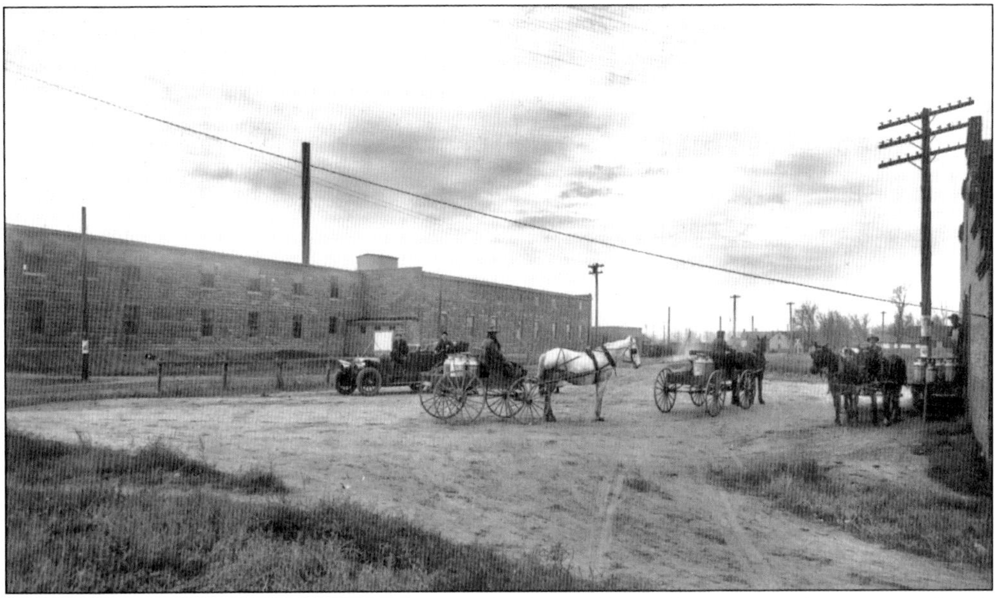

Early Morning Deliveries. Denver photographer Louis C. McClure captured this scene of early morning deliveries of milk to the Silver State Creamery in 1910. The building across the street still stands. In 1908, Wilmore's Canning Company built this factory out of locally produced hydrostone between the railroad tracks and North Main Street. The factory was later known as the Green Canning Company, the Blayney Canning Company, and the Platte Valley Canning Company, some of which the Frinks and Daisy Counter managed. During World War II, the building was used to house German prisoners of war who worked in the beet fields around Brighton. The Northern Dairy, successor to the Silver State Creamery, is pictured below. (Above courtesy of the Denver Public Library and Genealogy Department; below courtesy of the Brighton Historical Preservation Commission.)

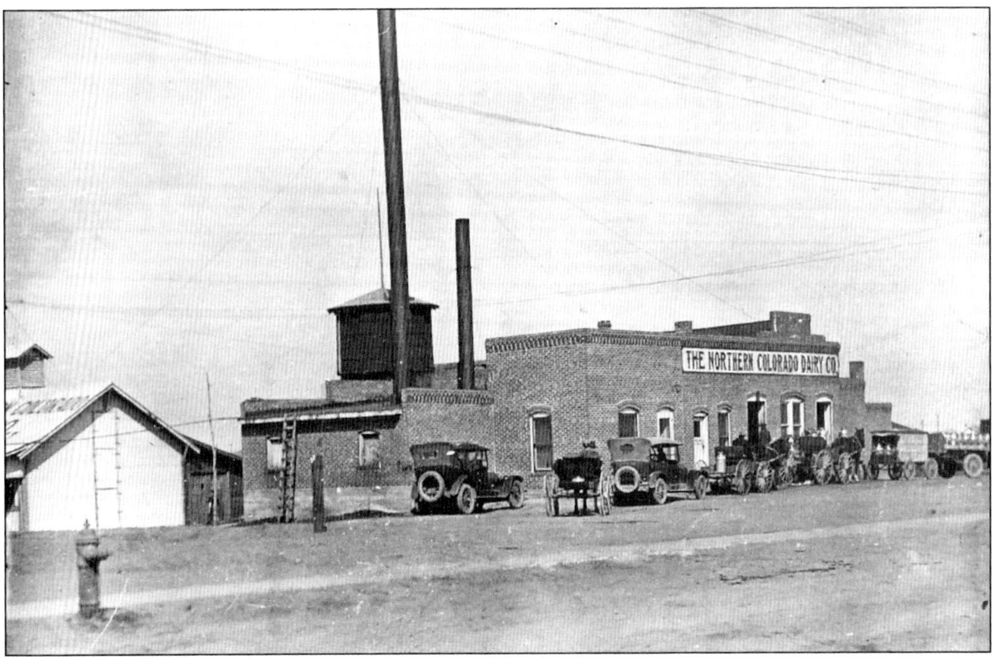

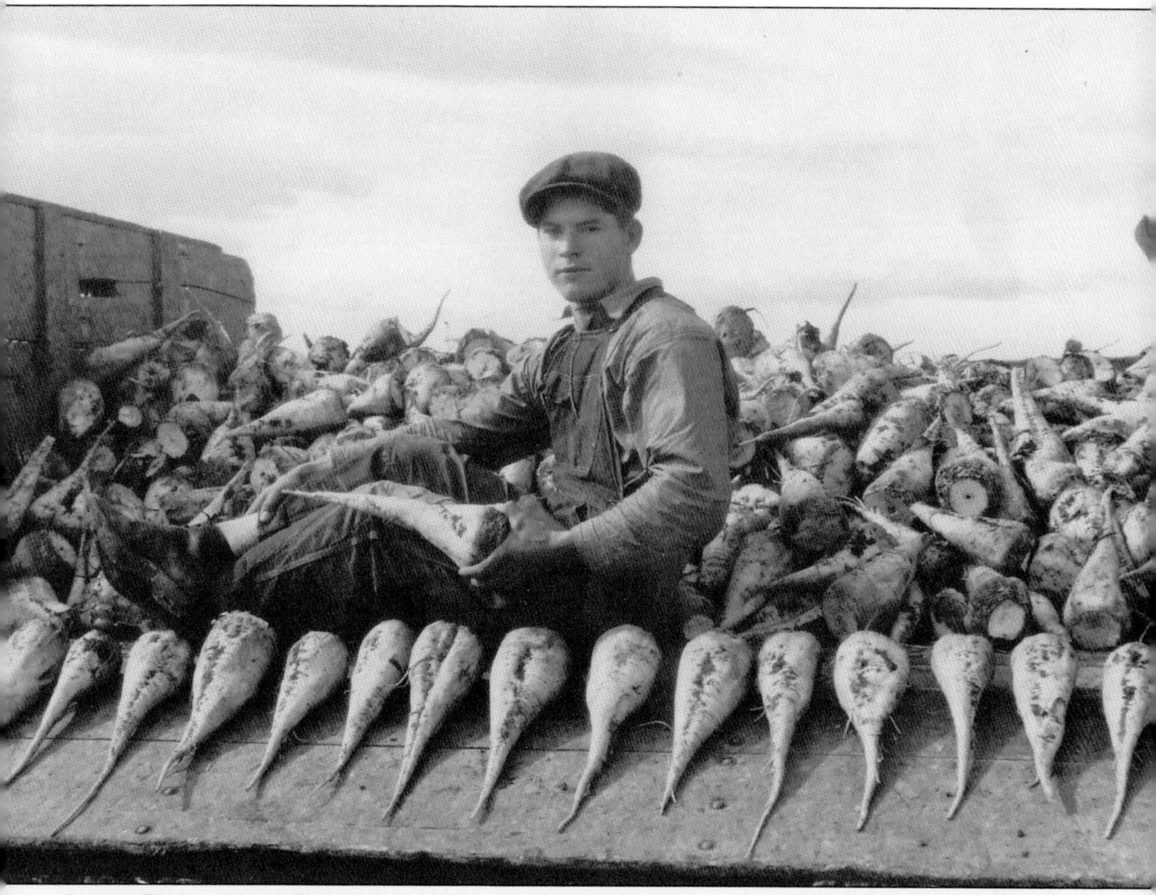

Sugar Beets: More Than Gold. "If we had sugar beet factories in Colorado, farmers would produce more gold than the miners in the mountains," predicted Littleton farmer Peter Magnes. The prophecy came true. Years later, sugar beets became the largest cash crop in the state. A truckload of sugar beets is seen in this 1931 photograph. Note how the beets are "topped" (leaves cut off) for processing. (Courtesy of the Denver Public Library Western History and Genealogy Department.)

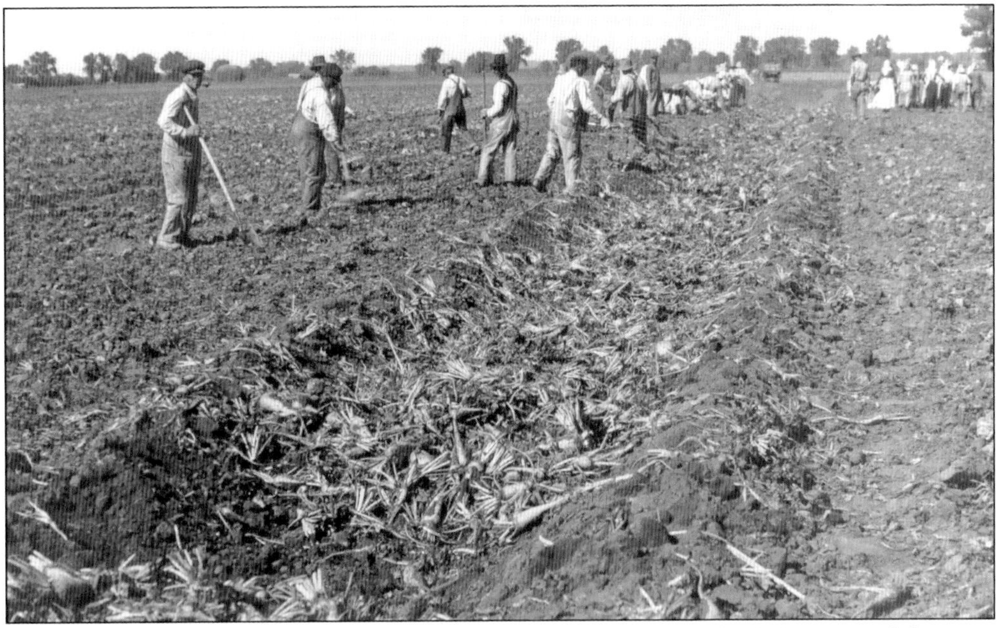

Beet Fields. Whole families, including children, worked in the beet fields, hoeing and thinning beets in the spring and summer and digging and harvesting beets in the fall. A group of Germans from Russia (above) was photographed in 1916 by Denver photographer L. C. McClure as they left the beet field. Note the beet tops and other tare placed in the trench to be covered up. (Courtesy of the Denver Public Library Western History and Genealogy Department.)

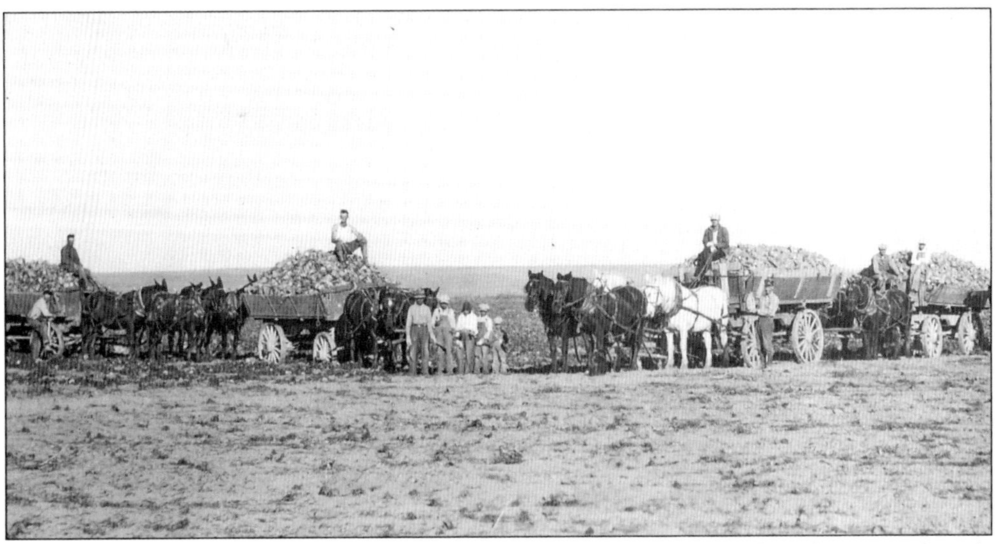

Beet Wagons. Harvested sugar beets were transported from the fields to "beet dumps" or directly to the sugar factory, first in horse-drawn beet wagons and later by trucks. Beet wagons were pulled by two horses in the field and four after being loaded on the way to the beet dump. Untrained horses sometimes spooked on the high platforms used at the beet dumps to unload the wagons. (Courtesy of the Library of Congress.)

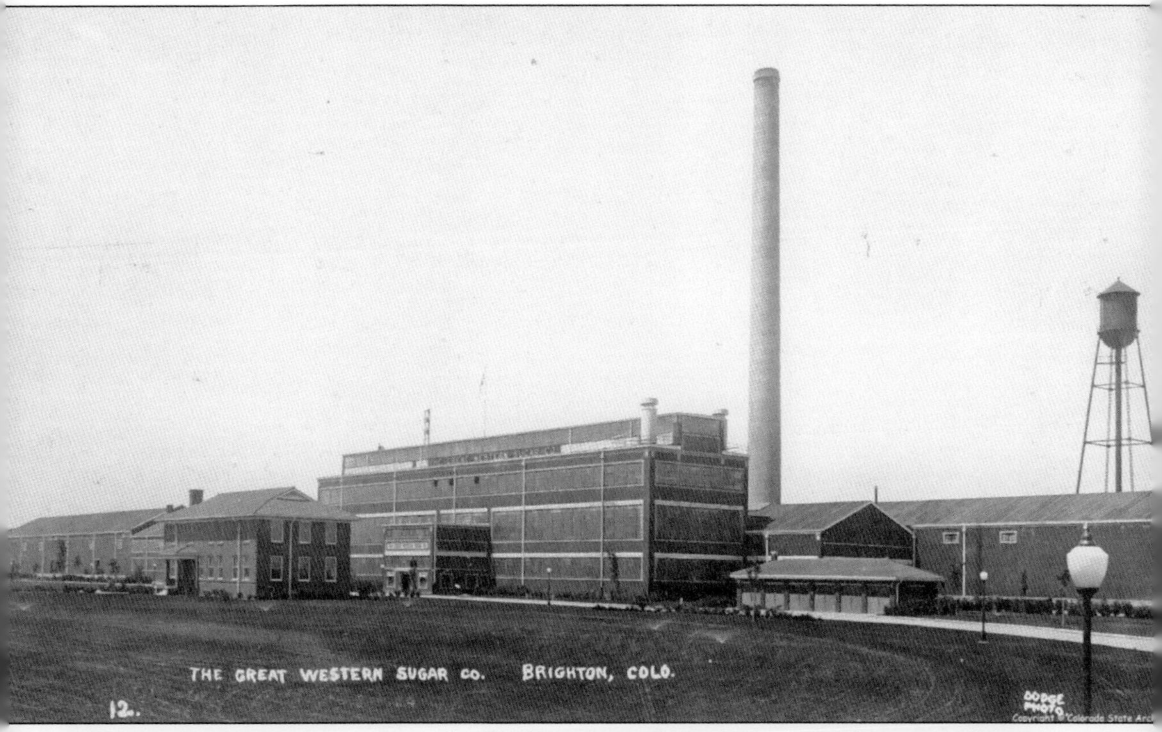

BRIGHTON SUGAR FACTORY, 1920. The Brighton Sugar Factory is seen in this postcard shortly after it was constructed. The Keyes Syrup Company built the first beet syrup factory in the West in Brighton in 1906 on 40 acres just north of the Boulder Valley tracks with a switch built directly to the factory. The venture was unsuccessful and closed after a few years. In 1916, the Farmers and Merchants Association of Adams County convinced the Great Western Sugar Company to build a factory in Brighton. The factory began operation in 1917. In 1947, the silo-style sugar bins were added to the factory. The company promised to make the factory a showplace. They kept their promise. Over the years, the factory was visited by many dignitaries, including Pres. Dwight D. Eisenhower, before it closed in 1977. (Courtesy of Colorado State Archives.)

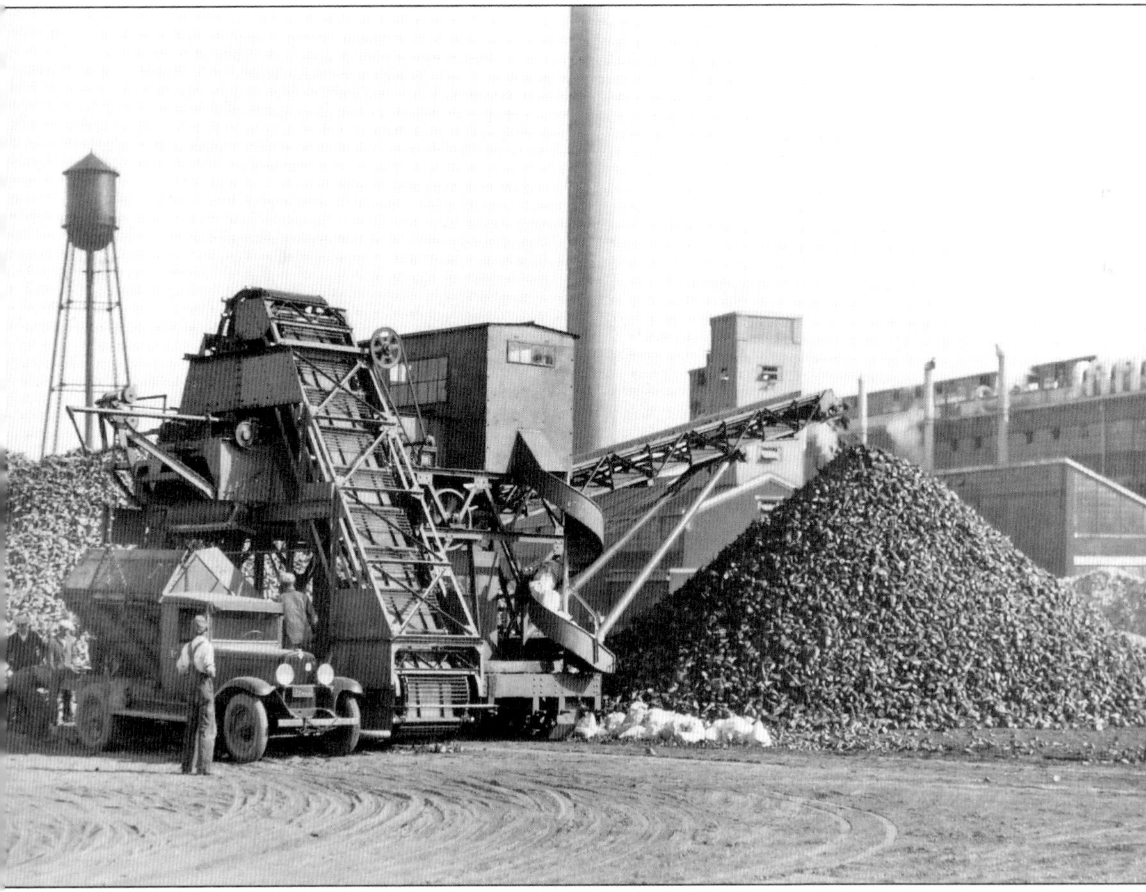

Beet Dump. The beet dump at the rear of the Brighton Sugar Factory is seen in this 1910 photograph by Denver photographer Louis C. McClure. The beet truck unloading sugar beets into the "piler" must have been one of the earliest dump trucks. In the early days, all beet wagons and beet trucks were emptied by hand. The white bags on the circular shoot on the side of the piler contain beet samples. The beets were tested and growers were paid according to the sugar content of the beets they delivered. (Courtesy of the Denver Public Library Western History and Genealogy Department.)

BEET HARVESTING EQUIPMENT. The sugar beet industry also sparked the development of several companies in Brighton that manufactured and sold beet harvesting equipment. One company, the Baby Beet Puller Company, located at the present site of Dailey's Warehouse on Kuner Road, manufactured a variety of beet farming equipment, including a beet puller (seen here) designed to unearth sugar beets. (Courtesy of Kenneth Wagner.)

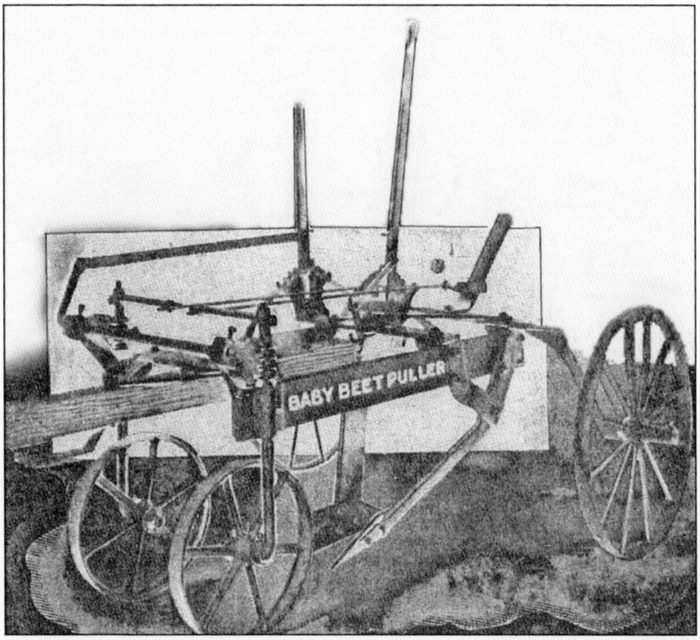

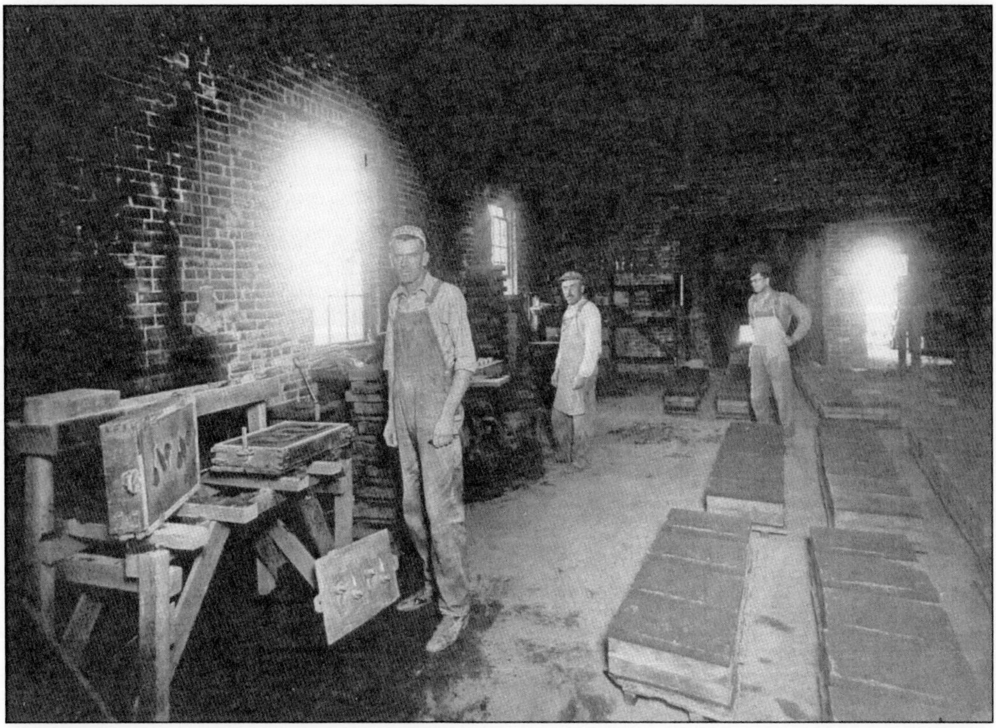

BABY BEET PULLER COMPANY. This 1929 photograph of the interior of the Baby Beet Puller Company factory shows the foundry operation of casting the metal parts for the machines they manufactured. From left to right are William ("Bill") Carlyle, Joseph ("Joe") Ford, and John Wagner. The factory closed down in 1939. (Courtesy of Kenneth Wagner.)

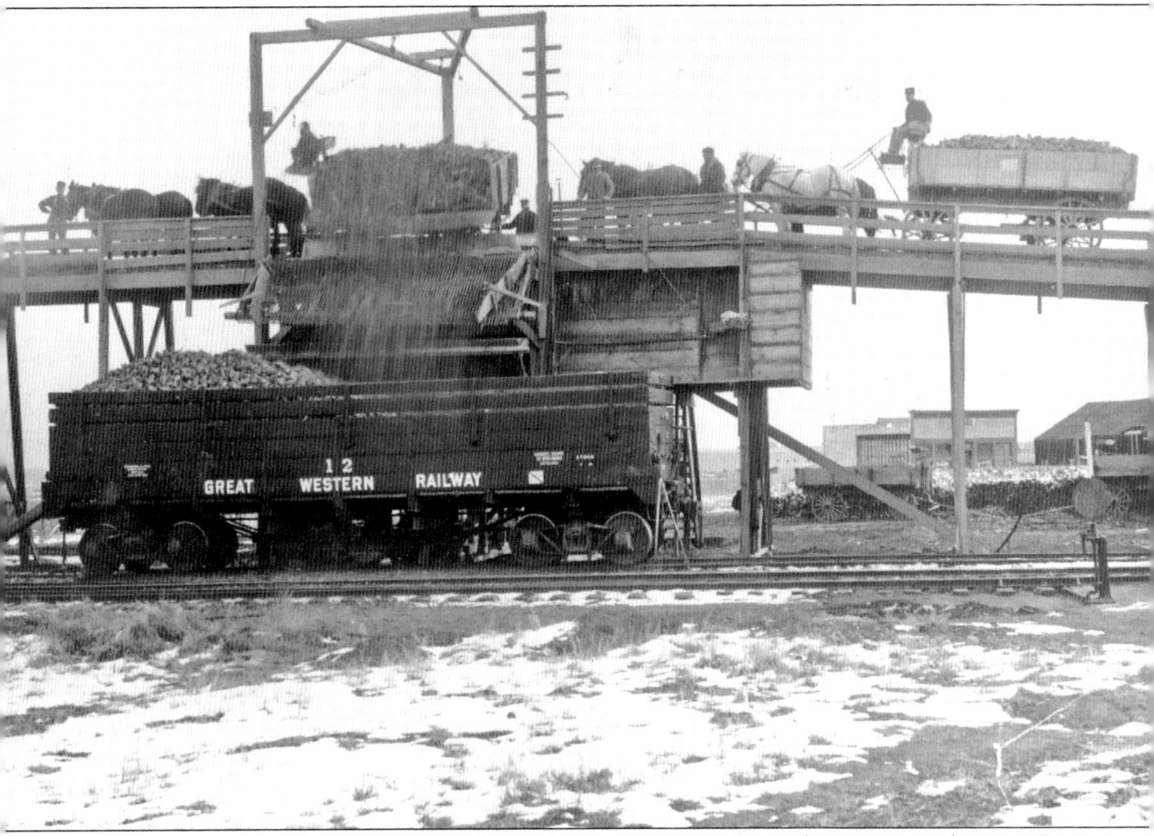

Great Western Railway. Horse-drawn beet wagons are shown being emptied into a Great Western Railway gondola car for transportation to the Brighton Sugar Factory. This photograph was taken by Denver photographer Louis C. McClure in 1910. The Great Western Sugar Company operated their own railroad company, the Great Western Railway, with a network of tracks throughout north-central Colorado to transport sugar beets to their various factories, along with a number of steam engines permanently located at the factories for switching cars. In 1911, the Great Western purchased the Denver, Laramie, and Northwestern Railway west of Brighton. The Great Western planned to maintain the 23 miles of railroad tracks north from the Union Pacific–Boulder Valley branch to the Milliken station near Greeley and to junk the 15 miles of tracks from Utah Junction to Brighton. (Courtesy of the Denver Public Library Western History and Genealogy Department.)

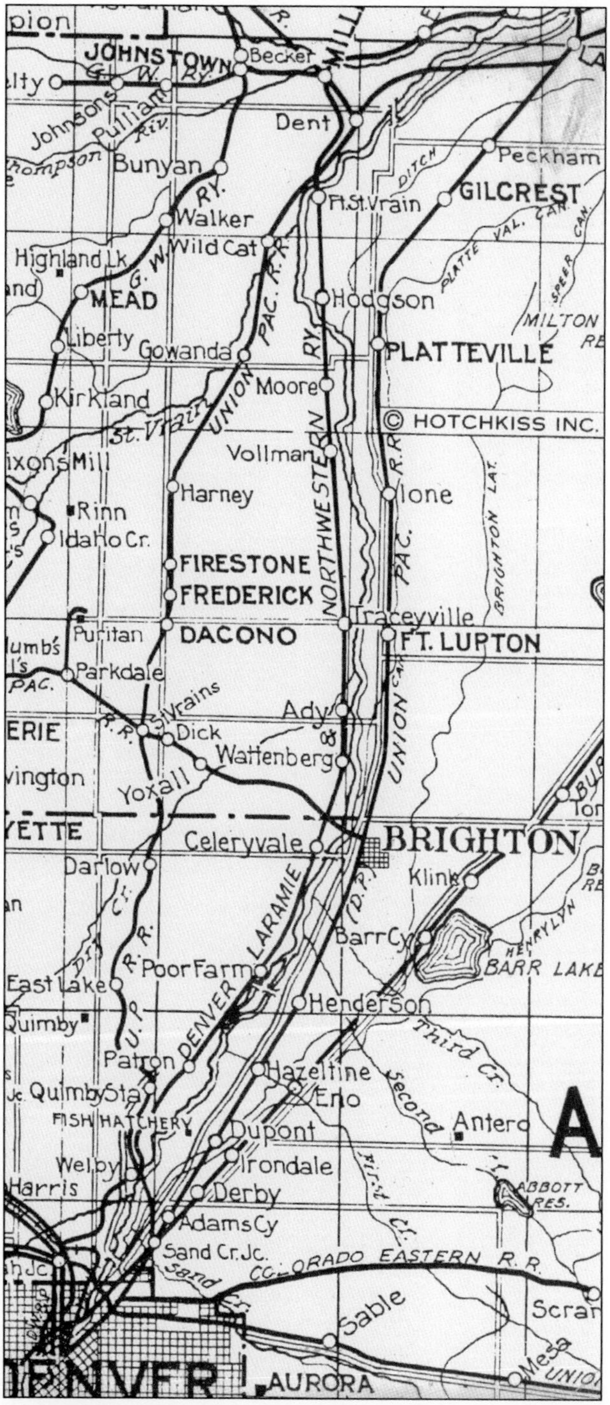

Denver, Laramie, and Northwestern Railway. The map of the Denver, Laramie, and Northwestern Railway shows the location of the railroad along the west bank of the South Platte River and the railroad stations in Adams County: Welby, Patron, Poor Farm (now the site of the Adams County Regional Park), and Celeryvale (Z. J. Fort's farm west of Brighton). The empty roadbed of the railroad can still be seen in places north of Adams County Regional Park.

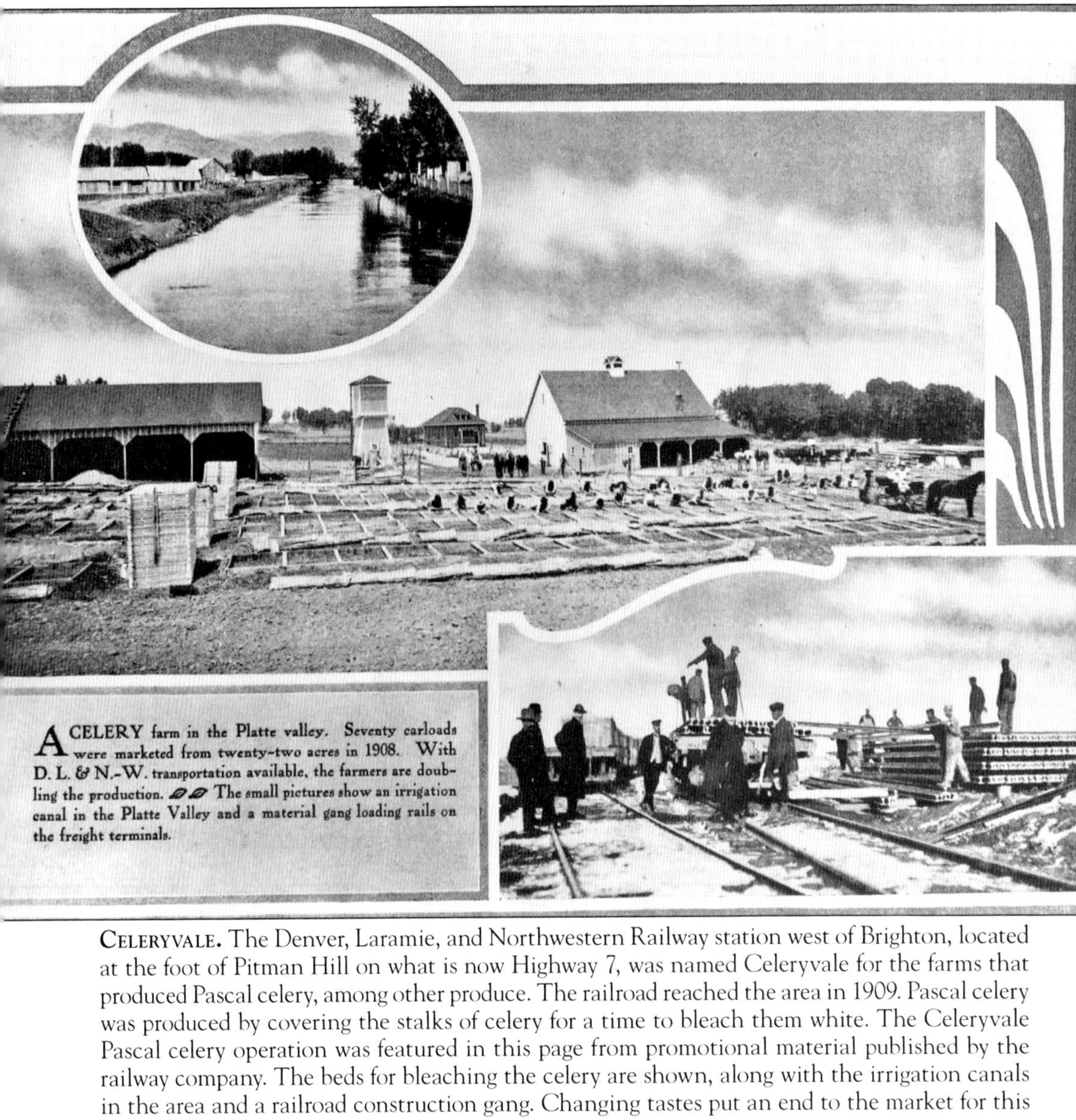

CELERYVALE. The Denver, Laramie, and Northwestern Railway station west of Brighton, located at the foot of Pitman Hill on what is now Highway 7, was named Celeryvale for the farms that produced Pascal celery, among other produce. The railroad reached the area in 1909. Pascal celery was produced by covering the stalks of celery for a time to bleach them white. The Celeryvale Pascal celery operation was featured in this page from promotional material published by the railway company. The beds for bleaching the celery are shown, along with the irrigation canals in the area and a railroad construction gang. Changing tastes put an end to the market for this type of celery.

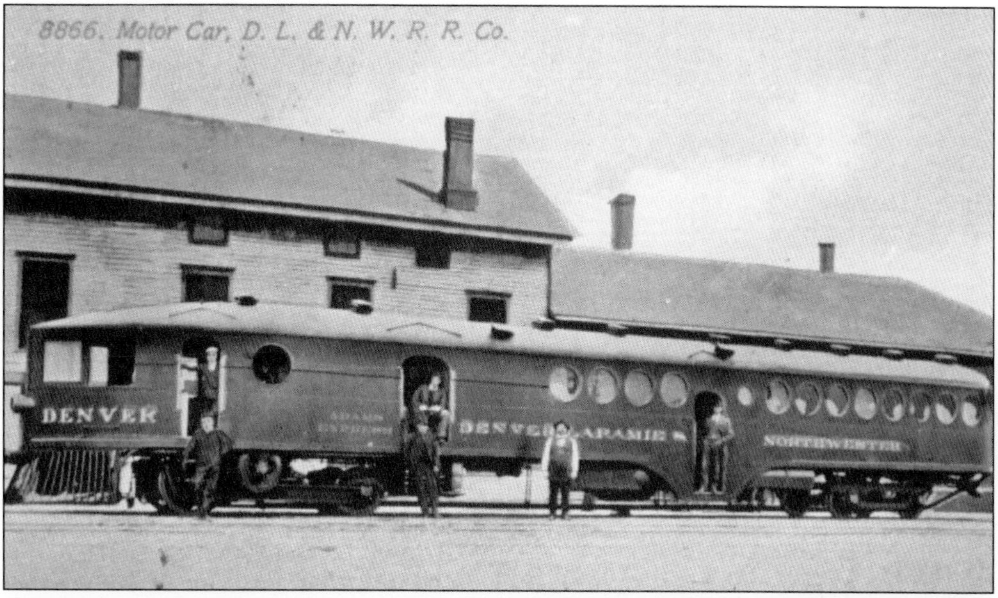

DENVER, LARAMIE, AND NORTHWESTERN RAILWAY MOTOR CAR. The motor car used for passenger service by the Denver, Laramie, and Northwestern Railroad between Denver and Greeley was featured on a 1912 postcard (above). The railroad company owned two of these modern McKeen cars. After the Great Western Railroad, owned by the Great Western Sugar Company, purchased the north half of the bankrupt DL&NW in 1917, the Great Western Railroad used these cars for passengers until 1927. The railroad advertised in the *Brighton Blade* in 1908 "Six Passenger Trains Daily" between Denver and Greeley. The DL&NW provided passenger service for several railroad stations in Adams County: Welby, Patron, Poor Farm (now the site of the Adams County Regional Park), and Celeryvale (west of Brighton). Residents of Brighton and the surrounding area frequently traveled into Denver on the train from the Celeryvale station on the west bank of the South Platte River. The Union Pacific introduced its own version of the motor car for passenger service (seen below). (Above courtesy of Greeley Municipal Museum; below courtesy of Beulah Barnard.)

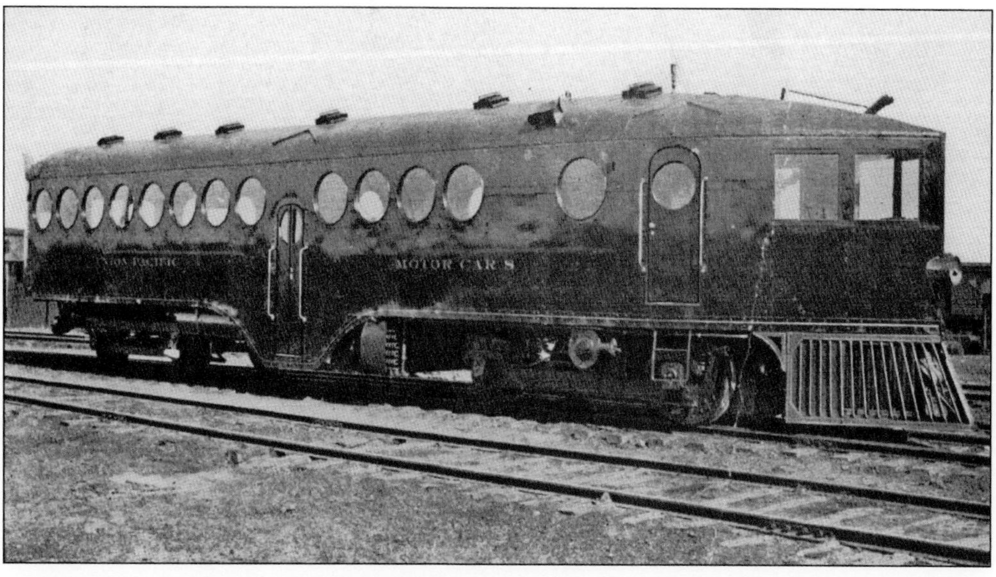

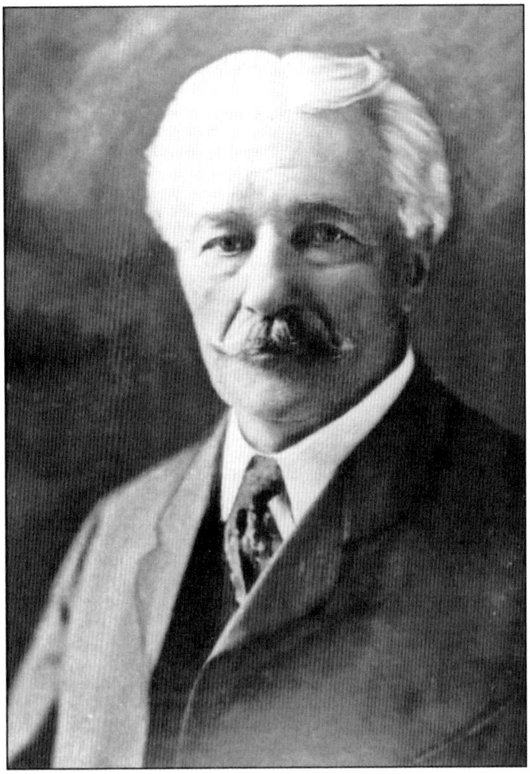

Max Kuner. Max Kuner (1824–1913) was born in Bavaria and came to the United States alone when he was seven years old. In 1873, he took over a pickle factory in St. Louis in 1873 for a debt. In 1883, he moved to Denver, where he started the Kuner Pickle Company. The company grew rapidly. In 1927, the Kuner Pickle Company merged with the Empson Packing Company of Longmont to form the Kuner-Empson Canning Company. Kuner was the active manager of the company until his death in 1913. (Courtesy of the Brighton Historical Preservation Commission.)

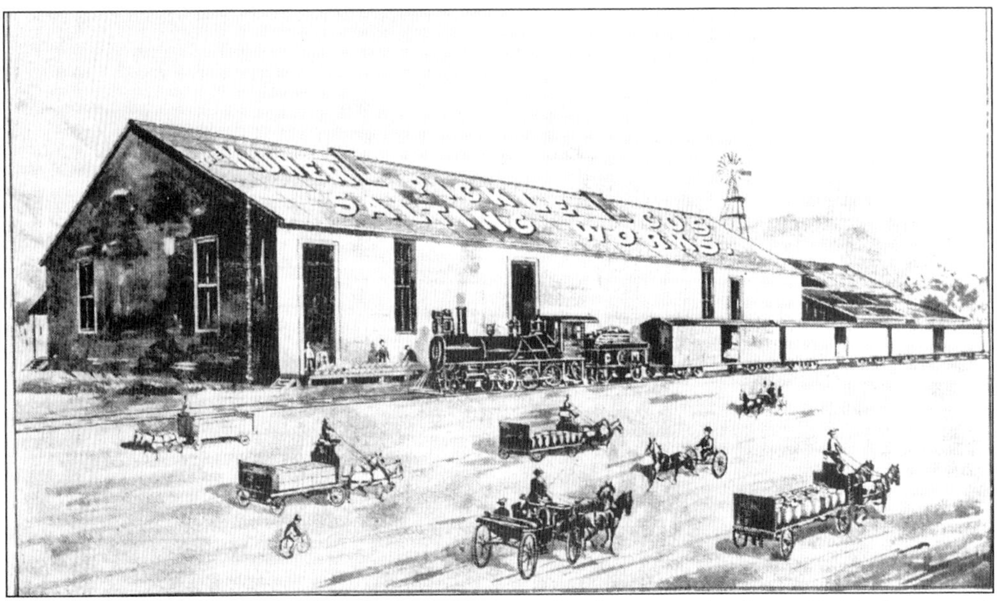

Kuner Salting Works. The first Kuner's factory in Brighton was the Kuner Pickle Company's Salting Works (seen here in a contemporary drawing from a Kuner's advertisement). The building, situated near the Union Pacific tracks, was moved to Brighton from Greeley "on account of the superior quality of tomatoes grown here." It was used for salting and storing cucumbers, cauliflower, onions, and other vegetables. It was also the principal source of cabbage for sauerkraut for the company.

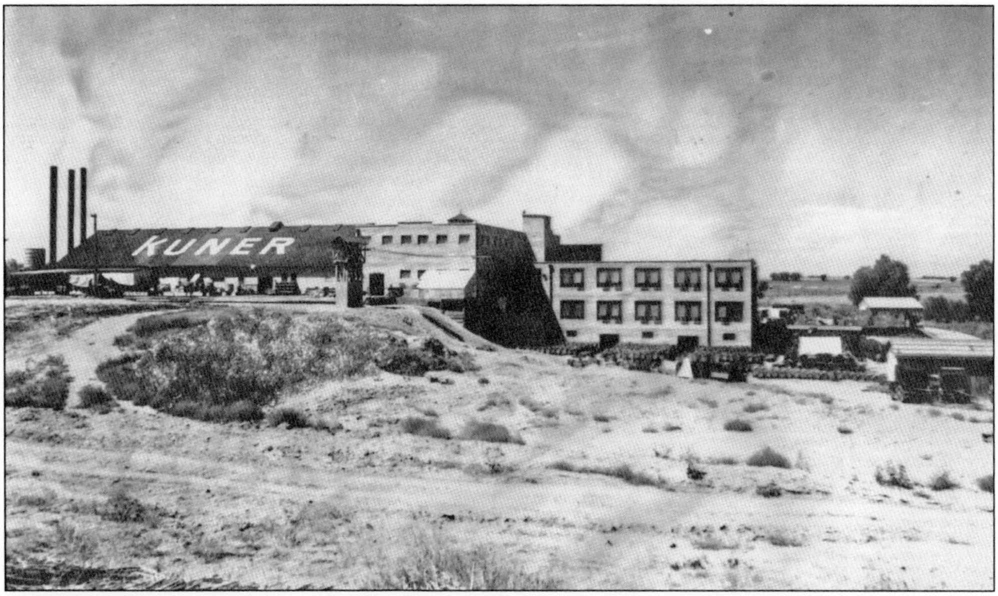

Kuner Canning Company. Brighton was the headquarters of the Kuner-Empson Canning Company for over 50 years. The company operated out of offices in Brighton from 1916, when the Kuner Pickle Company was moved from Denver to Brighton, until 1960, when the company was sold to Stokely–Van Camp, a national company. The factory buildings were demolished in the summer of 1987. (Courtesy of the Brighton Historical Preservation Commission.)

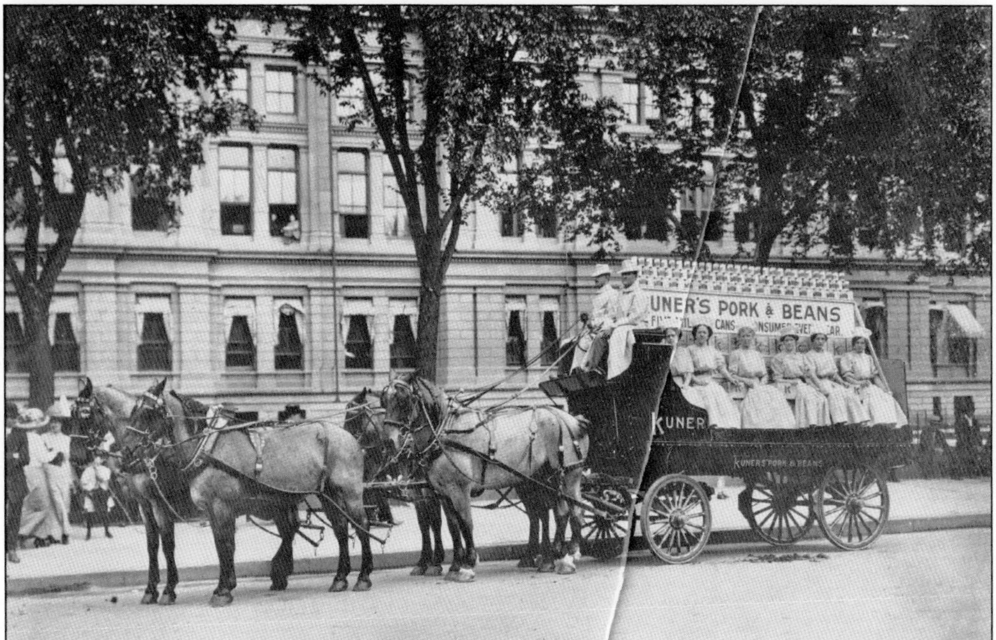

Kuner Float. The Kuner-Empson Company always had an active advertising campaign to promote its products. This float was in a parade in Denver. White clothing was required for women on the float to emphasize the purity of the Kuner products. (Courtesy of the Brighton Historical Preservation Commission.)

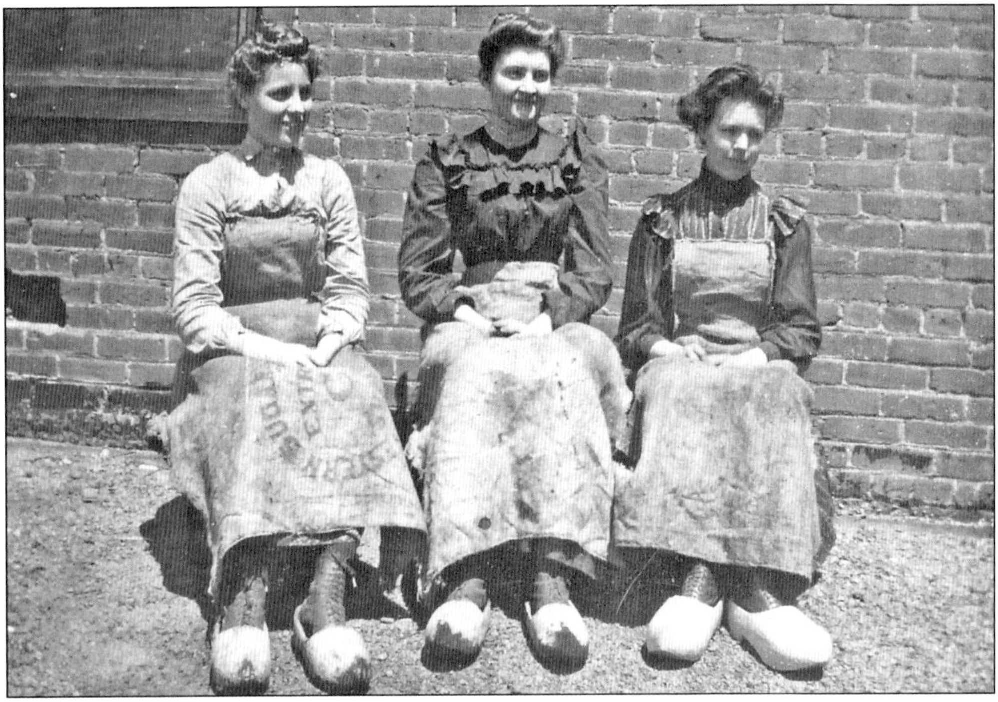

WOODEN SHOES. The Kuner "Bottling Room Girls" were issued wooden shoes to wear in the factory since the vinegar used in the pickle brine and many of the other processes would destroy leather shoes. As a result, the theme was carried on in the uniforms worn by the women employees, which had a Dutch appearance. (Courtesy of the Brighton Historical Preservation Commission.)

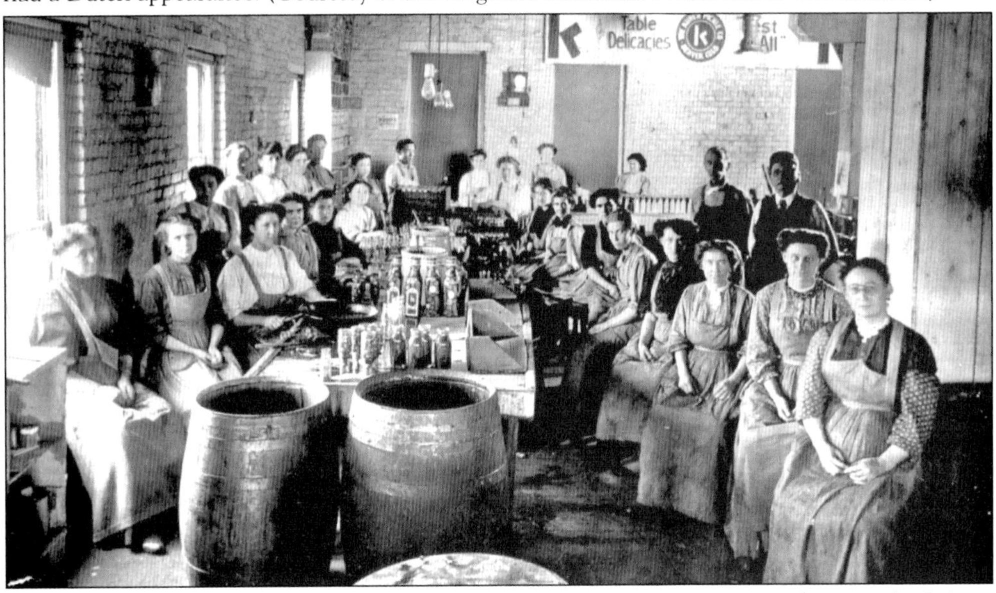

THE BOTTLING ROOM. The Bottling Room of the Kuner Pickle Company was photographed about 1900. The women took the pickles from brine-filled barrels in the foreground and packed them in jars on the tables. Note the Kuner "K" on the rear wall, and the motto, "Straight Goods and a Fair Deal." The company moved the main offices and factory to Brighton in 1917. (Courtesy of the Brighton Historical Preservation Commission.)

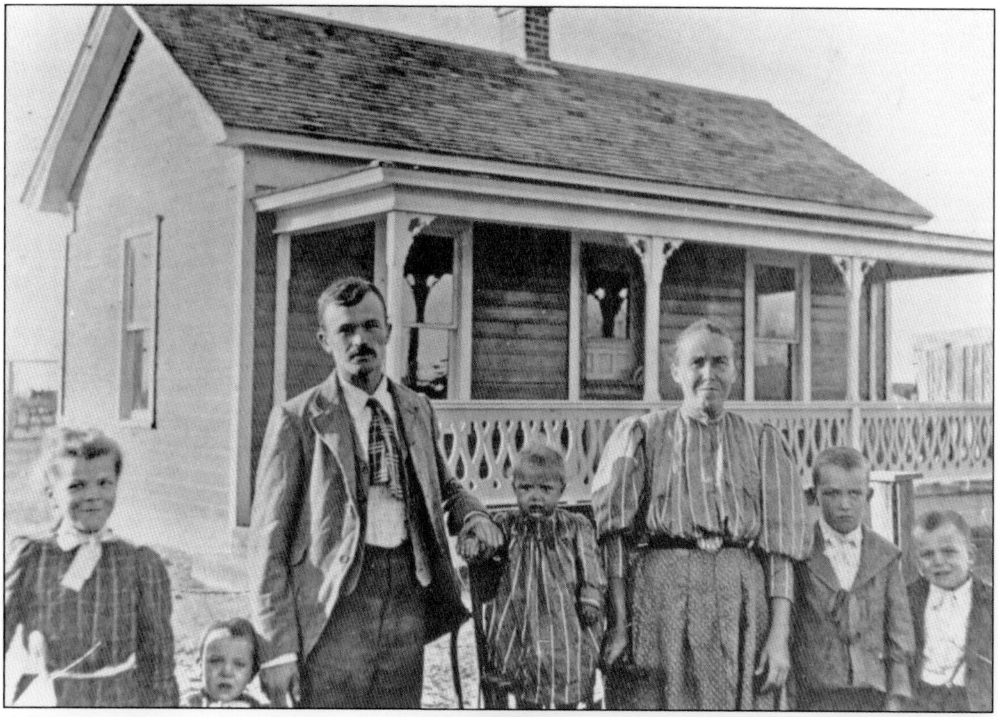

A Diverse Community. The development of a system of large irrigation reservoirs and canals and the resulting produce, sugar beet, canning, and dairy industries needed farm and factory workers. It created a diverse community of German, Japanese, Spanish, and English-speaking families and institutions. Many early settlers in Brighton were Germans. The Germans from Russia greatly added to that population. Seen in the photograph above is a family of Germans from Russia in front of a typical two-room house, including a *Wohnenzimmer* (living room) and a *Schlaffenzimmer* (bedroom). From left to right are Charlotte ("Lottie"), Karl, Jacob (Sr.), Mary, Katherine, Jacob (Jr.), and John Wagner. The group quickly assimilated. Jacob Wagner (Jr.) is pictured at right (left) with "Slim" in front of the county courthouse after becoming a naturalized citizen.

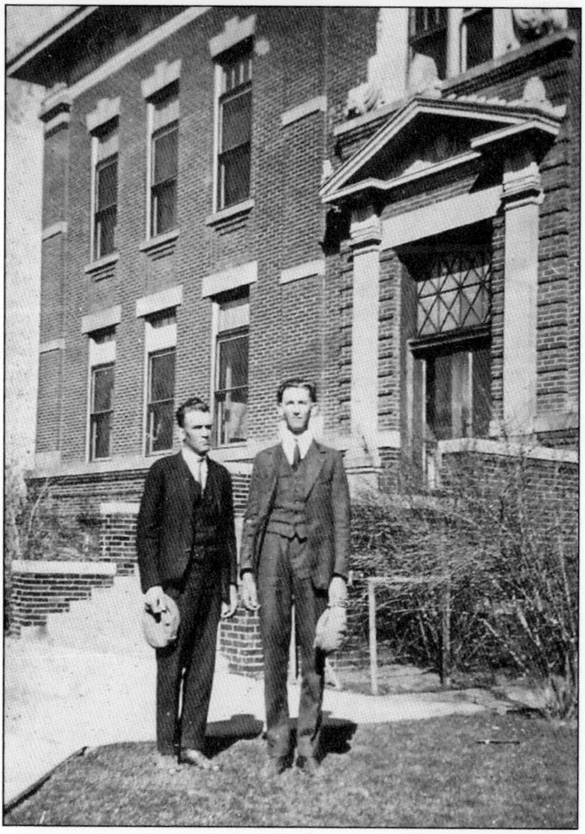

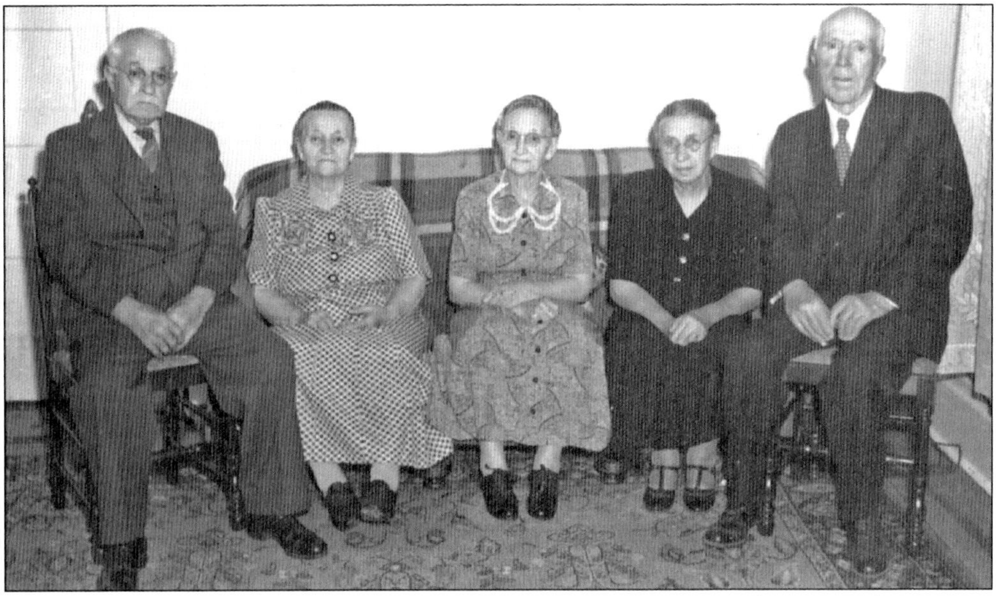

FOUNDERS. The charter members of the Zion Lutheran Church, organized on November 8, 1900, were Jacob and John Kramer, Herman and John Delventhal, Fred and John Lutz, William Lutz Sr. and John Lutz Jr., John Bauder, and Frederick Beach, some of whom are pictured here. Germans also helped to organize other churches in Brighton, including the St. Augustine Roman Catholic Church, the German Congregational Church, and Emmaus Lutheran Church. (Courtesy of the Brighton Historical Preservation Commission.)

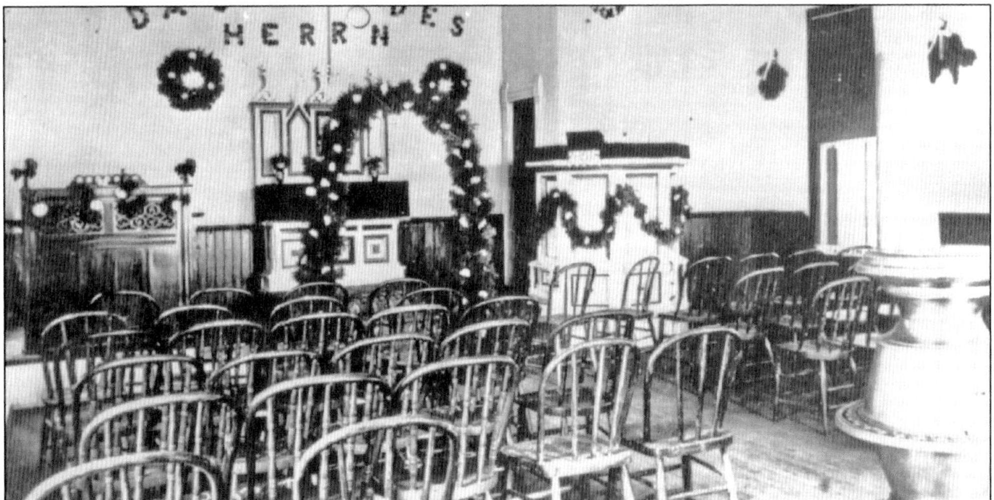

GERMAN LUTHERAN CHURCH. The newly formed Brighton School District No. 27 began construction of a schoolhouse on Front Street (now South First Avenue) in 1884. The schoolhouse was completed the next spring on Valentine's Day, February 14, 1885. It was the first school building in Brighton. The school district sold the schoolhouse to the German Lutheran Church (now Zion Lutheran Church), who used it for a church and school. Zion Lutheran built its own church in 1908 and a new school in 1915. The old schoolhouse was torn down to make a parking lot in November 1972. The German slogan on the wall means "The House of the Lord." (Courtesy of the Brighton Historical Preservation Commission.)

Zion Lutheran Church. Zion Lutheran congregation completed construction of their own church building on the northeast corner of North Fourth Avenue and Strong Street (now the location of the Brighton Post Office) in 1908. Some English worship services were introduced in 1918, and alternate English and German services began in 1926. In 1965, a new church was built at South Fourteenth Avenue and Skeel Street and the old property was sold.

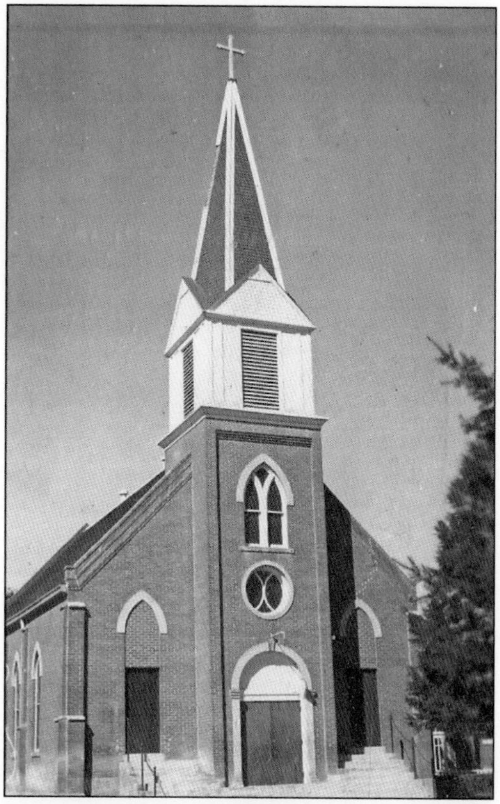

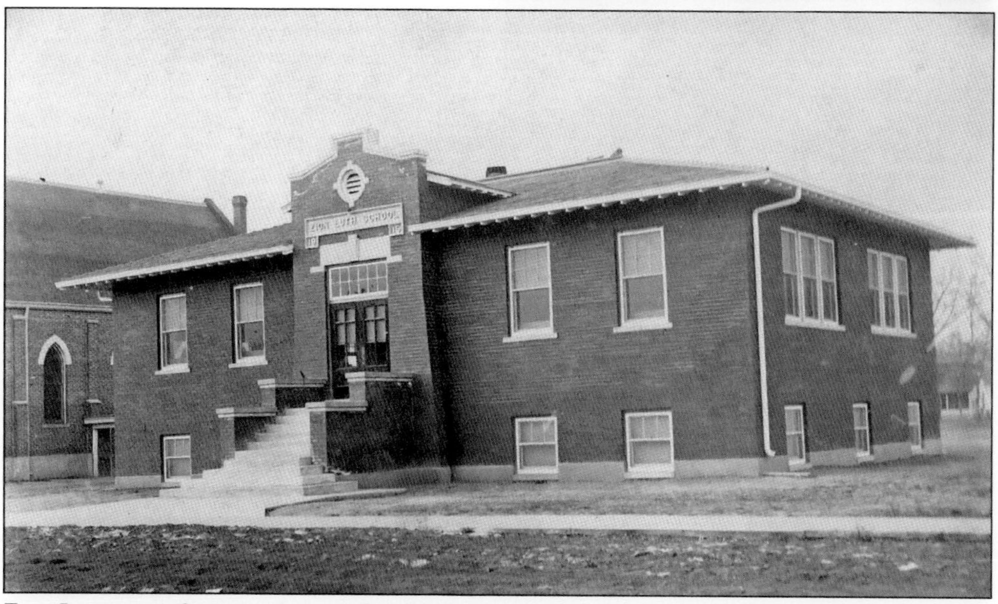

Zion Lutheran School. A new schoolhouse was built next to the church in 1915. As the school year began in September 1918, English was the only language used in teaching. The teacherage, constructed in 1917 as housing for the schoolteachers, was purchased by John and Nelda Gamble and moved to Bromley Lane when the new Zion Lutheran Church and school building was constructed in 1965. (Courtesy of Evelyn Tepe.)

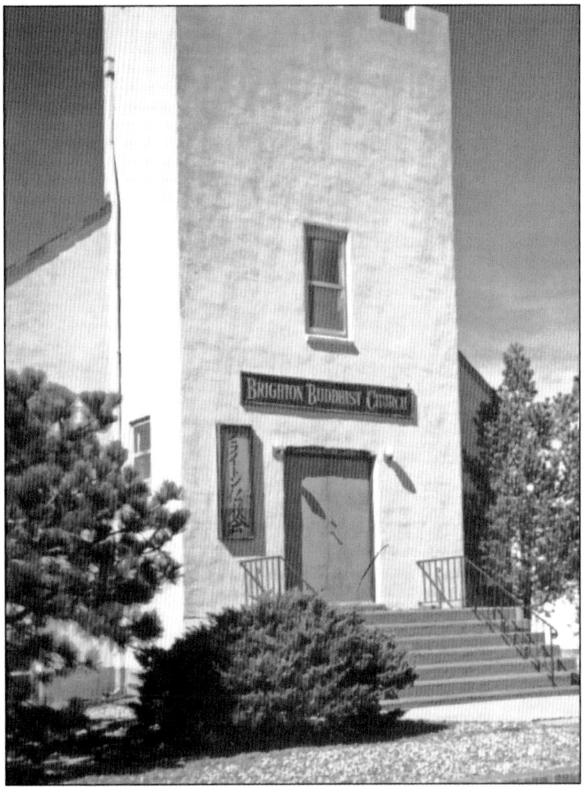

BRIGHTON BUDDHIST CHURCH. The Brighton Buddhist Church at 25 South First Avenue was completed in February 1940. Before completion of the building, the Brighton Kyudokai met in members' private homes, the Yomata Hall in Fort Lupton, and the Japanese Hall (the former Brighton Pavilion) in Brighton. Many Japanese were members of the Methodist church because of their active missionary program in Japan and work among the Japanese immigrants in America. (Courtesy of Dorene Kramer.)

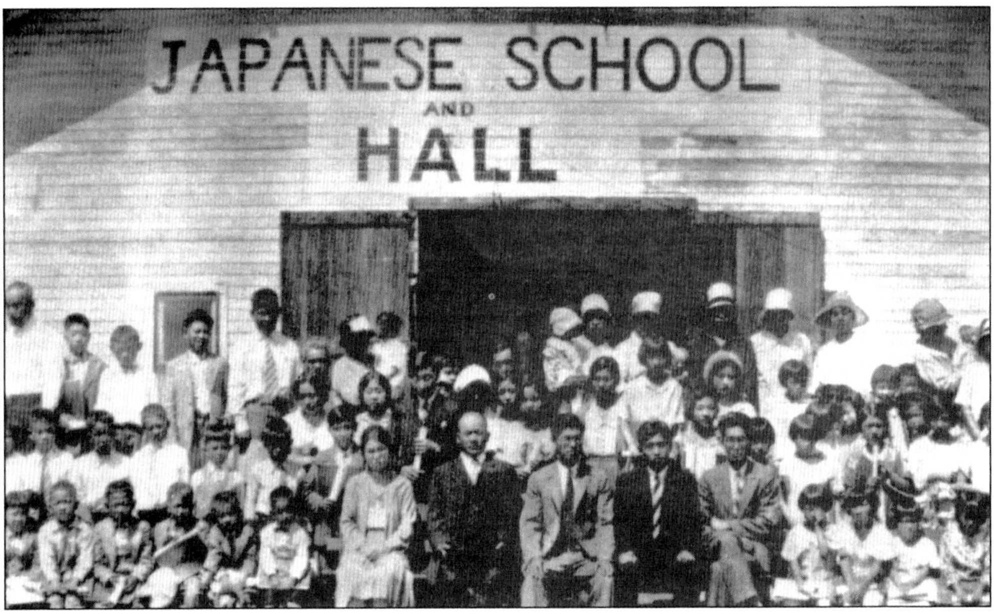

JAPANESE SCHOOL AND HALL. The Japanese Association purchased the old Brighton Pavilion, located between downtown Brighton and the river, in 1927. The Japanese Hall was used by the Japanese School, the Brighton Buddhist Church, and the Japanese Association. After the Brighton Japanese-American Association sold it in 1951, it became an apartment building. Money from the sale was used to purchase what is now BJAA Park. (Courtesy of the Brighton Historical Preservation Commission.)

Naoichi ("Harry") Hokazono. After arriving in Colorado in 1898, Naoichi ("Harry") Hokazono became a leading labor contractor. Hokazono imported 70 Japanese men to work the sugar beet fields and soon employed over 2,000 men on projects like the Moffat Tunnel and Barker Dam. A resident of Brighton, Hokazono was president of the Japanese Association of Colorado. In 1977, he was immortalized in a stained-glass window in the state capitol building.

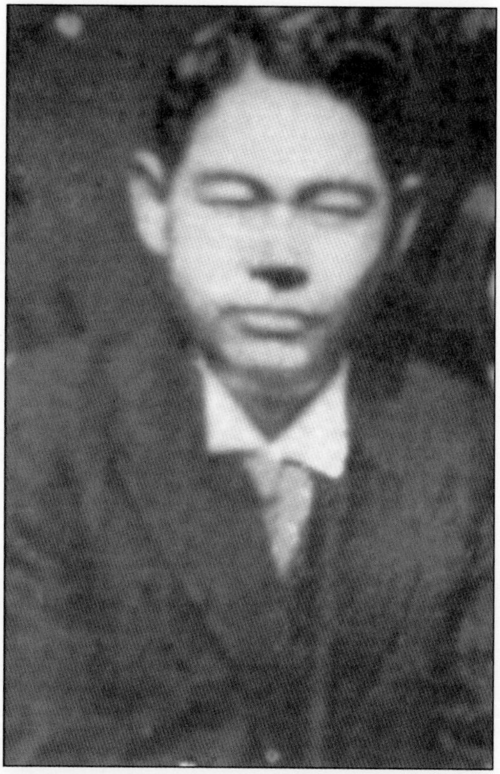

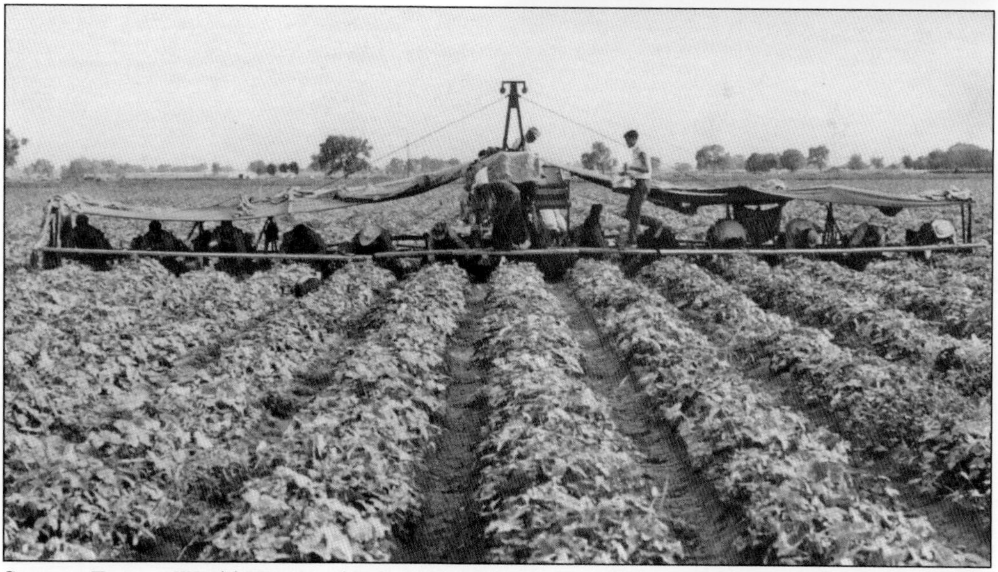

Sakata Farms. World War II added to the Japanese population of the Brighton area after the U.S. government moved all the Japanese families on the West Coast to "relocation camps." Many local Japanese sponsored individuals to farm here. One evacuee, Robert ("Bob") Sakata, developed a successful farming operation with his brother, Harry Sakata, headquartered at 900 South Fourth Street. Sakata was known for his inventions to automate farming processes, as in this photograph. In 1999, Sakata and his wife, Joanna, were inducted into the Colorado Agricultural Hall of Fame.

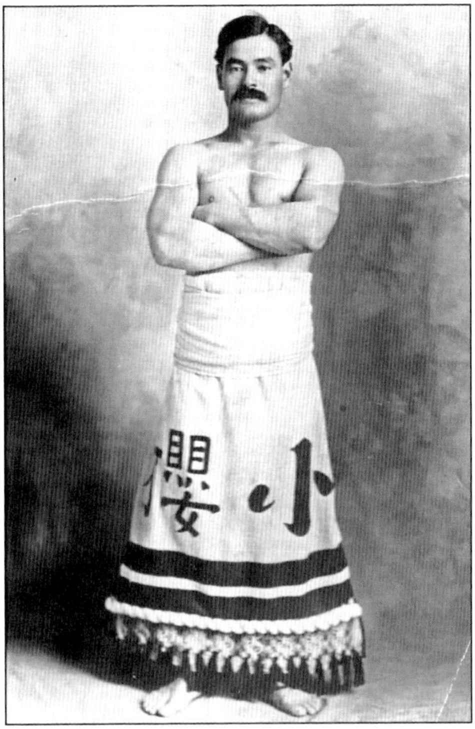

Japanese Wrestler. A famous professional Judo wrestler, Noda, was a performer at the Okamoto wedding in Brighton in 1910, seen here from his *carte de visite*. (Courtesy of the Brighton Historical Preservation Commission.)

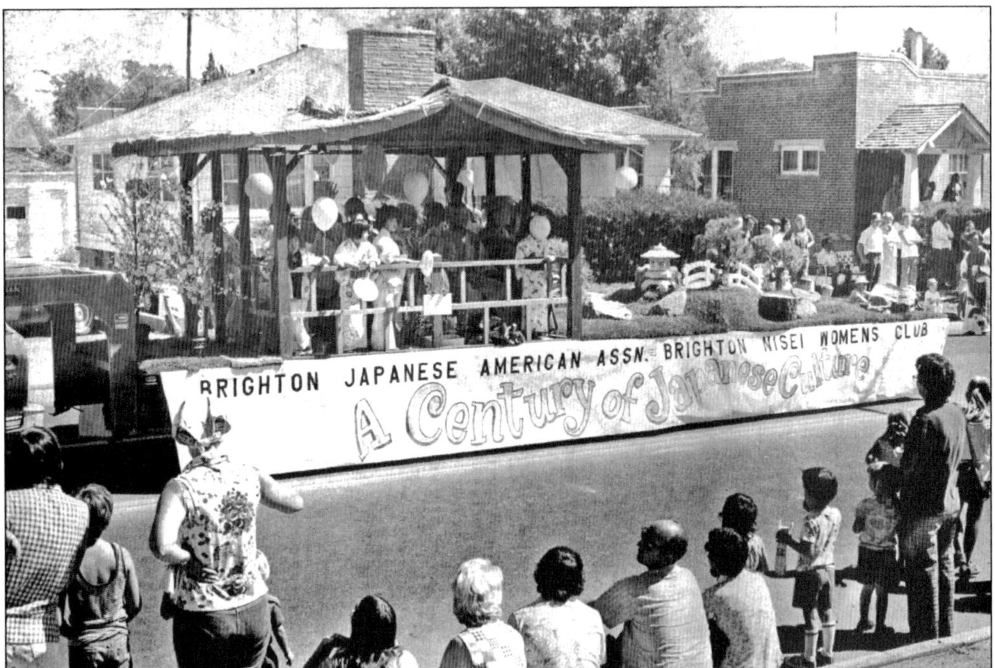

BJAA Float. The local Japanese community emerged from the war stronger than ever. In 1943, the Nesei Women's Club was formed in Brighton by the younger women. On February 3, 1950, the Brighton Japanese American Association (BJAA) was organized by the younger men. Both organizations have been active in the Brighton community, as evidenced by this parade float.

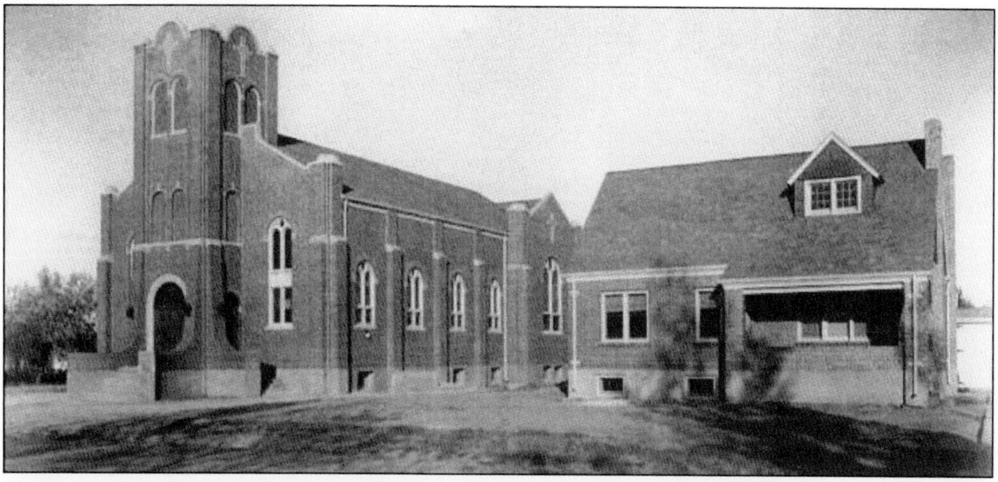

St. Augustine Roman Catholic Church. Oscar E. Lindeval photographed the St. Augustine Roman Catholic Church building on the corner of South Sixth Avenue and Bush Streets sometime between 1930 and 1940. The art deco–style brick church, built in 1930, has arched windows and an arched entrance, crosses on a central tower, and buttresses. The church served a diverse community. The Altar Society was formed in 1928. The Holy Name Society started in 1935. The St. Augustine Catholic School was built in 1956. (Courtesy of the Colorado Historical Society.)

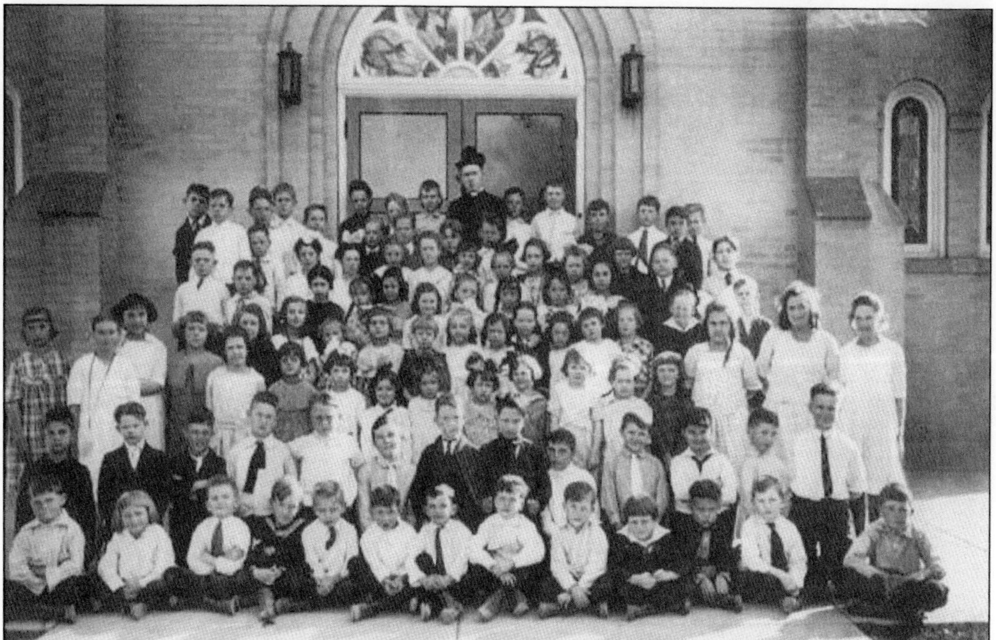

Father Verschraegen and His Flock. Father Emile J. Verschraegen, pastor of the St. Augustine Roman Catholic Church in Brighton (1929–1938), in vestments, poses behind his flock of children in 1930. A hand-written note on the back of the photograph said, "Youngsters pose with Father Verschraegen, who could tell them "to smile" in six languages," (Spanish, German, English, Latin, and two more). Note the brick construction of the St. Augustine Catholic Church in the background and the arched doors with a stained-glass fanlight and flanking lamps. The photograph is from the T. J. Noel collection. (Courtesy of the Denver Public Library Western History and Genealogy Department.)

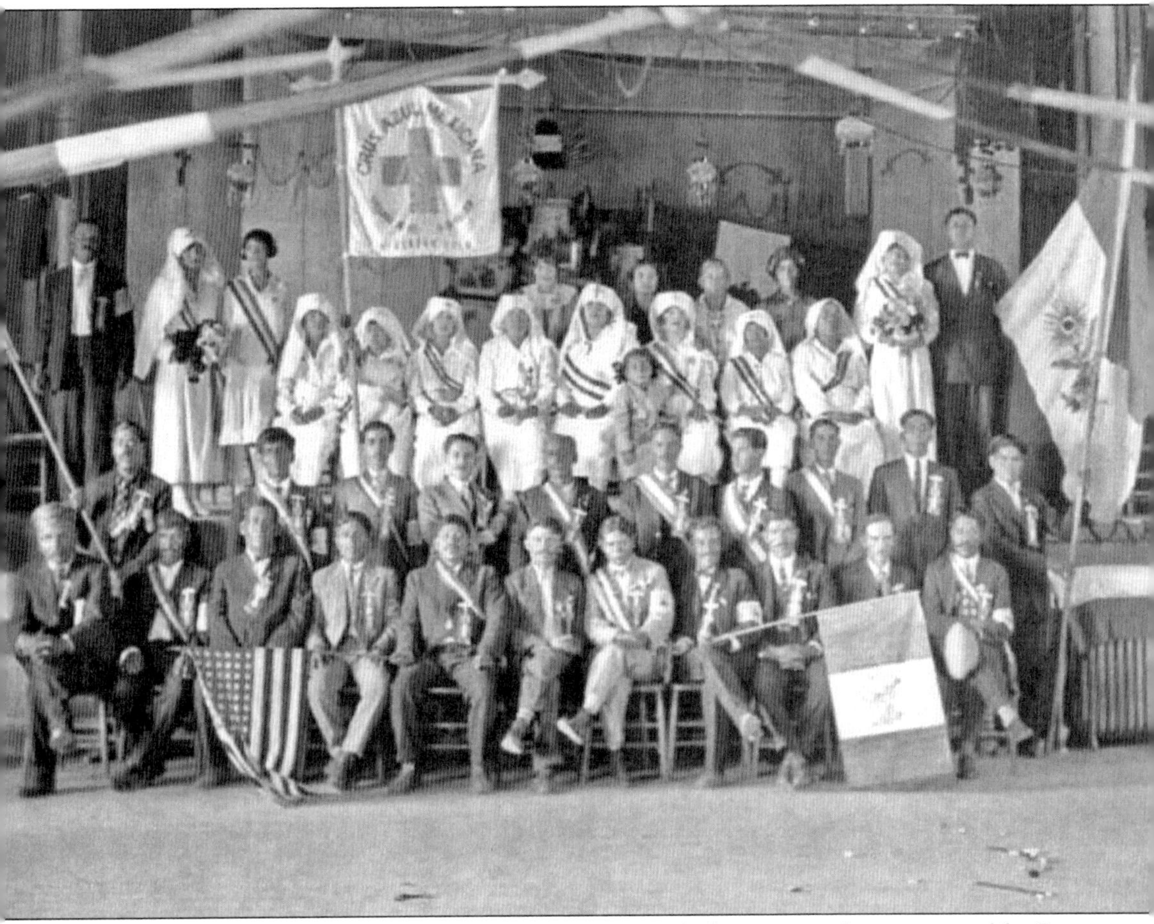

COMISION HONORIFICA MEXICANA DE BRIGHTON. In 1920, these men and women posed for Oscar E. Lindeval in 1920 with a banner for the "Cruz Azul Mexicana, Brigada No. 68, 3 Division, Brighton, Colo." on the front steps of the St. Augustine Catholic Church in Brighton. La Cruz Azul Mexicana was a charitable organization that provided assistance to low-income Mexican families. The women wear light-colored uniforms with striped sashes and crosses on habits. The men wear suits and ties, sashes, and ribbon pins with insignia and pose with flags that include U.S. flags and a Mexican flag. The society was only one of several charitable organizations in the Brighton area. The House of Neighborly Service (originally at 186 North Ninth Street) was built of adobe in the 1920s and served area Hispanics in need of help. El Buen Pastor Presbyterian Church was built next door in 1968. The House of Neighborly Service moved to the Heritage Community Center at 840 Bridge Street in 1984. (Courtesy of the Colorado Historical Society.)

Eight

Barr City
A Lost Dream

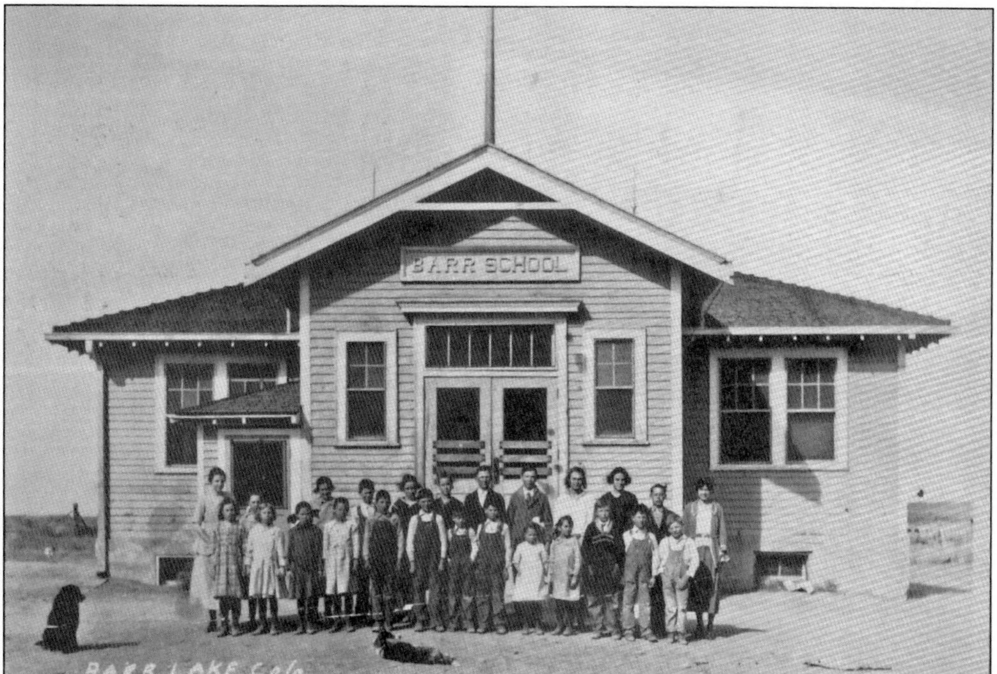

Barr School. The Barr schoolhouse was already showing signs of wear and tear when this annual class photograph was taken in 1920. The dream of Barr City had begun to fade. The grandiose plans for Barr City began when the Chicago, Burlington, and Quincy Railroad completed its branch there at Platte Summit in 1882. The name was later changed to Barr. Developers were quick to see the possibilities of the combination of the railroad and lake at that location. (Courtesy of Ester and Bruce Canterbury.)

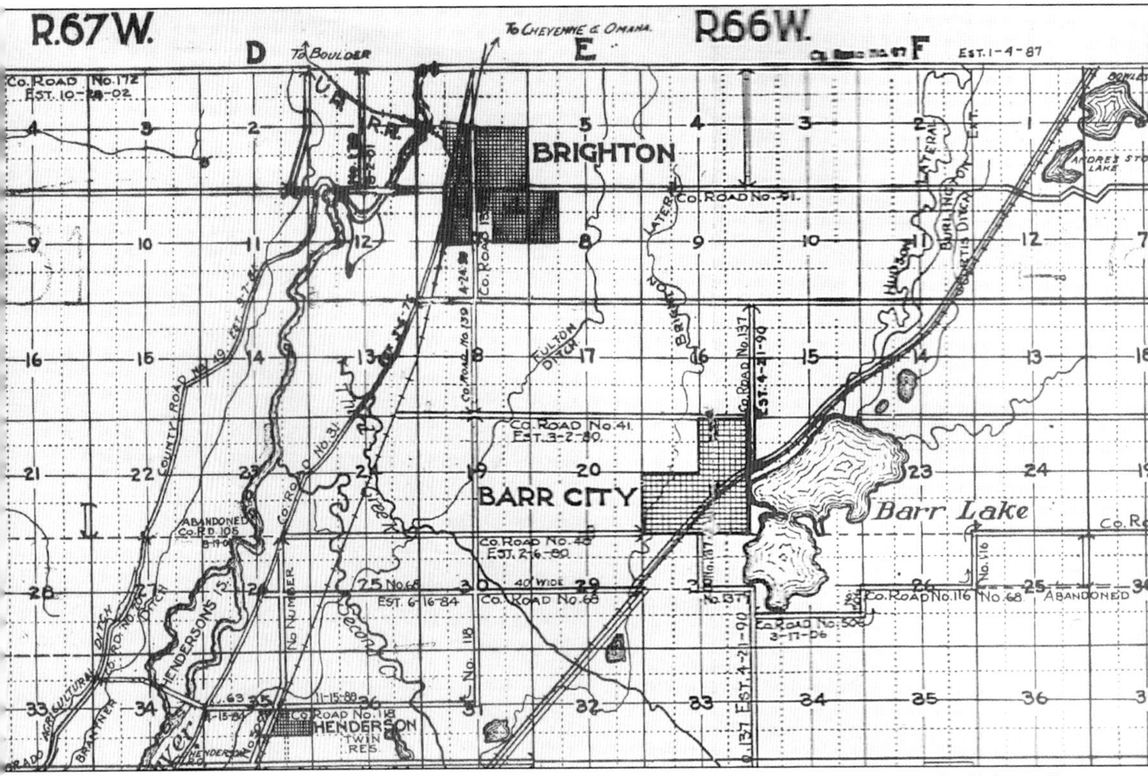

Barr City Map. The natural depression in which Barr Lake now lies was once a buffalo wallow. Farmers in the area viewed the old buffalo wallow as a natural location for storing water and formed the Burlington Ditch and Reservoir Company in 1884. They built a dam across the north end to contain water and constructed the Burlington Ditch, drawing water from the South Platte River at a headgate near the Riverside Cemetery. The lake that was formed was known as Oasis Reservoir. The combination of the lake and the railroad completed in 1882 created a unique opportunity for a town site, as seen on this map. The town soon boasted of its own creamery, brickyard, Presbyterian church, a grange, and a school. For a while, it even had its own newspaper, the *Barr City Gazette*. Plans for Barr City, like many Colorado enterprises, were hard hit by the Panic of 1893. In 1909, the Burlington Ditch Company enlarged the lake with a new dam, a new canal, and relocation of the railroad tracks, covering Oasis and Burlington Reservoirs on this map to create Barr Lake.

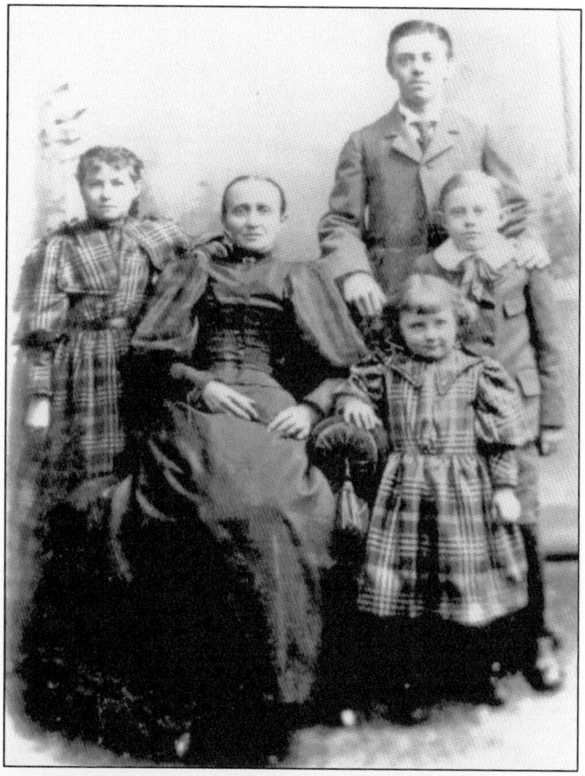

Emil Bruderlin Family. Many substantial homes were built in Barr City, including the Stone House, built in 1889 near the railroad tracks on the northwest edge of the lake by Emil Bruderlin, a Swiss bookbinder, seen here with his family. Bruderlin was killed when he fell under a train at the Barr depot. His daughter, Helen Crisp, was a longtime resident of Aurora. (Courtesy of the Rocky Mountain Bird Observatory.)

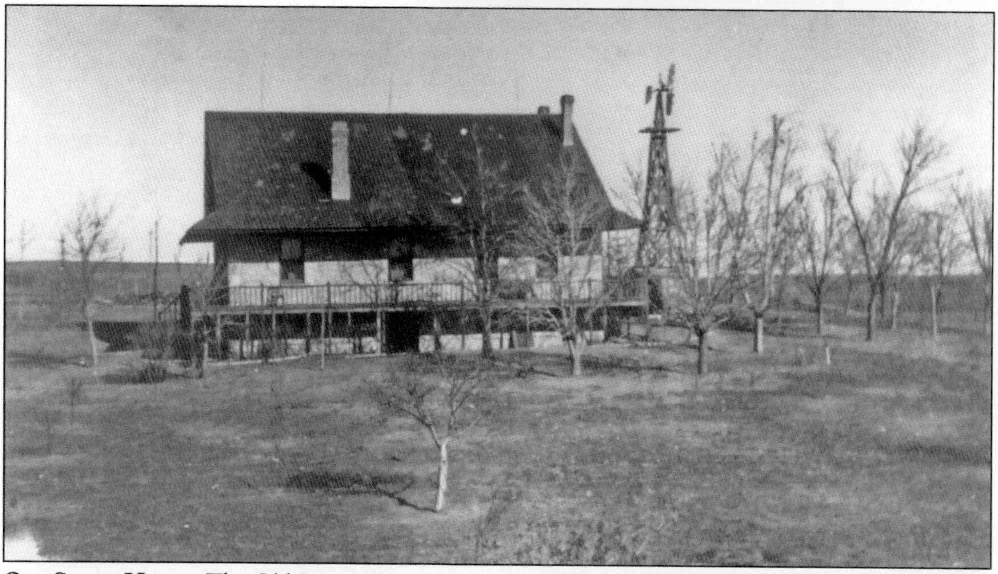

Old Stone House. The Old Stone House, now part of Barr Lake State Park, served as a farmhouse and originally housed the Bruderlin family and bookbinding business. The 1880 residence exemplifies Germanic building technique and style. Emil Bruderlin emigrated from Switzerland, and his house represents the application of design elements of his native land and the high plains setting of Colorado. After serving as a farmhouse for various families, the Old Stone House was abandoned and left to deteriorate. The house has been restored as the offices of the Rocky Mountain Bird Observatory at Barr Lake State Park. (Courtesy of the Rocky Mountain Bird Observatory.)

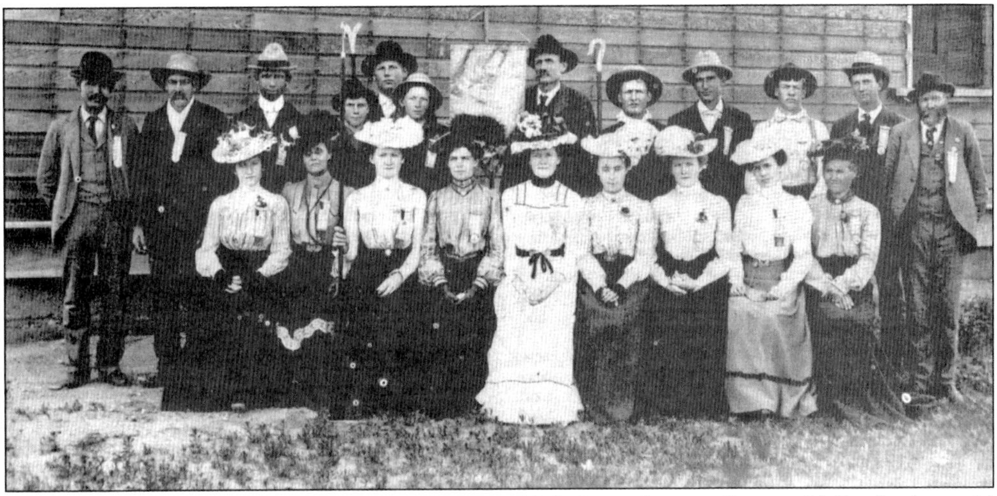

Barr Grange, 1902. In 1902, Barr Grange No. 133 dedicated a new Grange Hall, which would seat 300 people. Note the symbols of their offices used in the rituals of the fraternal organization. At its beginning, the Patrons of Husbandry (or Grange) was a fraternal organization—one of many formed during this period—with offices and rituals modeled along the lines of the Freemasons or the Odd Fellows. It included both men and women and emphasized social activities to lessen the isolation and loneliness of farm life by holding parties and picnics, lectures, and concerts. At first, the Grange had only social and educational objectives, but to meet the economic problems of the farmers, the Grange placed an increasing emphasis on cooperative enterprises in such ventures as creameries, warehouses, grain elevators, insurance, purchasing, and manufacturing farm equipment. (Courtesy of Esther and Bruce Canterbury.)

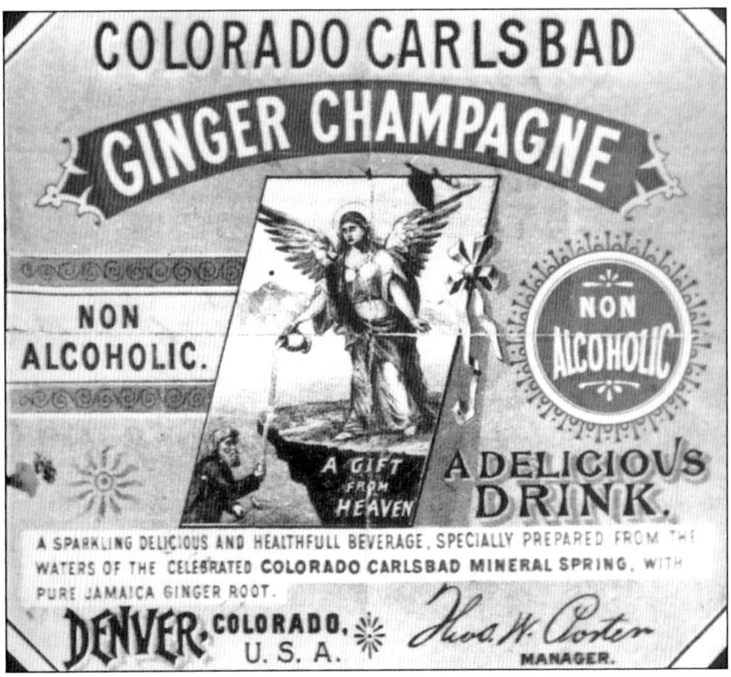

Colorado Carlsbad Mineral Spring. Carlsbad Springs were located at 144th Avenue at Barr Lake. The naturally effervescent waters of the artesian well were bottled and shipped throughout the region and even back East. In 1901, the Colorado Carlsbad Company planned a European-type spa at the springs and an electric railroad, but the plan never materialized.

BURLINGTON AND O'BRIAN DITCHES. The Burlington Ditch, named for the Burlington Railroad, was originally constructed in 1886 and enlarged over the years. The O'Brian Canal, named after company official Peter O'Brian, was constructed in 1909. The O'Brian Canal heads jointly with the Burlington at the South Platte River but has a higher grade that fills Barr Lake to a higher level. The Denver Reservoir Company acquired all the rights to the canals and reservoirs in the area in 1903. In 1909, the Denver Reservoir Company was reorganized as the Farmers Reservoir and Irrigation Company (FRICO). The company, headquartered in Brighton, still owns Barr Lake, as well as Stanley Lake and several other large reservoirs. The company constructed a new office building in Brighton in 1976. (Both courtesy of the Library of Congress.)

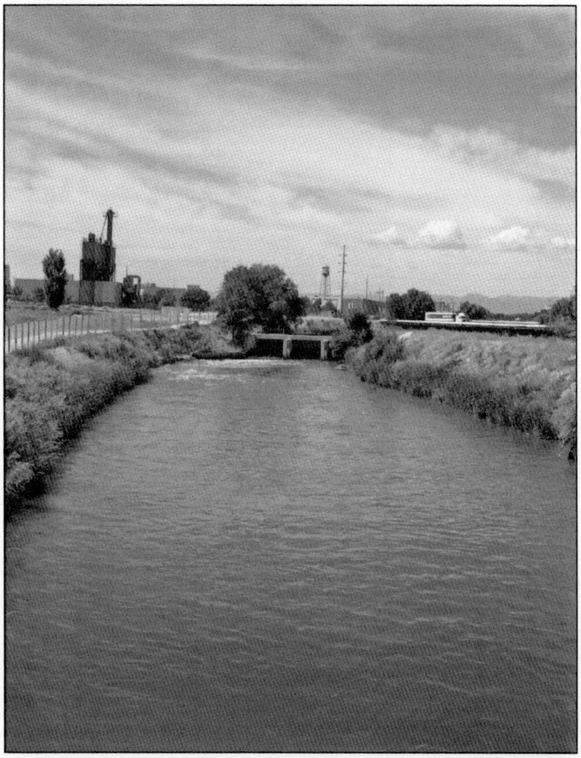

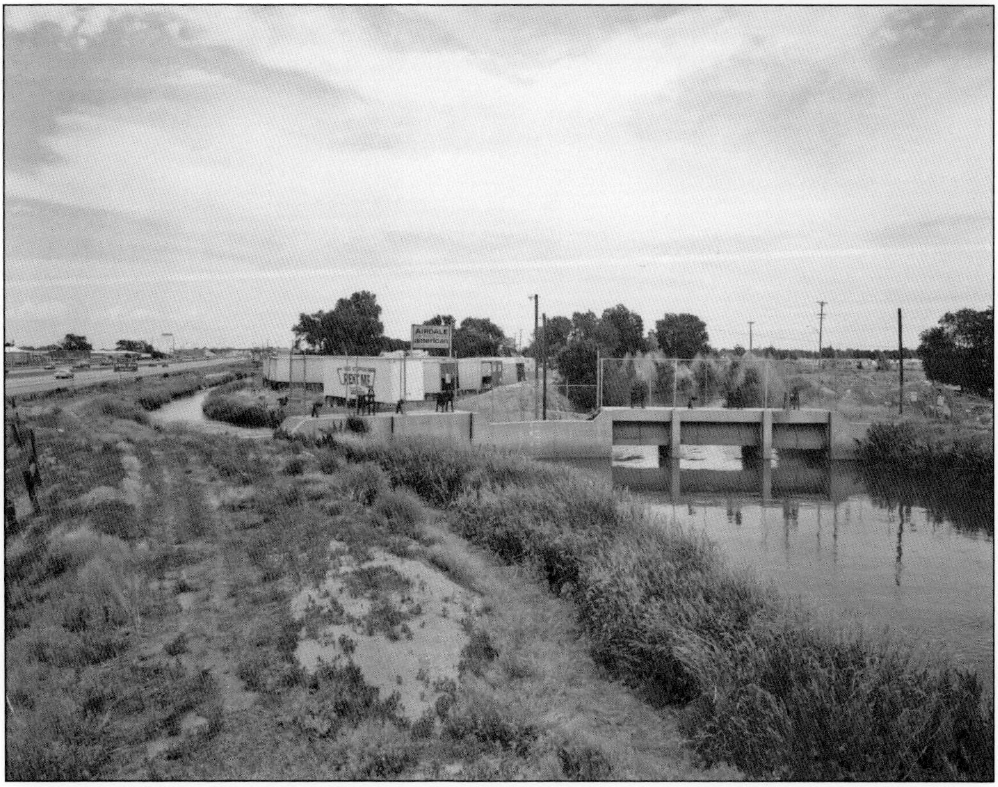

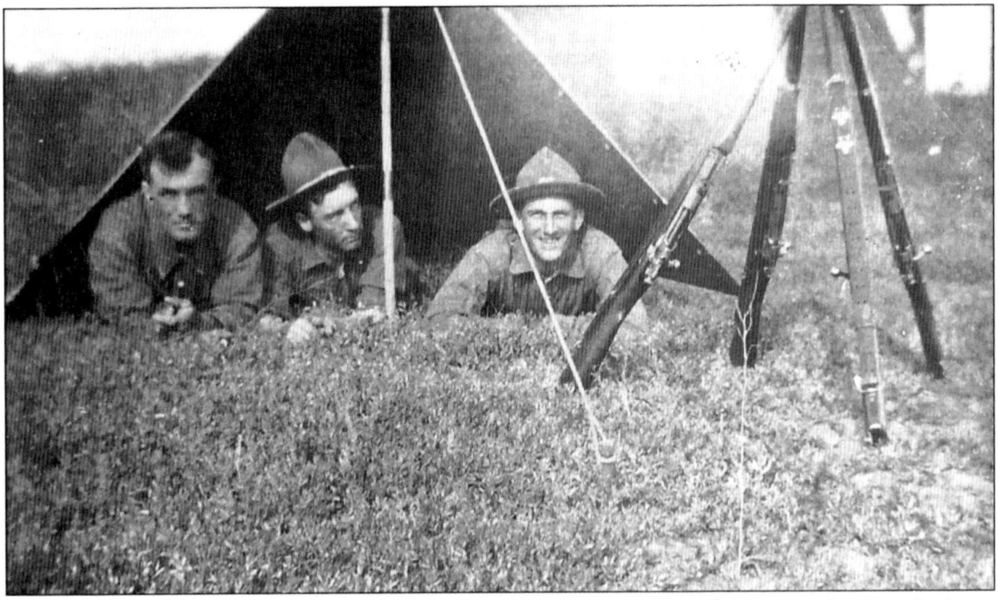

Guarding Barr Lake. Company K of the Colorado National Guard was posted at Barr Lake in 1918 during World War I to guard the dam and the water supply against any German saboteurs. The irony was that the lake was later polluted, not by enemy agents, but by the Denver Union Stockyards and Denver Sewage plant located just above the headgate of the Burlington and O'Brian Ditches on the South Platte River. Members of the local Company K are seen here at Barr Lake during the summer of 1918. (Courtesy of the Brighton Historical Preservation Commission.)

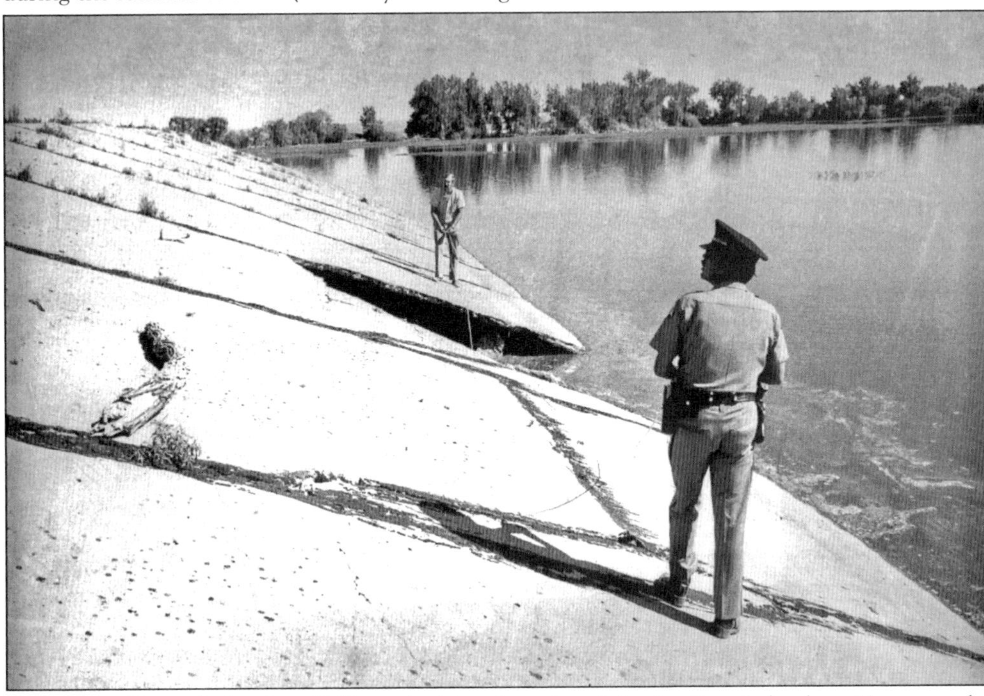

Barr Lake Dam. A flood in 1965 resulted in a large break in the Barr Lake dam. However, the disaster was a blessing in disguise since it flushed out the pollution in the lake and led to the creation of Barr Lake State Park, a wildlife sanctuary, in 1972. The park opened in 1977.

Nine

Bicycles, Baseball, Bands, and Fairs

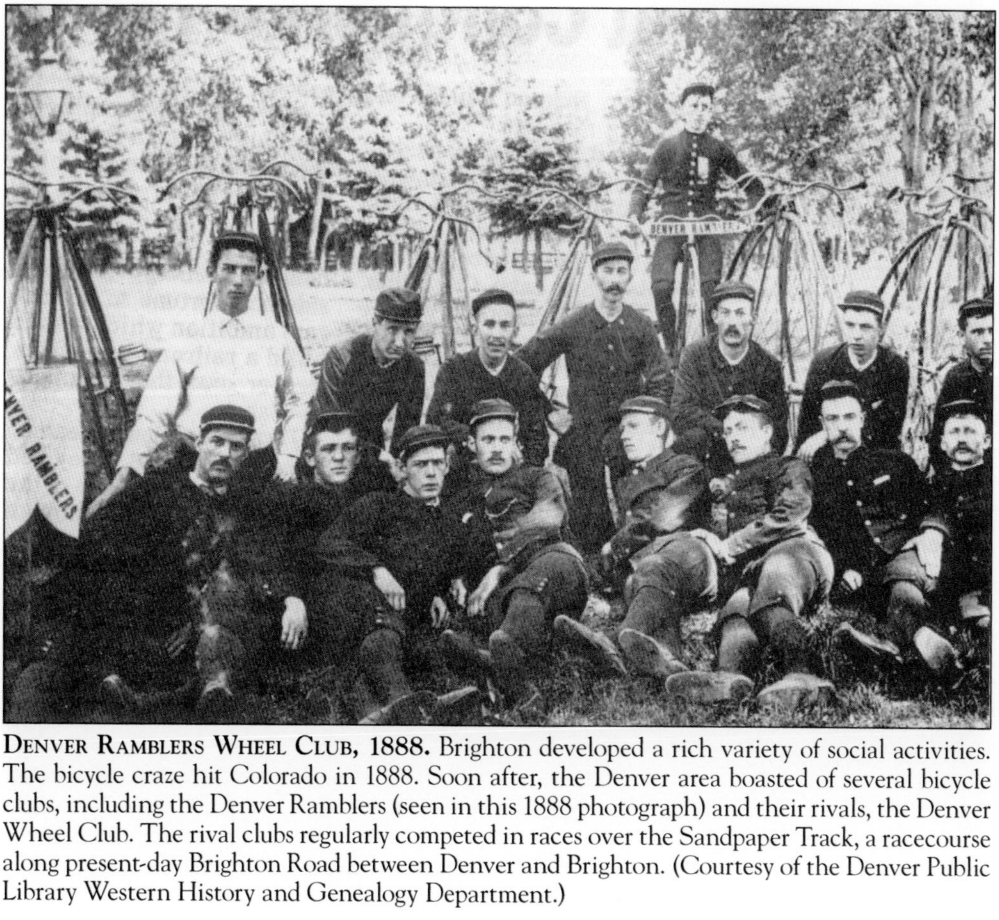

Denver Ramblers Wheel Club, 1888. Brighton developed a rich variety of social activities. The bicycle craze hit Colorado in 1888. Soon after, the Denver area boasted of several bicycle clubs, including the Denver Ramblers (seen in this 1888 photograph) and their rivals, the Denver Wheel Club. The rival clubs regularly competed in races over the Sandpaper Track, a racecourse along present-day Brighton Road between Denver and Brighton. (Courtesy of the Denver Public Library Western History and Genealogy Department.)

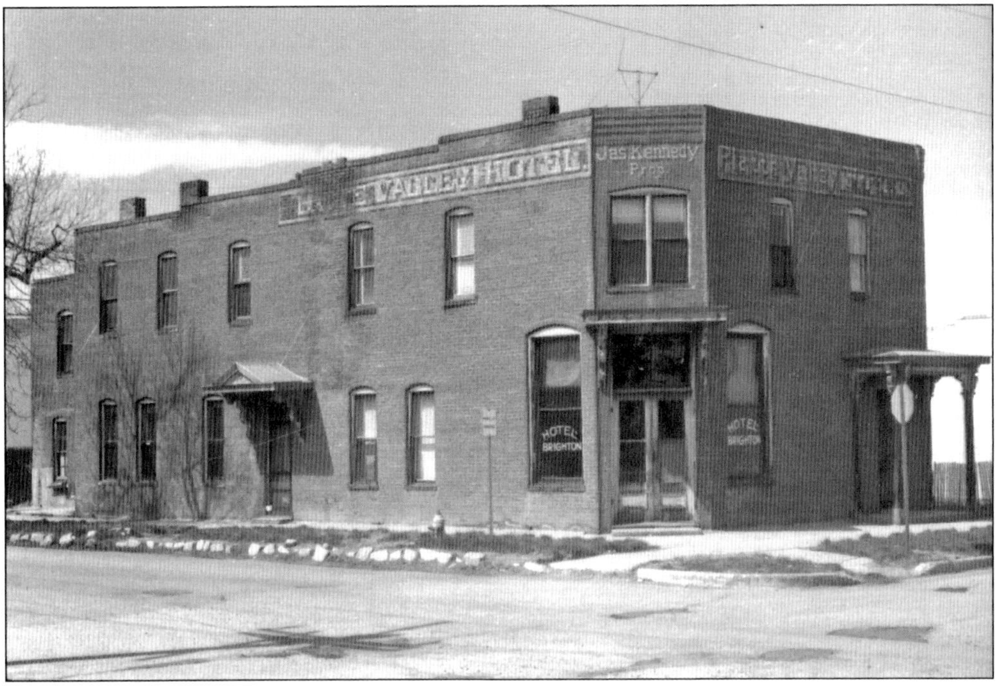

Brighton Hotel. The Brighton Hotel, built as the Platte Valley House in 1887, was the final destination of many bicycle races. Those who finished in the last half of the racers often had to buy the winners dinner at the hotel. Seen here shortly before its destruction, the Brighton Hotel was demolished in 1973 to make way for a parking lot at the northwest corner of Cabbage Avenue and Bush Street.

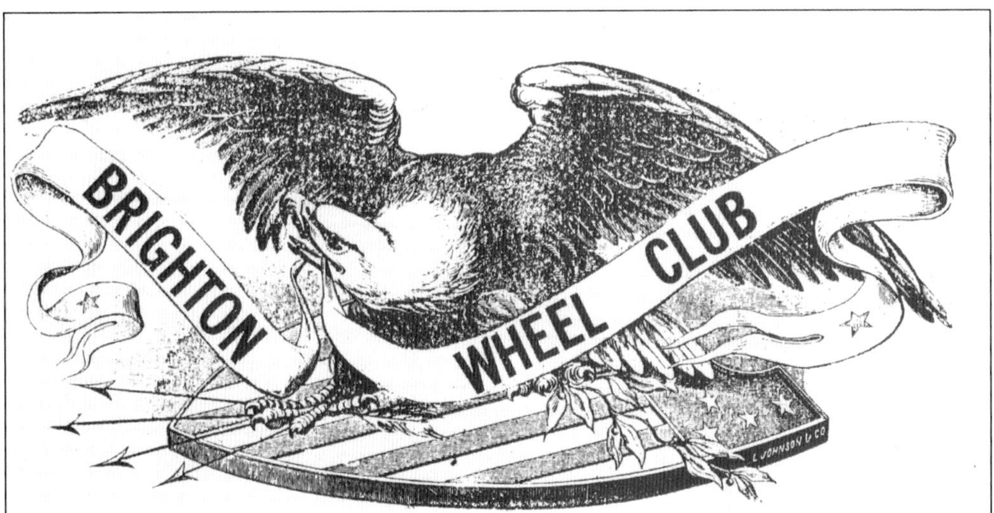

Brighton Wheel Club. The Brighton Wheel Club was founded in June 1897. Their club colors were red, white, and blue, as seen in the emblem of the club. The first events sponsored by the Brighton Wheel Club were bicycle races on the racetrack at the fairgrounds in Brighton on the Fourth of July, 1897.

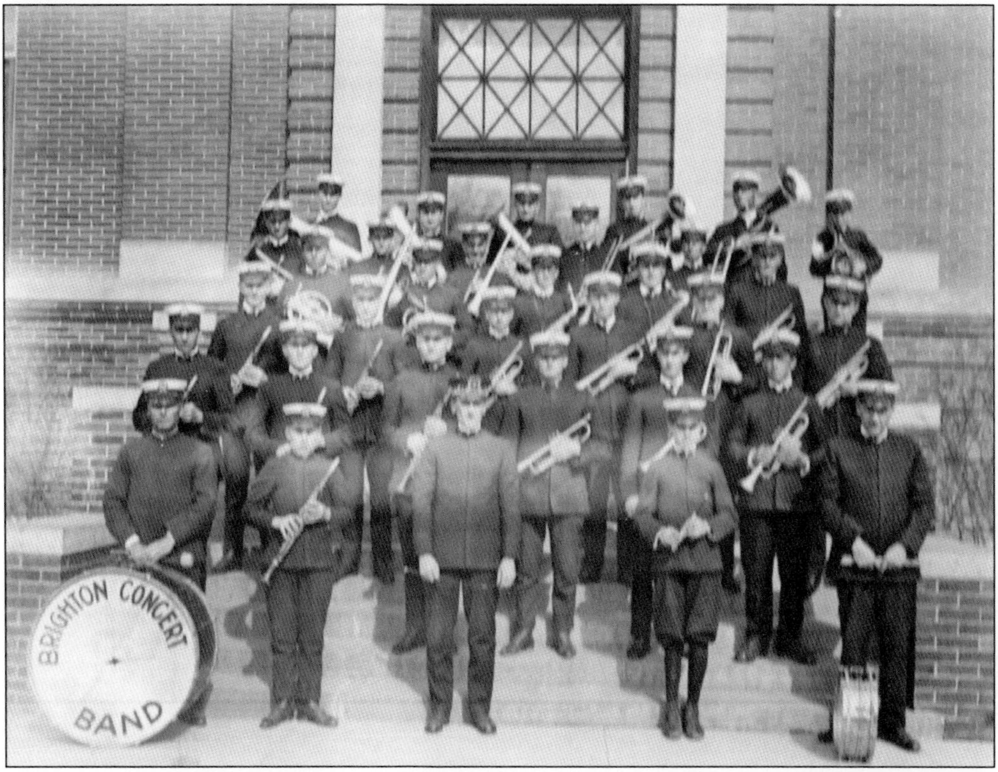

BRIGHTON BANDS. Brighton enjoyed a long musical tradition, including a number of local bands. Otto Rodekohr's Brighton Concert Band (above) held weekly summer concerts in the City Park at Bridge Street and South Sixth Avenue (now the location of North Elementary). Rodekohr is seen in the first row of the group above on the far right. He and his family also participated in the Mandolin String Band (below). The band members were, from left to right, (first row) Clara Kramer, Emma Lutz, Loretta Rodekohr, Bertha Kramer, and Loreen Rodekohr, accompanist; (second row) Herman Kramer, Otto Rodekohr, Martha Bredehoft, Leona Rodekohr, Ann Oelshlaeger, Louis Hiller, and Ernien Kramer. (Both courtesy of Evelyn Tepe.)

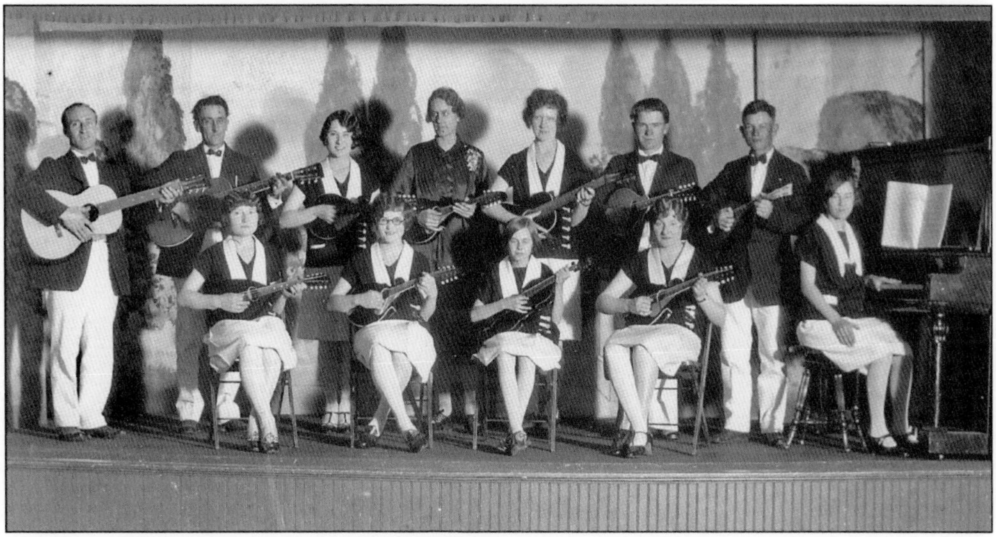

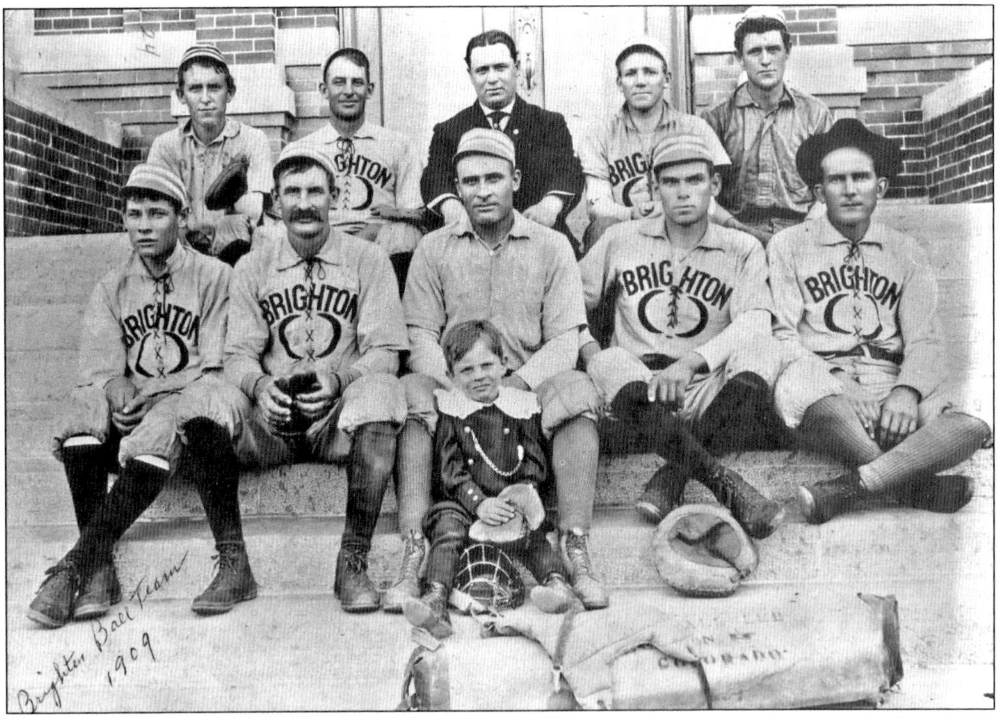

BRIGHTON BASEBALL TEAMS. The Brighton baseball team (above) was photographed in 1909 on the courthouse steps. The Brighton Boosters team (below) was photographed on August 22, 1920, in front of the grandstand at the Adams County Fairgrounds. From left to right, the Boosters are (seated) Duke White, Horace W. James (owner), "young" Higgins (batboy), Valentine ? (scorekeeper), and Walter P. Merrill (business manager); (standing) Ervin Hinds (second base), Fred Bauder (catcher), Howard Reidy (outfield), Eugene Kulow (catcher), James Morrison (pitcher), John Wall (shortstop), James Harmon (third base), Russell Merrill (pitcher and outfielder), Ralph Reidy (outfield), and James Higgins (pitcher). White was an umpire for 36 years, including umpiring for the Denver Bears (predecessors of the Colorado Rockies). In 1968, the Brighton High School dedicated the Duke White Field for his long service to the schools, Little League, and Pee Wee Baseball. (Both courtesy of the Brighton Historical Preservation Commission).

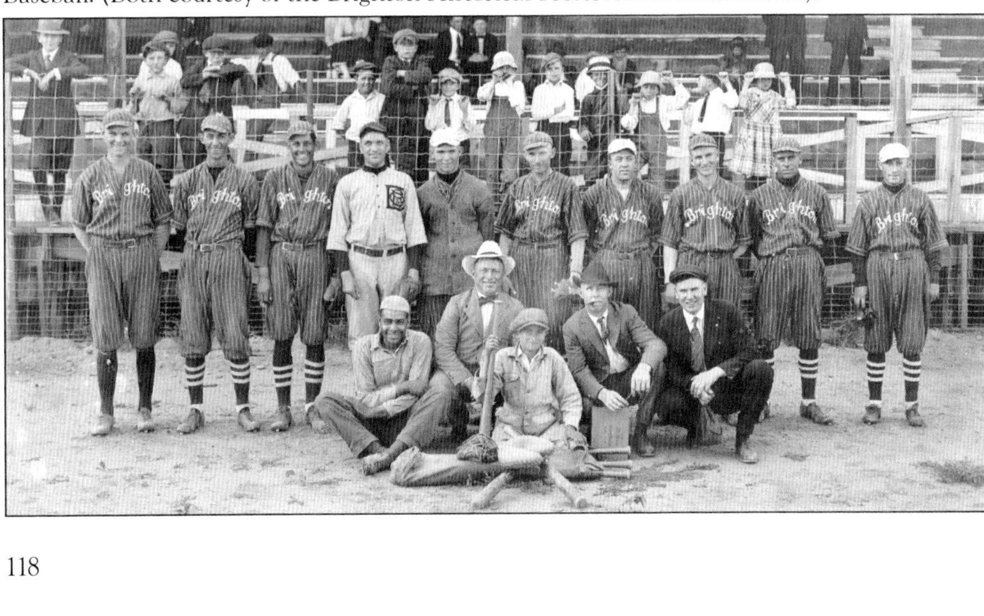

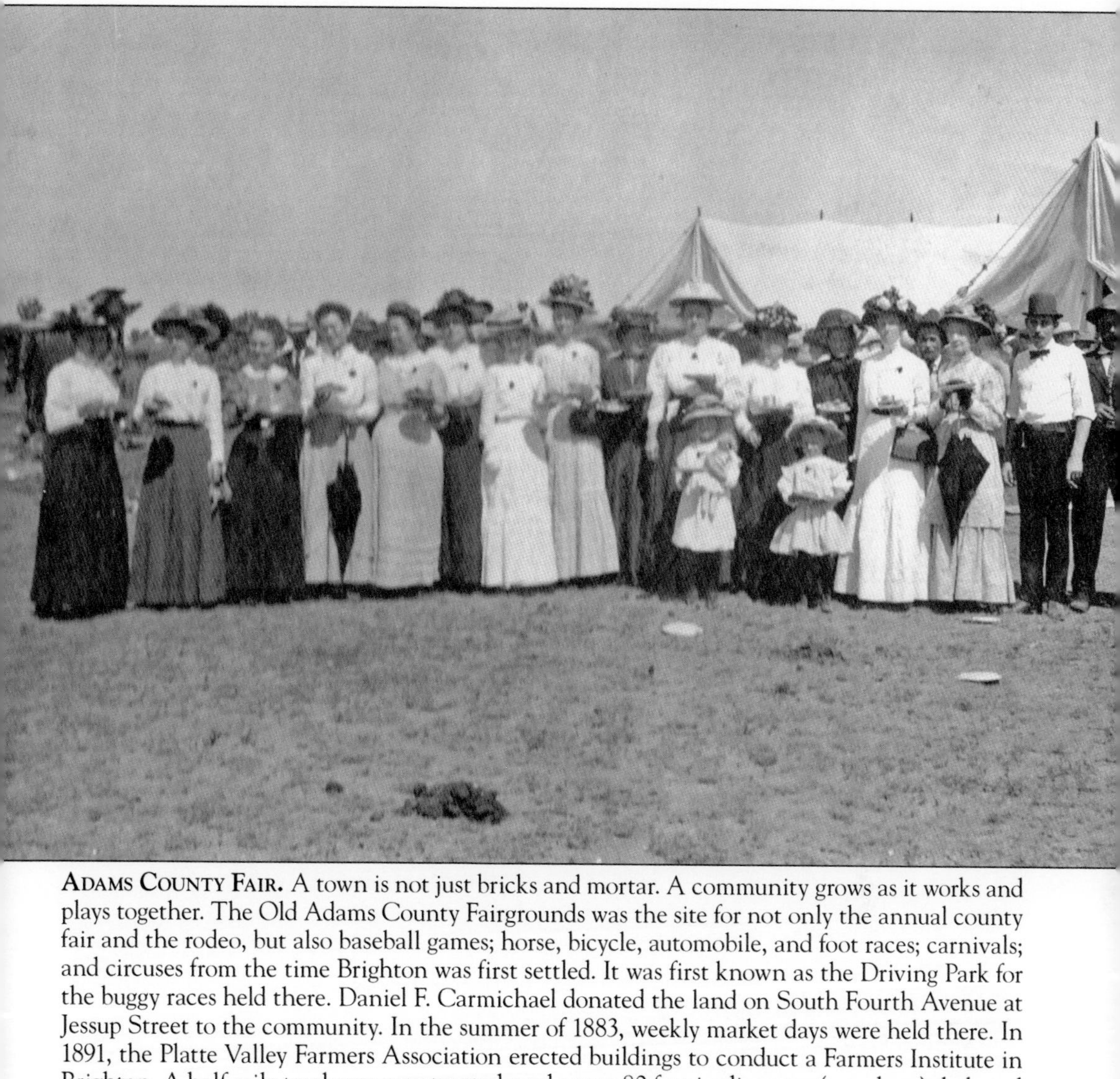

ADAMS COUNTY FAIR. A town is not just bricks and mortar. A community grows as it works and plays together. The Old Adams County Fairgrounds was the site for not only the annual county fair and the rodeo, but also baseball games; horse, bicycle, automobile, and foot races; carnivals; and circuses from the time Brighton was first settled. It was first known as the Driving Park for the buggy races held there. Daniel F. Carmichael donated the land on South Fourth Avenue at Jessup Street to the community. In the summer of 1883, weekly market days were held there. In 1891, the Platte Valley Farmers Association erected buildings to conduct a Farmers Institute in Brighton. A half-mile track was constructed, and a tent 80 feet in diameter (seen here) sheltered agricultural exhibits. On the south side of the track were stalls for horses, sheds for cattle, and pens for sheep and hogs. A violent wild storm or small tornado destroyed the tent, which led to construction of permanent buildings at the site. (Courtesy of the Brighton Historical Preservation Commission.)

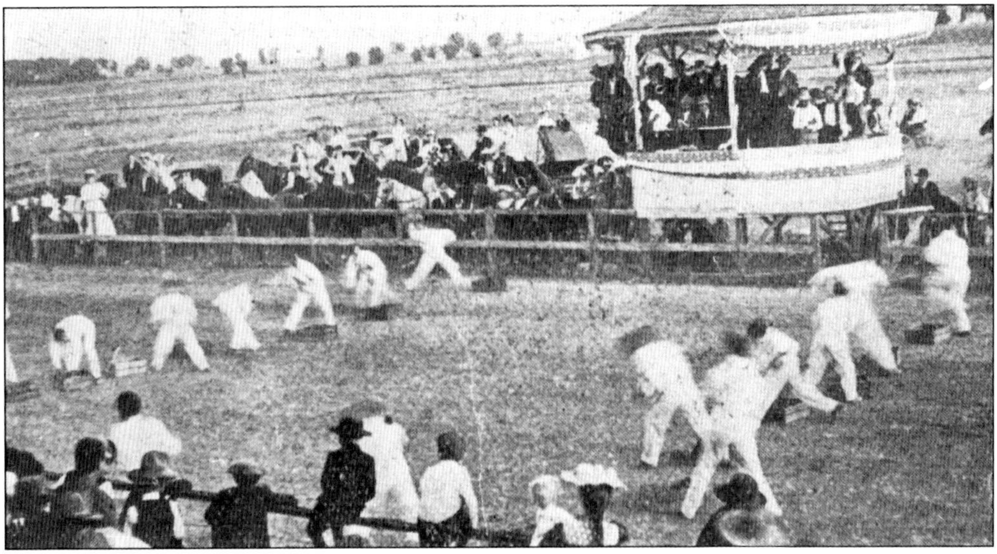

The Battle of Brighton. One of the most popular events in the early Adams County Fairs was the "Battle of Brighton" between two teams of white-clad, tomato-slinging contestants. On various years, the two teams represented rival Republicans and Democrats, residents of Brighton and Fort Lupton, or other combinations. The bandstand in the background once graced a small park on the northeast corner of Division (now North Main) and Strong Streets in Brighton, catty-corner from the D. W. Strong Mercantile Store, and hosted community concerts before it was moved to the fairgrounds. (Courtesy of the Brighton Historical Preservation Commission.)

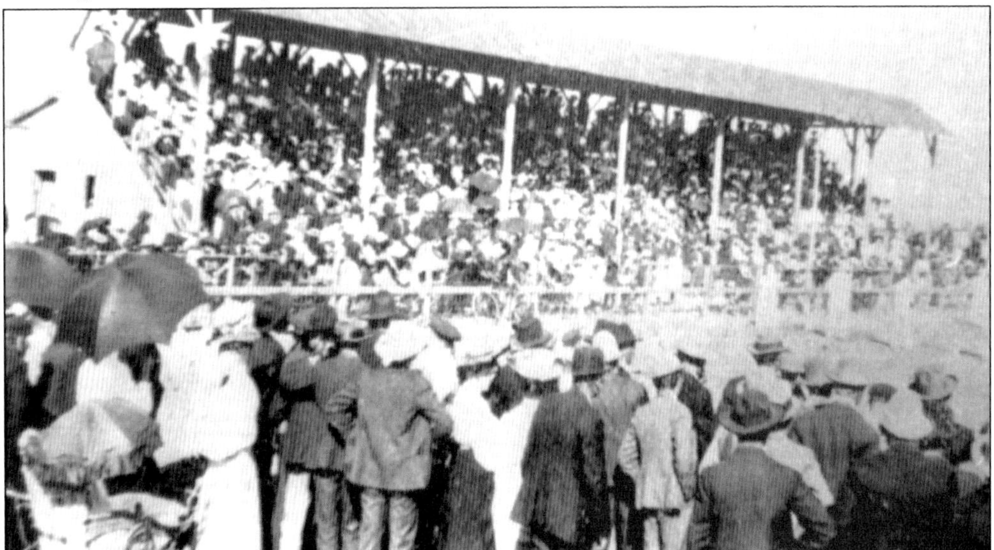

Grandstand. The grandstand at the Adams County Fairgrounds was located on the north side of the half-mile track. Constructed in 1892, it was capable of seating 500 people and had a "Fine Arts Hall" underneath the stands. In 1965, the county made the decision to move the fairgrounds to the former location of the Denver Poor Farm west of Henderson. The old fairgrounds were cleared, and a recreation complex was developed on the east end of the property. In 1975, a new six-story Adams County Administration Building was built, facing South Fourth Avenue, on the west side of the old fairgrounds.

Ten

Our Town

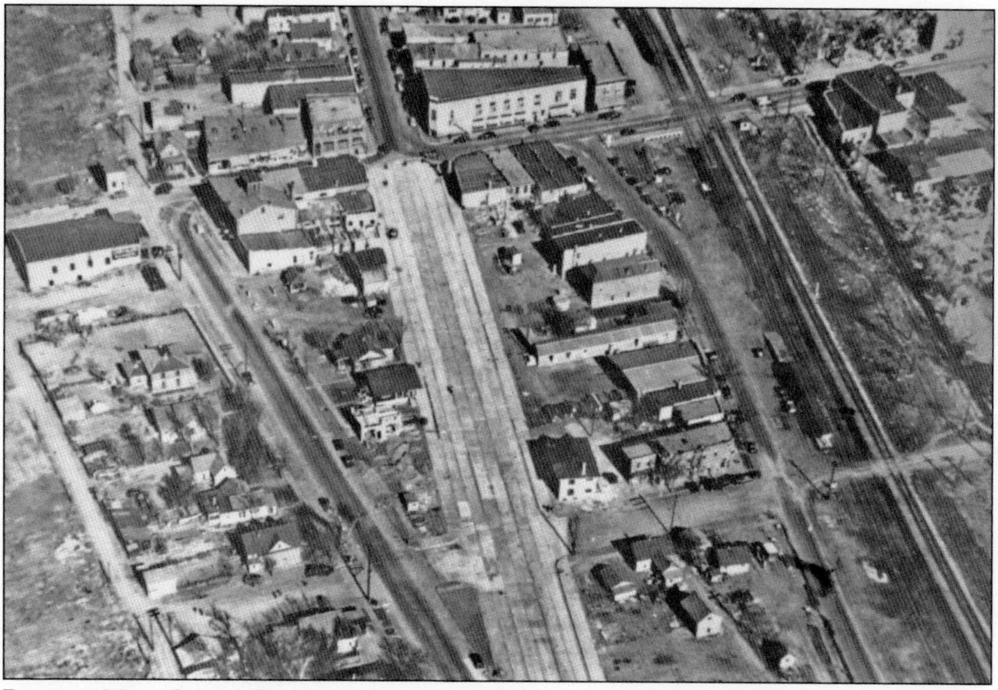

Putting Main Street Through. Downtown Brighton took on its familiar shape in 1935 when Main Street was extended south through the block between South First Avenue and Cabbage Avenue, south of Bridge Street, greatly altering Daniel Carmichael's original plat. The major portion of the Carmichael business block, including the original Carmichael Building, was demolished to extend Main Street through to the south edge of town. The action created a new business section on either side of the new street and solved downtown traffic patterns that had plagued the town since its beginning. A series of fires in the 1950s and 1960s, which destroyed the Rex Theater (1954), the Wire Building (1955), and the Nitske Building (1966), also greatly altered the appearance of downtown Brighton. (Courtesy of the Brighton Historical Preservation Commission.)

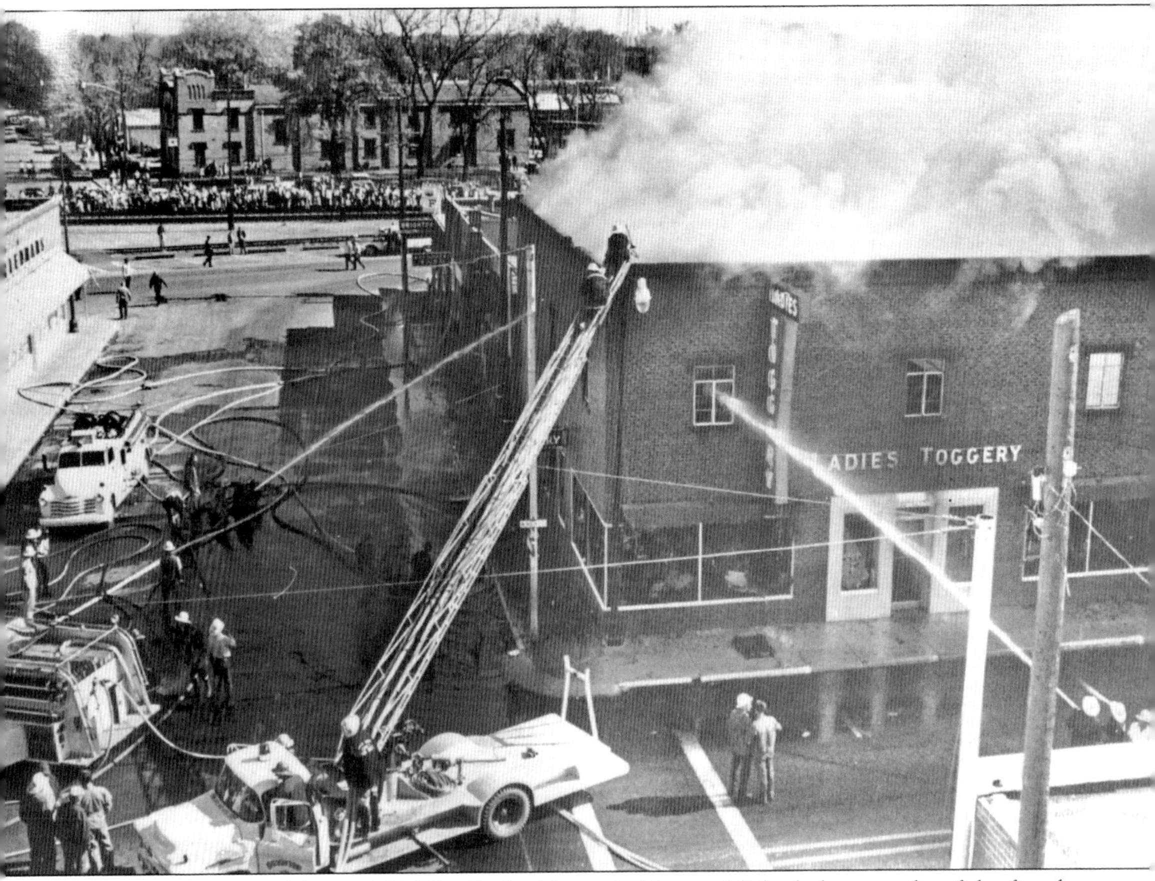

NITSKE BUILDING FIRE, 1966. The *Rocky Mountain News* published photographs of the fire that destroyed the Nitske Building at North Main and Strong Streets in October 1966. Note the Ladies Toggery, Friedman's Grocery Store, and the crowd of people gathered along the railroad tracks in front of the American Legion Philip Wade Post No. 46 (formerly the Colorado National Guard Armory in Brighton). The Brighton Armory was built at 300 Strong Street, just across the railroad tracks from the Union Pacific Railroad station in 1921 for Company K, 157th Infantry, Colorado National Guard, when they were moved to Adams County. The American Legion Post bought the armory in 1946. Activities held at the Legion Hall included church bazaars, teen dances, pro wrestling, boxing, gymnastics, roller skating, agricultural banquets, and the Great Western Sugar Company's annual "Sugar Tramps Ball." The Legion sold the armory to the United Lumber Company and purchased the former post office building at 105 Bridge Street as a new Legion Hall. United Lumber used the old armory building as a warehouse until it was sold in 2007 to become part of the new Brighton Public Library complex. (Courtesy of the Denver Public Library Western History and Genealogy Department.)

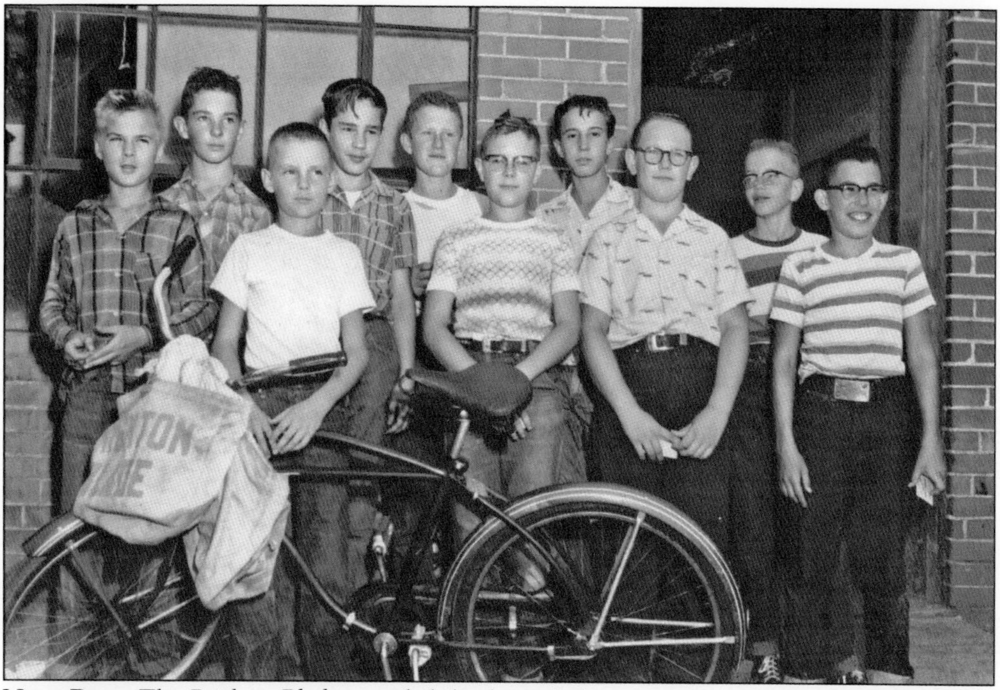

News Boys. The *Brighton Blade* provided the first job for several generations of boys delivering the newspaper. The boys in this photograph have been tentatively identified. From left to right are (first row) Ronald "Ronnie" Read; unidentified; Gary White; Bernard Coble; and Gordon "Gordie" Reed, son of Wally Reed, manager of the Public Service Company (PSCO); (second row) the Lehr brothers (or possibly Leon Schmidt or Mike Stathem and Benjamin "Ben" Schiefelbein), Alfred "Al" Lempke, Dennis Mead (student body president), and George Ott. Note the *Brighton Blade* bags on the handlebars of the bicycle. (Courtesy of the Brighton Historical Preservation Commission.)

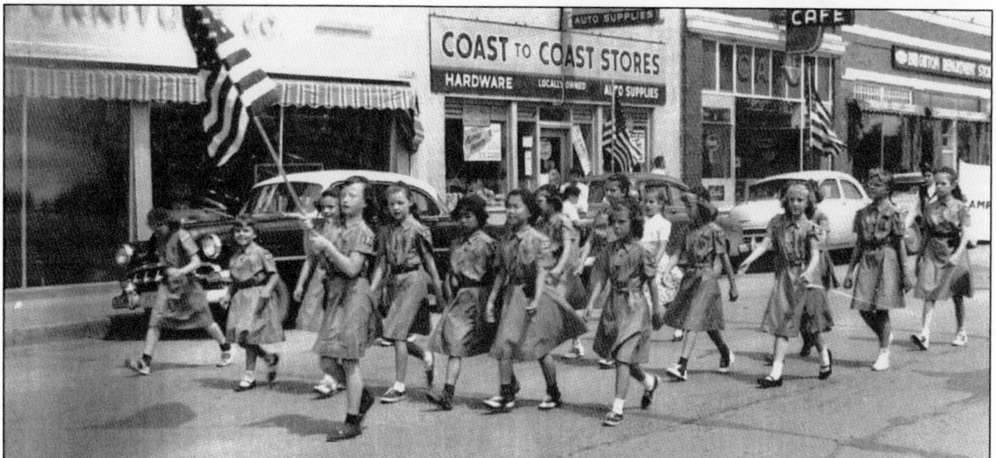

Girl Scouts on Parade. The Girl Scouts and other organizations provided training for young people. Here the Girl Scouts are, from left to right, Sharon Foos, Kathy Zeiler, Sydney Hutherson, Nancy Strode, S. Okubo, Norma Murata, Ruth Ann Silver, Beverly Rosenbrock, unidentified, Donna Chambers, Anne Meehl, unidentified, and Kitty Dodd, marching past the Benedict Furniture, Coast-to-Coast, Sportsman Café, and Brighton Department stores (117, 119, 121, and 123 North Main Street). (Courtesy of the Brighton Historical Preservation Commission.)

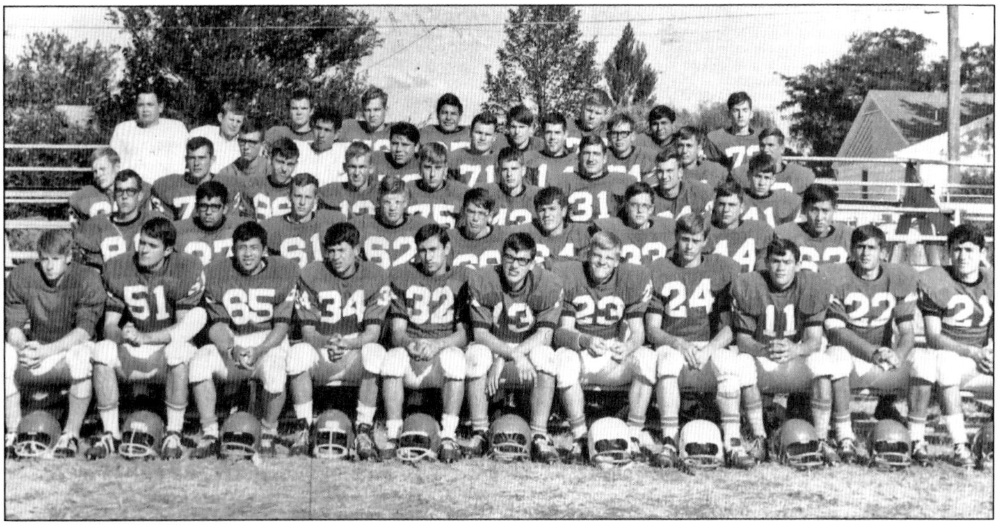

Brighton Bulldogs, 1967. Like many communities, the high school sports were an important part of the community life. Brighton High School has been no exception. Over the years, the Brighton High School teams have won championships in basketball, wrestling, and other sports. Many of the members of the 1967 Brighton High School football team are now, 40 years later, prominent members of the community. (Courtesy of the Brighton Historical Preservation Commission.)

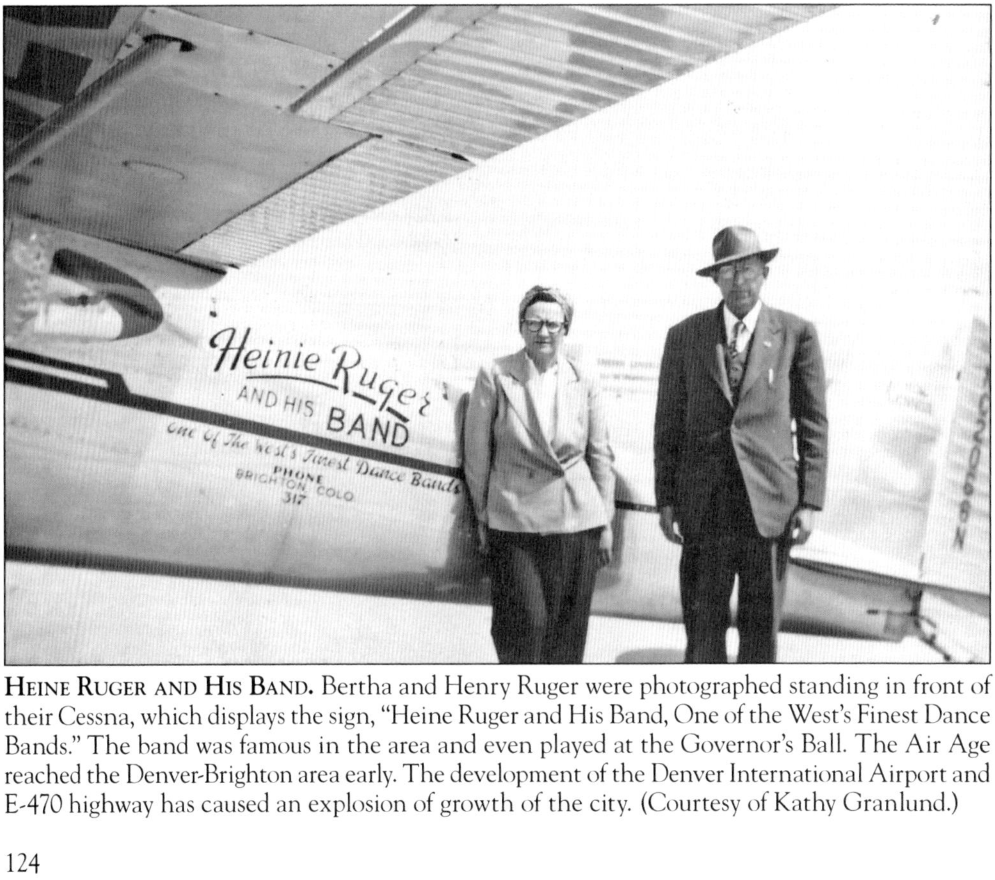

Heine Ruger and His Band. Bertha and Henry Ruger were photographed standing in front of their Cessna, which displays the sign, "Heine Ruger and His Band, One of the West's Finest Dance Bands." The band was famous in the area and even played at the Governor's Ball. The Air Age reached the Denver-Brighton area early. The development of the Denver International Airport and E-470 highway has caused an explosion of growth of the city. (Courtesy of Kathy Granlund.)

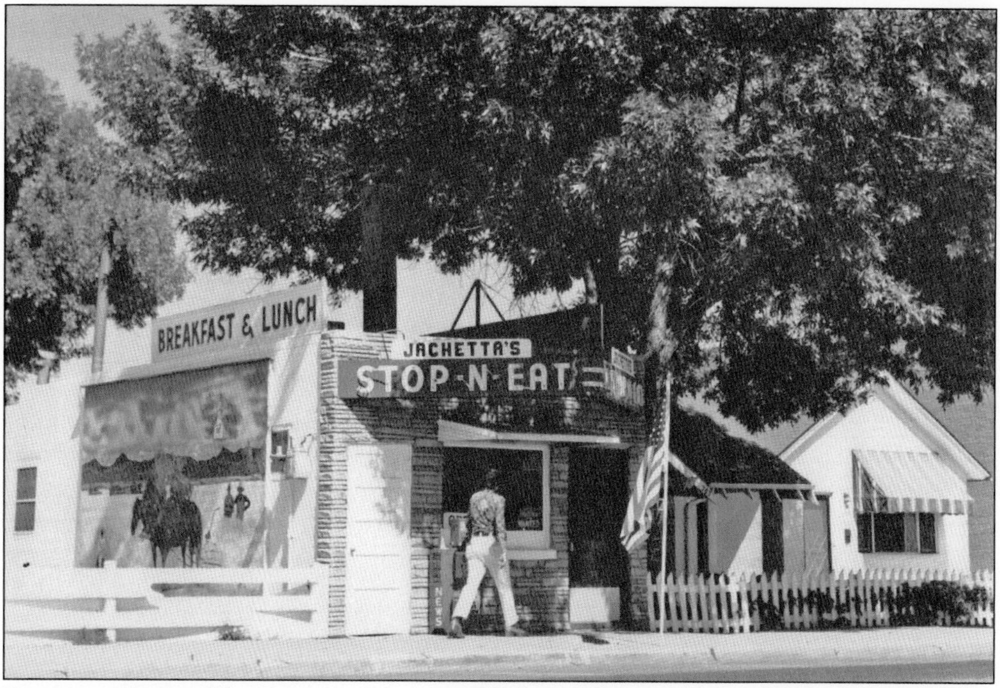

BRIGHTON DEPOT. The Brighton Depot was built in 1907 to replace earlier railroad stations constructed at the same location in 1870 and 1882. The depot sat on the west side of the railroad track at the end of Strong Street until it was moved in May 1981 to a new site (below) just west of the tracks on Bridge Street, the former location of the Jachetta family's Stop-N-Eat diner (above), where it was converted into a restaurant. The Brighton Armory seen in the background as an antique steam engine passes the relocated railroad depot is a fitting summary of the history of Brighton and the changes it is experiencing.

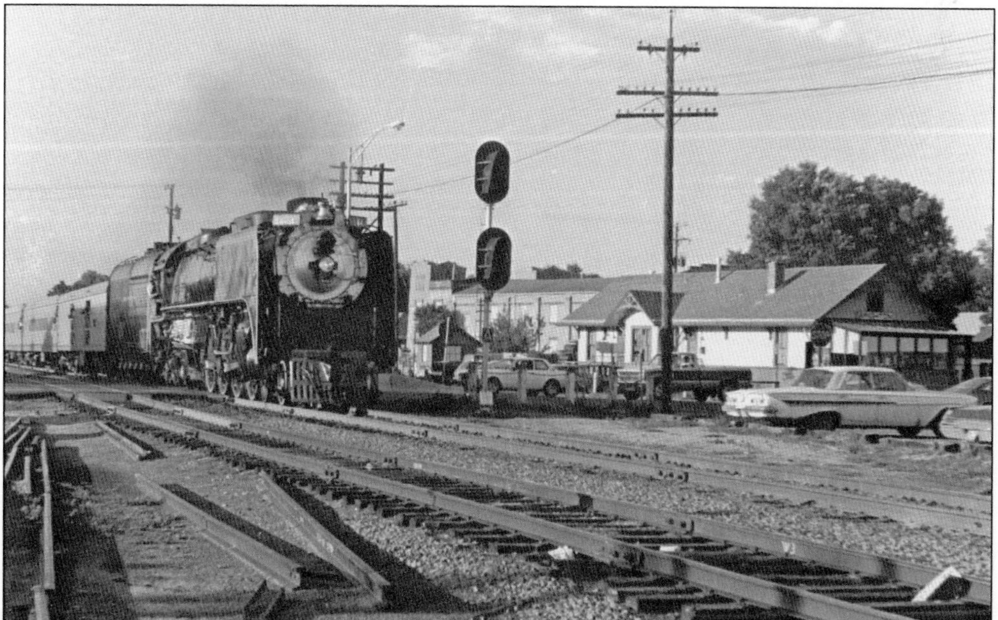

BIBLIOGRAPHY

Brown, Seletha. *Rivalry at the River in Colorado's Fur Forts*. Boulder, CO: Johnson Publishing Company, 1959.

Dorr, W. Carl. *History of Adams County, Brighton and Fort Lupton, Colorado*. Brighton, CO: Brighton Publishing Company, 1955.

———. *Looking Back: A Historical Account of the Development of Brighton and the Surrounding Community from 1859–1976*. Brighton, CO: Brighton Centennial-Bicentennial Committee, 1976.

Foster, Jack. "The Story of Barr Lake." *Rocky Mountain News*, Denver: October 5, 1952.

Hafen, Leroy R. *Colorado and Its People*. New York: Lewis Historical Publishing Company, 1948.

Lindstrom Frandsen, Maude. *All the Way: An Account of the Development of a City and a Church*. Brighton, CO: Methodist Episcopal Church of Brighton, 1963.

Long, Margaret. *The Smoky Hill Trail*. Denver: W. H. Kistler Stationery Company, 1947.

Marcy, Richard, ed. *The Forgotten Past of Adams County*. Vols. 1–4. Thornton, CO: Thornton High School, 1978–1981.

Riesel, Annette Rinkler, ed. *Brighton—Fort Lupton at the Dawn of the Millennium, 2000*. Brighton, CO: MetroWest Newspapers, 2000.

Reither, Patricia L., ed. *History of Brighton, Colorado and the Surrounding Area*. Dallas, TX: Curtis Media Corporation, 1987, reprinted, Brighton, CO: Brighton Historical Preservation Commission, 2006.

Rathgeber, Harold E. "The Public Life of Alva Adams." Master's thesis. Denver: University of Denver, 1954.

Wagner, Albin. *Adams County, Colorado: A Centennial History, 1902–2002*. Virginia Beach, VA: Donning Company, 2002.

———. Adams *County: Crossroads of the West*. Vols. 1 and 2. Brighton, CO: Adams County Board of County Commissioners, 1977.

———. *Brighton Reflections: The Bicentennial Years, 1776–1976*. Brighton, CO: Brighton Federal Savings, 1976. (Reprinted as *Brighton Reflections: Brighton City Hall 100-Year Commemoration, 1906–2006*. Brighton, CO: Brighton Historical Preservation Commission, 2006.)

West, Elliott. *The Contested Plains: Indians, Goldseekers and the Rush to Colorado*. Lawrence, KS: University of Kansas Press, 1998.

Index

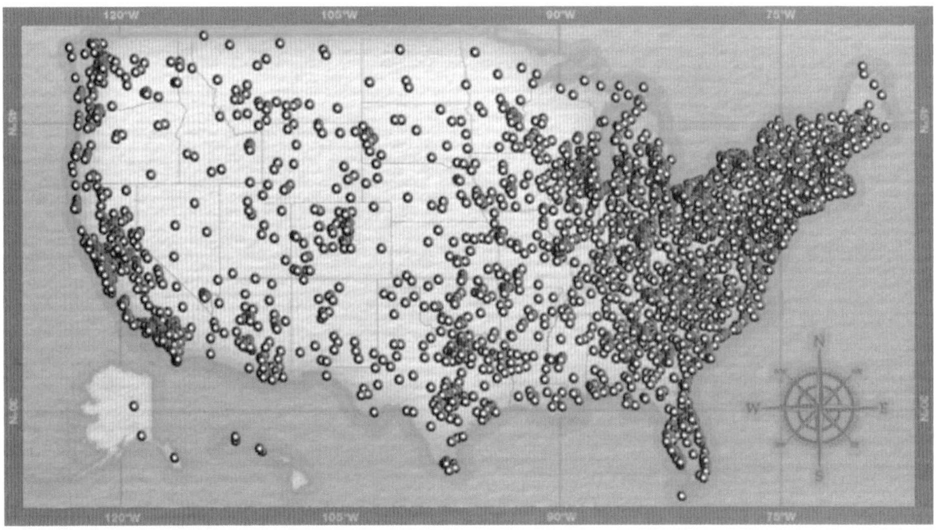